PRAISE

"The turbulence in the world today underscores the need for clear, agile and thoughtful strategy. Kraaijenbrink's approach is distinct from the thousands of available books on strategy, as it is founded on the assumption that organizations will always face uncertainties and provides a pragmatic and actionable approach to moving forward."

Stuart Read, Professor of Strategic Management, Willamette University (Retired) and Co-Author of *Effectual Entrepreneurship*

"Dr Kraaijenbrink has given strategizing managers, strategy consultants, and even some academics, a really useful book. Strongly recommended."

J.C. Spender, Research Professor, Kozminski University and author of *Business Strategy*

"Fantastic strategy playbook, ready-to-implement, while at the same time meeting rigorous academic standards."

Dr. Gunther Wobser, CEO of Lauda and author of *Agiles Innovationsmanagement*

The Strategy Handbook is clear, precise, organized, and readable. At the same time, it is challenging, thought-provoking, demanding, and status quo disturbing.

Rick Orford | investor, and mentor.

Execution in strategy is critical. Consumption of concepts without implementation is elementary in theory yet few are able to move from concept to action to deliver results. This is a wonderful tool take concepts to action and have a written measure to later review while proceeding to execute for future success. Lessons learned from the writer or this shows in the methods presented in the handbook and will be useful to all to reference this book.

Paul L Gunn Jr | Founder, KUOG Corporation

Throughout my years in business, I have seen first-hand the complexities in executing strategy even when said strategy is sound. People often overlook the necessary preparation, which allows for successful implementation and that is where Jeroen comes in. *The Strategy Handbook* explains how to find the best path for strategy implementation through user-friendly charts, tools, case studies and step-by-step processes. Jeroen also shares how these processes can be used by people of all backgrounds, not just those in high level business settings.

John Rovani | Managing Partner, Ponterra Business Advisors, LLC

Kraaijenbrink uses real-world examples to make his points. This book isn't just theory, it's concepts validated by real people making real designs.

Glenn Hopper | CFO, Sandline Global, Author of *Deep Finance*

Reading this wonderful book on strategy one gets to know Jeroen's source of intellectual power. His secret lies in 'knowing by doing'. This book is a beautiful synthesis by a creative mind, immersed in the corporate world. You need not unbox this book because his out-of-box concepts flow freely. The unique feature of this book is that the concepts developed in the Western world are equally relevant in the East. I don't want my students to miss this valuable book and am going to adopt it during my next strategy class in India.

Dr. Ajit Patil, Top-75 Global Marketing Professor, and LinkedIn Top Voice

I have been a huge fan and supporter of Dr. Kraaijenbrink's work since I first discovered "The Strategy Handbook" several years ago. As a continuous student and professional practitioner of strategy execution, I have found him to be one of the few voices who truly understand the interrelated yet tenuous relationship that exists between those two disciplines. This new edition of the book will help any organization and leadership team understand the shift taking place and the increased role that execution now plays in making strategy successful. This is a very practical read, well written, and applicable to all that I highly recommend.

Monte Pedersen, Principal, The CDA Group LLC

In The Strategy Handbook, Kraaijenbrink stresses the importance of being able to implement the strategy so that you can execute and achieve your vision. He takes an action-oriented approach and demonstrates the effectiveness of measurable actions.

David Martin, Co-Founder, Execution360

Is your strategy starting to get stale? Stop deliberating and start getting action-oriented with The Strategy Handbook. Kraaijenbrink does a wonderful job covering the varied aspects of strategy development and execution.

Akhil Kohli, Founder, and CEO, MindStrength

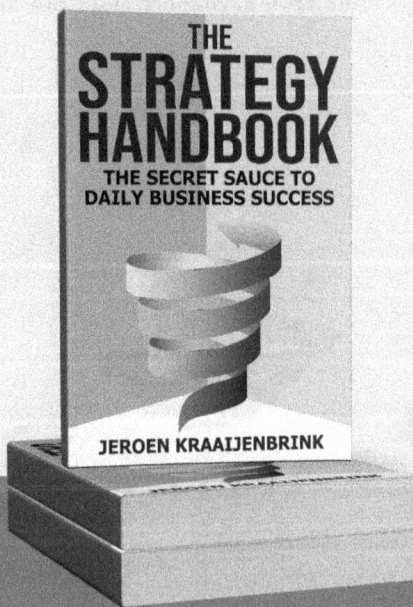

THE
STRATEGY
HANDBOOK

THE SECRET SAUCE TO
DAILY BUSINESS SUCCESS

JEROEN KRAAIJENBRINK

CONTENTS

Preface to the Second Edition xi

PART I. INTRODUCTION 1

Chapter 1. Motivation 3
- • The Challenge: Putting Strategy into Action 3
- • Recipe for a Handbook 5
- • Three Ways to Use This Book 7

Chapter 2. Getting Ready 9
- • Defining Strategy 9
- • The Ten Elements of Strategy 12
- • Defining Strategy Generation 17
- • Defining Strategy Execution 21
- • Strategy as a Nine-Step Process 24
- • The Right Mindset: Ten Mottos 29
- • Strategy as a Participative Process 34
- • Introducing the Four Examples 40

PART II. STRATEGY GENERATION 43

Chapter 3. Step 1: Activating Key Stakeholders 45
- • The Activation Challenge 45
- • Excuses and Causes for Strategic Inactivity 47
- • Six Activation Tactics 52
  - ○ 1. Open people's minds 52
  - ○ 2. Reveal the urgency 54
  - ○ 3. Sell the benefits 56

○   4. Take away risks 59
○   5. Just start 62
○   6. Enforce action 63
•   The Four Examples 65

Chapter 4. Step 2: Mapping Strategy 69
•   The Meaning and Role of Mapping Strategy 69
•   How to Use the Tools..70
•   The Ten Elements of Strategy 71
○   1. Resources & competences 71
○   2. Partners 73
○   3. Customers & needs 76
○   4. Competitors 79
○   5. Value proposition 81
○   6. Revenue model 84
○   7. Risks & costs 87
○   8. Values & goals 90
○   9. Organizational climate................................93
○   10. Trends & uncertainties...............................96
•   The Four Examples 98

Stepping Back for a Moment 109
•   A Brief Summary of What We Have Seen So Far ...109
•   A Fast and Frugal Strategy Generation Format.......110

Chapter 5. Step 3: Assessing Strategy 111
•   Why and When to Assess Your Strategy 111
•   Ten Strategy Checks..112
○   1. Coherence check 113
○   2. Efficiency check 115
○   3. Effectiveness check......................................116
○   4. Uniqueness check 119
○   5. Flexibility check...122
○   6. Robustness check 124
○   7. Scalability check 125
○   8. Responsibility check 126
○   9. Actionability check 129
○   10. Energy check 130
•   A Quick Strategy Checklist....................................132

- How to Use the Strategy Checks 133
- The Four Examples 135

Chapter 6. Step 4: Innovating Strategy 139
- Defining Your Strategic Innovation Appetite..........139
- Five Strategic Innovation Approaches 144
  - 1. Elementary innovation 146
  - 2. Amplifying innovation.............................147
  - 3. Routed innovation....................................150
  - 4. Projective innovation 154
  - 5. Freestyle innovation.................................156
- Generating and Selecting Strategic Options 159
- The Four Examples 160

Chapter 7. Step 5: Formulating Strategy 163
- The Strategy Formulation Challenge 163
- The Core and Structure of Your Strategy 166
- Formulating Strategy in Words 168
- Writing a Strong Strategic Plan 175
- The Four Examples 176
- Formulating Strategy in Pictures 181
- Pitching Your Strategy.......................................186

PART III. STRATEGY EXECUTION 191

Chapter 8. Step 6: Bridging Gaps 193
- The Bridging Challenge 193
- Bridging Information Gaps..................................198
- Bridging Implementation Gaps............................208
- Closing the Bridging Step 214
- The Four Examples 215

Stepping Back Again..223

Chapter 9. Step 7: Organizing Strategy............................225
- The Organizational Challenge..............................225
- The Organizational Map 226
- A Quick Organizational Fitness Scan 231
- How to Use the Tools 232

- ○ 1. Leadership 234
- ○ 2. Controls 236
- ○ 3. Motivation..239
- ○ 4. Commitment..243
- ○ 5. Expertise..246
- ○ 6. Information technology 249
- ○ 7. Structure..252
- ○ 8. Communication 255
- ○ 9. Processes..259
- ○ 10. Policies 262
- • Connecting Bridging and Organizing 266
- • The Four Examples 267

Stepping Back Once More 273

Chapter 10. Step 8: Planning Strategy 275
- • The Planning Challenge......................................275
- • Completing the Strategy Backlog........................277
- • Assembling the Realization Team 281
- • Prioritizing and Scheduling................................284
- • Meetings and Briefings..288
- • Committing to the Plan.......................................290
- • The Four Examples 293

Chapter 11. Step 9: Realizing Strategy 297
- • The Realization Challenge....................................297
- • Managing Relevance 298
- • Managing Progress..303
- • Managing Emotions..308
- • The Four Examples 317

Conclusion 323
- • The Complete Strategy Process............................323
- • How to Implement the Process in Practice............325
- • What It Asks from Leaders...................................329
- • A Final Recommendation 331

PREFACE TO THE SECOND EDITION

The Strategy Handbook started as a two-volume book of which Part I (Strategy Generation) was published in 2015 and Part II (Strategy Execution) in 2018. Because the two parts are inseparable and refer to one and the same strategy approach, I wanted to merge the two books into one integrated handbook for this second edition. Furthermore, while working with the books over the past years, I have identified various ways in which their contents could be fine-tuned and improved. For this reason, I felt the urge to update the book. With this second edition, you now have everything you need to know to successfully generate and execute strategy combined in a single handbook.

This integration into one book is one of the two major changes that I've made compared to the first edition. Since its original publication, the Strategy Sketch and the nine-step approach to strategy have proven their value to numerous executives and organizations. In my executive teaching and consulting, as well as in the experiences that executives, managers, entrepreneurs, and consultants have shared with me, the structured and down-to-earth approach of the book has proven its value in a wide range of very different types of organizations–startups, SMEs, large firms, and non-profits. Therefore, while integrated into one volume, and although improvements have been made to all chapters, the core approach of the book has remained unchanged.

The other significant change is that I've simplified the book by leaving out parts that are not absolutely necessary in practice. While the first edition was already targeted at being as practical as possible, it still had a bit of "textbook" flavor by referring to various models and tools. It still contained details that complicated the approach more than illuminated it. The main question that I kept in mind all the time while preparing this second edition is whether or not I had used what I had written before at any point in the past five years in my work with clients. If not, those parts were removed.

The result is a book that is more focused, more coherent, and even more practical than the first edition–while still maintaining its core, depth, and rigor. The result is also a book that even more clearly shows that strategy generation and execution are two inseparable parts of the same process and that it is only their combination that can lead to systematic, daily business success.

I intentionally say "daily" here to emphasize the everyday nature of the strategy approach outlined in this book. Strategy is not something done every couple of years, concerned only about the long term, or something reserved for high-level executives. A good strategy approach is an inherent part of an organization's normal activities. It drives these activities on a day-to-day basis, and involves people from all over the organization in an ongoing process of thinking and doing. Practiced in that way, strategy is not something special or exceptional, but *the* core process that drives an organization's business success, every day.

Indeed, *the* process. This may sound like an overstatement. One might argue that an organization's primary process, through which it creates and delivers its products and services, is the core process. It is in some ways. It is that process which, if done well, leads to satisfied customers and generates revenues. As such, it is core to the organization and its survival. However, it is not the process that drives an organization's success over time.

In a world that is dynamic and complex, an organization's products, services, and the processes that produce them require constant change. The same applies to an organization's resources and competences, which require constant development, or even reinvention. This makes them not a very solid basis for long-term success. After all, what can be seen as an organization's strength today, can be outdated or a weakness tomorrow.

It is the strategy process that is responsible for keeping your organization up-to-date, for making sure you keep on creating unique value for your customers tomorrow, and the day after tomorrow. It is this process through which you keep track of the internal and external developments and evaluate their impact on your organization. And it is this process that drives change in your organization and that enables it to catch up or stay ahead of competitors. This is why I firmly believe that the strategy process is indeed *the* core process in 21st century organizations to achieve daily business success in the long term.

A WORD OF THANKS

I could never have written this book on my own. Over the past few years I have discussed ideas, texts, chapters, and models with numerous entrepreneurs, experts, managers, directors, academics, students, friends, and the like. Some of them were my clients, others were participants at my strategy and entrepreneurship courses at the University of Twente, Amsterdam Business School, and TSM business school, and still others participated in various seminars, workshops, and conversations. It would go too far to name all of them personally—if only because I would certainly forget some of them. So, pardon my generic "Thank You!" here, but it is meant just as sincerely.

There are a few people I want to thank personally though, since they took the effort to actually read through the drafts of this book and provide comments. Stuart Read, thank you for confronting me with the lacking personality of earlier versions of the book and your extremely fast and to-the-point feedback. Jeroen Sempel, thank you for comparing the book to other books, pointing out its underdeveloped normative message, and taking the time to discuss all nine steps with me in detail. J.-C Spender, thank you for your ever critical and unconventional view on strategy and for sharpening me up in the journey towards this book. Jason Weller, thank you for your detailed comments and for also pointing out the parts you particularly liked. Björn Kijl, thank you for your precision, for contrasting the book with the business model literature, and for your continuously supportive comments. Saras Sarasvathy, thank you for inspiring me with your work on "effectuation" and for bringing in the idea of exercises. Scott Newbert, thank you for reviewing the book and for your creative way to use the Strategy Sketch in your teaching. This has been inspirational. Dick Korenhof and Rogier Cazemier, thank you for having the guts to adopt this book in your teaching before the part about strategy execution was written. This has given me an important incentive to finish it. Also, thank you for your detailed feedback and push to keep the book practical. Paula Ravensbergen, thank you for your meticulous reading and attention to detail, which has helped me reduce the number of errors.

I also want to thank the team at Leaders Press for supporting me in creating and publishing this new paperback version of the book and for helping me integrate what previously were two separate parts. You've made it a better book and helped me share its message with a wider audience.

And finally, Caroline Smeets, thank you for reading the entire book word for word, for telling me where it was boring, superfluous, or incomprehensible, for supporting me with everything else that made it possible to write this book. Your intuitive feedback has made sure that the book stayed close to myself. And thank you for being and staying my wife.

I am grateful to all of you and really appreciate that you've bothered to help me in writing this book. Your contributions have made it a much better book than it was. Any remaining ambiguities or errors are mine.

To close this preface, I want to emphasize that the book is not meant to be a blueprint that you follow dogmatically. You should use it as a source of inspiration and background to create your own approach to strategy—one that fits you and your organization. Maybe you need to skip parts of it, change them, or add stuff. Perfect. Do so. And if you have made a change of which you are proud, let me know so that I can use it in a next edition ☺.

Jeroen Kraaijenbrink

PART I.

INTRODUCTION

1

MOTIVATION

This first chapter explains why this book was written, what you can expect, and how you can use this book in different ways. Altogether, these three topics should give you a sense of the purpose and nature of this book.

THE CHALLENGE: PUTTING STRATEGY INTO ACTION

This book was written with one purpose in mind: supporting you in making strategy work. To achieve this, I wanted to write a practical handbook that you can use to generate and execute strategy yourself on a day-to-day basis. Perhaps you still need some support after reading it, but the overall idea of this guide is that it should be self-explanatory so that it can be used independently.

I felt I had to write this book because the way strategy is generated and executed in the average organizations I've observed is not particularly compelling. To say it less politically, the majority of organizations have substantial problems with strategy generation and execution. Often there either a) is no strategy, b) it isn't clear enough, or c) it doesn't get executed. In the first case, strategy just isn't on the organization's agenda. Such organizations are typically too involved with survival and running their daily business to pay attention to strategy. In the second case, there is attention to strategy, but the organization isn't able to get beyond vague mission and vision statements, quantitative goals, or abstract formulations that are otherwise not actionable. And in the third case, strategy remains a paper vehicle of which only a small part ever gets executed. All three result in unsuccessful strategy.

These are not just my own observations. Numerous studies in recent decades confirm that strategy generation and execution are cumbersome processes. Dependent on the exact design of the studies, astonishing failure rates of 70-90% have been reported. This means that just one out of every three to ten strategies are successfully executed. Even though strategy is a complex matter, that's a poor statistic. Typical problems that have been found in such studies are vague strategy, conflicting priorities, overoptimism, a lack of addressing market needs, mismatch with the organization, lacking guidelines for implementation, lack of commitment, and so on.

These problems with strategy generation and execution certainly don't occur due to a lack of strategy books. On the contrary, a quick search on Amazon.com reveals that there are already over 100,000 books on strategy. So, could another book like this make any difference? I hope so and I'm optimistic that it could. To find out how, we need to see how this book tries to be different from existing books. Of course, I haven't read all 100,000+ of them, so I might have missed something. However, from what I've seen, we can roughly divide the existing books into two categories: broad strategy books and focused strategy books.

> *"The majority of organizations have substantial problems with strategy generation and strategy execution."*

Broad strategy books, such as strategy textbooks, typically try to cover the entire scope of strategy by offering a collection of tools. Some of these tools are known under acronyms such as PESTLE, SWOT, 5FF, 7S, VRIO, 4P, BCG, or BSC. These tools are useful and the books are too. They support strategic analysis and making generic choices, but they hardly facilitate designing and developing concrete new strategy that can be executed. They're good at telling you *what* you should pay attention to when generating and executing strategy. However, they don't give much guidance on *how* to do it. Although not entirely *im*practical, they are not practical enough.

On the other hand, there are focused books that are also valuable and often more practical. Such books typically try to make a specific point and a focused contribution to existing strategy approaches. I want to name five specifically, since they have been a great source of inspiration for me while writing this book: Chan Kim and Renée Mauborgne's *Blue Ocean Strategy*, Alexander Osterwalder and Yves Pigneur's *Business Model Generation*, Saras Sarasvathy's *Effectuation*, Eric Ries' *The Lean Startup,* and A.G. Lafley and Roger L. Martin's *Playing to Win.* These five are all practical books on strategy and entrepreneurship that provide new and different insights into how to generate new strategy. However, they offer partial solutions, not complete strategy approaches.

So on one side we have rather complete but less practical strategy books, and rather practical but less complete strategy books on the other. In order to be successful in practice, though, you need both. In this book, I have tried to take the best of both worlds and turn that into a guide that outlines a practical approach to strategy.

The Goal of this Book

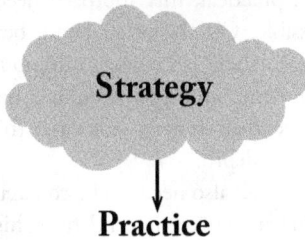

Strategy

↓

Practice

RECIPE FOR A HANDBOOK

But what should a practical strategy handbook look like? For one thing, it needs to put strategy back on earth. If we look at how it's treated by textbooks, MBA programs, scholars, consultants, and organizations generally, strategy is too often put on a pedestal, as some sort of mystical and elite boardroom thing made bigger than it actually is. Of course strategy is extremely important for organizations. However, as I hope to show you in this book, strategy can also be approached in a practical, down-to-earth manner. And it needs to be, if you want it to result in daily business success.

A strategy handbook also needs to be rather complete without becoming bulky. If we want to foster successful strategy generation and execution, we have to make sure that all important steps and elements of strategy are covered. This means that this book does not just cover strategic analysis and decision-making, but also less honorable tasks such as turning strategy into a communicable message and getting people to actively work on strategy in the first place. It also means that a strategy handbook should cover strategy generation *and* strategy execution. Both are needed for successful strategy.

> *"A strategy handbook needs to put strategy back on earth."*

Since strategy is a complicated matter, a handbook should also be structured and thorough. On the one hand it should provide you with a clear step-by-step approach that leads you through the strategy process and makes sure that you don't skip essential steps. In order to remain practical, this approach needs to be as clear and simple as possible. On the other hand, because strategy is a complicated matter, there is no use in dumbing things down. Strategy is just difficult and you wouldn't benefit from this handbook if it pretended strategy was easy; this book aims to balance simplicity and depth.

A strategy handbook also needs to be concrete and hands-on. Concrete means that it has to descend from high-level mission and vision statements and from generic strategies and objectives towards the concrete elements of which strategy is composed. Only in that way can we make sure that we actually understand what is meant by strategy and assess whether it's good or not. Hands-on means that it provides you with information and tools that you can immediately apply in your own situation. A handbook should be action-oriented and stimulate *doing* strategy rather than just thinking and talking about it.

Finally, a practical strategy handbook needs to be realistic as well. I certainly don't mean that it should limit your ambition and creativity and narrow down strategizing to small incremental changes. On the contrary, a strategy handbook should foster creativity and push you to come up with radically new ideas that go beyond the status quo without ignoring what is already there. Even in startups, but especially in existing organizations, there is always a current strategy that is lived by the organization and its people today. Whether we want it or not, this current strategy will have a large impact on any future strategy. This means that a strategy handbook has to embrace it and give it a proper place.

THREE WAYS TO USE THIS BOOK

Of course it's completely up to you how you use this book. You might read it page by page and from cover to cover. However, when actually using it as a handbook, I guess you also might want to skip parts, or move back and forth between different parts of the book. To guide you a little I have anticipated three ways of using this book. These three ways vary in the extent to which they actively make use of the process and content that are provided.

CHECKLIST APPROACH

The lightest of all three, the first approach is to use the book as a checklist to make sure that you pay attention to all the elements of strategy and all the steps of strategy generation and execution. You might want to follow this approach when you are already knowledgeable about strategy and basically know how to generate and enact it successfully. If you aim for this approach, you can immediately jump to the sections "The Ten Elements of Strategy" and "Strategy as a Nine-Step Process" in Chapter 2 (pages 12-27).

FAST AND FRUGAL APPROACH

The fast and frugal approach covers the core ideas of this book in a quick way. If you want limited efforts but still want significant results, I suggest using this approach. Start with Chapter 4, step 2 (Mapping strategy). Based on the main tool of this book, the

Strategy Sketch, it contains a set of questions, exercises, and inspirational checklists that you can use to quickly understand your current strategy and innovate it. After that, immediately work towards a brief action plan, which outlines the most important next steps to take in order to make the strategy work. For this approach, you focus on Chapters 8 and 10 (Bridging Gaps and Planning Strategy). The basic idea outlined there is that you complete a gap analysis in which you identify and prioritize the most important gaps between your current and aspired strategy, and then develop a prioritized action plan for bridging these gaps.

"You might want to skip parts or move back and forth between different parts of the book."

UNABRIDGED APPROACH

The most comprehensive way of using this book is the unabridged approach. With this approach you read the entire book carefully and use as much of it as possible during the strategy generation and execution process. There are two reasons why you may want to do this. First, it's the best guarantee that you will be successful in generating and implementing new strategy. The effort is larger than with the other approaches, but the payoff will also be larger. If you aim for maximum results in your daily business success, this is your approach. The second reason for following this approach is that it helps you in building up your own strategy expertise. By reading all the chapters and going through all the tools you can develop a deeper understanding of strategy generation and execution.

Thus, the most obvious way to use this book is to follow it from chapter to chapter and perform all the steps that are described. This is the most complete approach, and it will make sure you cover everything that might be relevant.

Enough about the book and its background. Let's get started!

2

GETTING READY

Whereas the first chapter has mainly given you some background to this book, this second chapter prepares you for the actual work. It defines and explains what strategy is and what the strategy process looks like. Also, to help you translate the ideas of his book into your own practice, the chapter introduces you to the four examples that will be used throughout this book and shows you the mindset needed for effective strategy generation and execution.

DEFINING STRATEGY

An important thing to know upfront is that this book is mostly about what is called "business level strategy." Business level strategy is strategy at the level of business units and small to medium-sized firms. Typically it concerns organizations with a limited portfolio of products and services and that are run as single businesses. "Corporate level strategy," on the other hand, is strategy for larger organizations with multiple business units or divisions. Although important too, corporate level strategy is not covered in this handbook. So, keep in mind that, whenever I use the word "strategy," I refer to business level strategy. Let's now turn to the meaning of that word.

> *"Stripped down to its essence, a strategy is a unique way of sustainable value creation."*

There are almost as many definitions of strategy as there are people writing about it. Some focus on long-term planning, others on differentiating the organization from its competitors, and still others on an organization's actual decisions and actions. That there isn't a universal agreed-upon definition of strategy doesn't really matter. However, I should be clear about what is meant by strategy in this book because it has a substantial impact on how you generate and execute it.

I will start by providing a short definition of strategy to provide you with an idea of its role and purpose. In the next section, I'll move on by presenting the elements strategy is made up of. This is needed to make sure that we actually understand and are talking about the same thing when we use the word *strategy*.

A SHORT DEFINITION OF STRATEGY

Stripped down to its essence, a strategy is *a unique way of sustainable value creation.* So, if we ask someone what the strategy of their organization is, we ask them about the organization's unique way of sustainable value creation. To understand what this means, let's look part by part at this definition.

VALUE CREATION

Strategy aims at creating something that has value and that matters to at least a number of people or organizations. This means that a strategy expresses what value an organization has and for whom. Organizations primarily create value through their products and services, and this can be seen as their main reason for existence. Accordingly, value creation is about the value an organization creates through its products and services.

Customers buy these products or services because they fulfill a particular need or desire. And since customers may buy them for very different reasons, value is subjective. People may buy a watch, for example, because it tells the time, because it's beautiful, or because it's expensive. This means that there is no absolute way of defining or measuring value. Of course, we can see the price of products and services, but this is not the same as their actual value for a specific customer. Furthermore, people may strongly disagree about what is valuable and what is not. Because of this subjectivity, a strategy needs to express for whom value is created.

UNIQUE

A good strategy aims at doing something different from others. This doesn't have to be 100% unique (it shouldn't be, because no one will understand what you are offering), but it should have at least some unique elements. This uniqueness may come from anywhere. You can think of, for example, your location, the specific history of the organization, the friendliness of your employees, or your pricing. Uniqueness is important because without it you can't distinguish yourself from others. And if you want to compete with them, or convince customers to buy your products or services, you need to be able to tell what is special about you.

SUSTAINABLE

Strategy aims at value creation that is sustainable over time. This implies first that a strategy should be hard to copy or circumvent by others. Protection by patents might be the first thing you think about, but there are other ways as well. Think of, for example, secrecy, or having a unique and hard-to-imitate competence or network.

Second, sustainable also means that an organization receives something in return for the value it creates. Usually this is money—if no one pays for the value that is created, an organization will have a hard time sustaining itself. It can also be information or other goods, though. Think about, for example, Facebook or Google, which are "free" because you provide personal information in exchange for their products.

Third, to be sustainable a strategy also shouldn't rely too much on resources that are easily depleted. This is both ethical and practical: if a strategy relies on resources that are soon gone, this strategy cannot be sustained.

Finally, to be sustainable, a strategy should take into account the interests of important stakeholders. These are the people or organizations that influence your organization or are influenced by it. Examples are customers, suppliers, or interest groups. If your strategy doesn't take care of your important stakeholders, it will be hard to sustain.

WAY

Strategy is not a fixed product, a set of goals, or a long-term plan that remains stable over time. Neither is it a statement or a slogan or limited to what is written down in official documents. All of that we could call an organization's *explicit* strategy–the strategy as it's officially communicated. But that is not an organization's *true* strategy.

An organization's true strategy appears more implicitly in what it *does*, in its processes, actions, and routines. That strategy is an ongoing and active process that is lived by the organization on a daily basis. Much more than a piece of text, strategy is a way of *doing* something–a unique way of sustainable value creation.

> *"An organization's true strategy appears implicitly in what it does; in its processes, actions, and routines."*

THE TEN ELEMENTS OF STRATEGY

The above definition helps us to get at the essence of strategy and *what* it aims for, which is important. To see *how* an organization can offer a unique way of sustainable value creation, we need to look more in depth at the elements strategy is made of. A reading of the strategy literature and feedback during the writing process revealed ten core elements of strategy. Throughout this book I will frequently refer to these ten elements. In brief, they comprise the following.

1. **Resources & competences.** *What you have, what you are good at, and what makes you unique.*
    Your resources and competences reflect what kind of unique means your organization has and what it's capable of. Resources are the things that you *have*, such as machines, people, information, location, money, and so on. Competences are the things you *can do*. These are the

skills, capabilities, and processes you're good at. Together, these means determine to a large extent what kind of products and services an organization can offer.

2. **Partners.** *Whom you work with and who makes your products or services more valuable.*
Not only are your own resources and competences important for your strategy but also those of the organizations and people you work with. Think of, for example, suppliers, universities, logistics services, or any other type of organization that could support you in offering something unique. Also, think of your own or other people's personal networks, since these can give you access to valuable information or other means that the organization doesn't have.

3. **Customers & needs.** *The organizations and people you serve and which of their needs you fulfill.*
Obviously, no organization can do without customers. Therefore, a strategy needs to specify who they are and what needs they have. To do this properly you do so on two levels. On the surface level you specify the kind of organizations or people you are targeting and which of their needs you're trying to fulfill. On a deeper level, you're also looking at the specific people that are involved. Think of those who *use* the product, those that *pay* for it, the people *deciding* about it, and those who *influence* and *initiate* that decision. They are all your customers and all their needs are relevant.

4. **Competitors.** *Others that your customers will compare you to in deciding whether or not to buy your products or services.*
Partners are the ones you work *with* and customers are the ones you work *for*. Competitors, on the other hand, are those people and organizations you work *against*. While you don't necessarily need to fight them aggressively, you have to deal with them somehow, if only because your customers compare you to them. Your competitors obviously include those organizations that do something similar to your organization. But don't forget substitutes, potential future competitors that might enter your industry soon or any alternative that

customers may consider. You are competing with these as well.

"A reading of the strategy literature and feedback during the writing process revealed ten core elements of strategy."

5. **Value proposition.** *What products and services you offer, how you offer them, and what added value they have for the customer.*
Your resources and competences and your partners determine what value you *can* create. Your customer and needs and your competitors, on the other hand, tell you what value you *should* create. With these inputs we can now move on to the core element of your strategy: your value proposition. A good value proposition consists of three closely connected parts: 1) the *products or services* that you offer, 2) the *way* you get them to the customer, and 3) what they do to create *value* for the customer. The value proposition is the heart of your strategy, the linking pin between all elements of which it is composed.

6. **Revenue model.** *What you receive in return for your offer, from whom, how, and when.*
When you create value you probably also want to get something in return. This is reflected in the sixth element of strategy, your revenue model. In plain terms, your revenue model shows how your organization makes money. A good revenue model explains *who pays* (this could be people other than your customers, such as a sponsor), *for what* (for example, for owning the product or for just using it), *how much* (the price level), and *how* (such as paying in advance or a subscription). Don't take payment too literally here. As we saw in the definition of "sustainable" on page 11, it can also consist of information or any other type of goods.

7. **Risks & costs.** *What financial, social, and other risks and costs you bear and how you manage these.*
No strategy comes for free. Good strategy, therefore, makes clear what costs and risks there are and how the organization

deals with them. Costs can be predicted and controlled relatively well. They include financial but also other costs such as time, effort, pollution, or reputation damage. Risks, on the other hand, cannot be easily predicted or controlled. They reflect "potential costs," the bad things that could happen as a result of your strategy. Think of product risks, safety risks, technological risks, or financial risks.

8. **Values & goals.** *What you want, where you want to go, and what you find important.*
   Together, the first five elements explain how your organization creates value and the sixth and seventh element reflect what you get in return. These cover an important share of your strategy. However, these elements don't say anything about the organization itself yet. For that reason, we need two further elements that represent your organization's identity. The first are your values and goals. Values indicate what is important to you and your organization and what you stand for; the guiding principles the organization is based on. Goals reflect your organization's aspirations, its ambitions or objectives that express where it wants to be in the future.

9. **Organizational climate.** *What your culture and structure look like and what is special about them.*
   The second part of your identity is the organizational climate. This covers the structure and culture of the organization. The organizational *structure* is the way tasks are divided and coordinated. Think of the organization's chart, job descriptions, and the way things are communicated. The organizational *culture*, on the other hand, reflects the attitudes and behaviors that are characteristic of the organization. You find it in, for example, the organization's symbols, dress code, stories, or habits. The organizational climate is important for your strategy because it can be an important enabler or barrier. An innovative "boutique" strategy, for example, asks for quite a different climate than a large-volume, low-cost strategy.

10. **Trends & uncertainties.** *What happens around you that affects your organization and what uncertainties you face.*

    The tenth and last element of strategy concerns the relevant trends and uncertainties that are happening in the direct or broader environment of your organization. *Trends* are changes in your environment that are relatively clear and inevitable and that you will somehow have to deal with. You might think of increased automation or a shrinking market. *Uncertainties* are the changes in your environment with as yet unknown outcomes. Think of, for example, a new law that might or might not be passed and that will have a direct impact on your strategy.

THE TEN ELEMENTS IN A PICTURE: THE STRATEGY SKETCH

With ten elements, this is quite a list. But now you have all the key elements of strategy. Together, they give a much more detailed and concrete idea of the meaning of the term *strategy* than the definition gave. As a list though, it might still look somewhat unstructured. Inspired by the Business Model Canvas, I've developed a visual tool that combines the ten elements in a structured and coherent way and that will be used throughout this book: *the Strategy Sketch*.

The Strategy Sketch

7 Risks & Costs
6 Revenue Model
2 Partners | 1 Resources & Competences | 5 Value Proposition | 3 Customers & Needs | 4 Competitors
8 Values & Goals
9 Organizational Climate
10 Trends & Uncertainties

On the left-hand side of the Strategy Sketch we find the organization's *means*–its resources and competences and its partners. These tell you what value the organization is able to offer. On the other side we find the organization's *market*–its customers and needs and its competitors. These show you the kind of value that is being asked for. Together with strategy's core element–the value proposition, these elements show how the organization creates value.

> *"The Strategy Sketch: a visual tool that combines the ten elements of strategy in a structured and coherent way."*

Above the value proposition we see what the organization gets in return for the value it creates through its combination of revenue model and risks and costs. Below the value proposition we find the organization that is doing all of this and that drives and supports the value proposition–represented by its values and goals and its organizational climate.

Finally, around these nine elements we find the trends and uncertainties that form the wider context of the organization.

DEFINING STRATEGY GENERATION

Now that we have seen what strategy is and what it's composed of, we can move on to defining strategy generation (this section) and strategy execution (next section). I'll start by discussing the relationship between strategy generation and strategy execution and then move on to discussing the three key features of strategy generation.

THE RELATIONSHIP BETWEEN STRATEGY GENERATION AND STRATEGY EXECUTION

Strategy generation and strategy execution are two intertwined but different processes. Both are needed for a strategy to be successful, but they are also distinct. Simply put, strategy generation is about *developing ideas* and strategy execution is about *realizing* those ideas.

The most common way of seeing the relationship between them is to present them as two sequential stages in a process: you generate strategy first, and then execute it. While this is intuitive and easy to understand, I find it more useful to see strategy generation and strategy execution as two parallel processes (see the figure below). Strategy generation is a *conceptual* process in which strategy is thought up, imagined, talked about, etc. Strategy at this level exists in people's minds, and in words and pictures that can be shared. Strategy execution, on the other hand, is a process in which strategy is actually *realized* through people's actions and by doing something with "stuff"–technology, materials, buildings, etc.

The Relationship Between
Strategy Generation and Strategy Execution

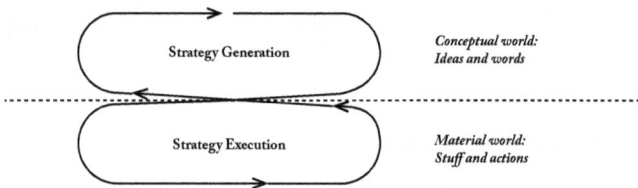

Strategy Generation — *Conceptual world: Ideas and words*

Strategy Execution — *Material world: Stuff and actions*

Strategy generation and strategy execution influence one another. This is important because it means that not only does strategy generation influence strategy execution, but also the other way around. Of course, strategy generation may come before strategy execution, and your organization might separate them into two stages. However, it's also possible that strategy execution precedes strategy generation–you might do something first and only later think about it and learn from it. And even if strategy execution comes formally after strategy generation in your organization, it still influences strategy generation: you will usually somehow take into account whether the strategy you generate can also be executed.

"Strategy generation and strategy execution are two intertwined but quite different processes."

KEY FEATURES OF STRATEGY GENERATION

When you engage in strategy generation, it's good to understand what kind of process you're getting yourself into, the kind of activities you'll mainly be doing. From reading the average strategy textbook, you might get the idea that strategy generation is primarily an analytical and rational process. Strategy generation as presented there typically relies heavily on information gathering, thorough analysis, systematic decision-making, and careful planning. If we want strategy generation to be practical though, we also need to take into account that strategy generation is a *creative*, *interactive*, and *emergent* process.

Strategy generation is creative. It's about using your imagination, intuition, and judgment to come up with original insights and ideas. You shouldn't over-rely on "objective" information and "rational" analysis but combine it with a good dose of your own and others' individual and subjective input. Since your competitors probably have access to the same "objective" information and use the same kind of "rational" analysis, only in this way can you expect to come up with something unique.

That strategy generation is creative also means that it's a process in which you *create* new things that weren't there before. This includes creating new products, services, customers, markets, and even creating (or at least influencing) your broader environment. Rather than making yourself over-dependent on your environment, try not taking it too seriously. Next to analyzing it, also try to influence it and focus on those actions that are within your own control rather than those that depend on where the environment might or might not go. This is often more useful than relying on some market research that might tell you whether there is a demand for your product or not. Expert entrepreneurs work this way, so why shouldn't you?

Finally, "creative" also means that you should try to have some fun during the strategy generation process. Of course, strategy is a serious matter for your organization, but if you can have some fun during this process it will boost your creativity and increase your chances for better outcomes.

> *"Expert entrepreneurs work this way, so why shouldn't you?"*

Strategy generation is interactive. If done well, strategy generation is an interactive process. From traditional books on strategy you might get the idea that you can strategize effectively by locking a few people up in a room with some models and a lot of information. I haven't seen this work very often or very well. If you want to be more successful, especially on a day-to-day basis, you should make your strategy generation process more interactive. Instead of relying on "hard" paper-based information, you might want to see the people around you as your main sources. They have worked for the organization for a while and maybe even much longer in the industry, so you can assume that they actually know a lot about it.

It's important to include people from within your organization (managers, staff, or other employees) and from outside (particularly customers and suppliers). After all, you need them to turn your strategy into practice, so why not include them early on? It can also help to deliberately include people who might present a very different or critical view. This increases variety and thereby the chance that you come up with unique and new ideas.

Strategy generation is emergent. Strategy generation is also an emergent process. It doesn't follow a strict linear step-by-step logic and usually leads you to a different place than you originally anticipated. So, although you might plan to go from A to B in a more or less straight line following the plan, the reality is that you might end up at place E because B doesn't exist, C didn't work out, or you stumbled unexpectedly at D. Since E could be a much better place than B, it's generally a good idea to embrace unexpected twists rather than systematically avoiding them.

Another way in which strategy generation is emergent is that it requires some trial and error. This doesn't mean you should just blindly try something new and see what happens. It means that rather than only trying to predict up front what will happen or what customers will need, you should also test your ideas in practice and learn from that. Based on what you learn you can then redirect and adjust your initial strategy.

> *"Strategy generation is as much about making adjustments and letting things go than about starting something new."*

The fact that strategy generation is emergent also means it's an ongoing process. Both strategy generation and strategy execution run the entire lifetime of an organization. Whatever new strategy you develop, there is usually a large part of the organization and the strategy that doesn't change, that follows an existing path. This is important–strategy generation is as much about making adjustments and letting things go as about starting something new. This is depicted in the following picture, which shows how strategy changes as a result of new ideas coming in and old ideas leaving.

Strategy as an Emergent Process

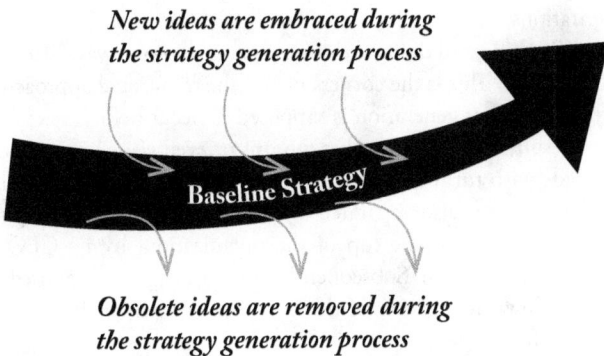

New ideas are embraced during the strategy generation process

Baseline Strategy

Obsolete ideas are removed during the strategy generation process

DEFINING STRATEGY EXECUTION

In essence, strategy execution means *doing* strategy. Given the definition of strategy above, strategy execution is the actual creation of unique and sustainable value. Strategy generation takes place in the conceptual world, focusing on ideas and aspirations. Of course, throughout the strategy generation process, these ideas are also confronted with the real world to assess and improve them. However, the main emphasis is still on generating a concrete idea about the new strategy. Strategy execution, on the other hand, happens in the material world. As such, it's about the actions and stuff involved in realizing strategy in practice. Along those lines, I define strategy execution as the process of closing the gaps between the actual and the aspired strategy.

> *"Strategy execution is the process of closing the gaps between the actual and the aspired strategy."*

STRATEGY EXECUTION AND THE GAP BETWEEN THINKING AND DOING

In many ways, strategy execution is about closing the gap between thinking and doing, between ideas and actions. What you aim for in strategy execution is to minimize the gap between the aspired strategy and the realized strategy without lowering your aspirations.

Thinking and doing are often separated in two ways. The first is over time. This is the cornerstone of the traditional approach to strategy, in that generation is supposed to occur before execution. As a result, it sometimes takes months or even years before a start is made with turning the strategy into practice. Second, thinking and doing are also separated within organizations. Strategy is often generated at the top of the organization, by its CEO or management team. Subsequently, the strategy is supposed to trickle down to the rest of the organization, which should then execute it.

This separation between thinking and doing over time and in organizations is one of the core reasons why there is so much failure in strategy. This book aims to help you close the gap between these two. As you'll see throughout this book, closing the gap implies an iterative process in which strategy generation and strategy execution go hand-in-hand and in which people from various levels and roles in the organization should be involved.

STRATEGY EXECUTION AS EMERGENT GAP CLOSING

Defining strategy execution as the process of closing the gap between the actual and the aspired strategy may, at first sight, seem like a fairly planned and static approach. Strategy, though, is inherently dynamic. While executing the strategy, important things may have changed inside or outside the organization, or you may have learned new things and want to adjust the strategy that you are trying to execute. To embrace such dynamics in the strategy execution process, it should be seen as a process of "emergent gap closing." The gaps that you have identified at the start will change during the execution process and new gaps will emerge.

A good metaphor for this process is driving a car in fog. You have an idea where to go, but you can only see a few car lengths ahead. Just like intersections, traffic lights and traffic appear while you are driving, so do new situations, challenges, and gaps appear during the strategy execution process. This means you have to adapt to the things that you're facing while on your way. It may even mean you have to change course, stop for a while, or look for a different destination.

To think about this process of emergent gap closing more systematically, we can make a distinction between three types of gaps that you will encounter during strategy execution.

1. **Manifest gaps.** These are the gaps you can identify upfront once you have generated a strategy and mapped out the differences between the actual and the aspired strategy. For example, your new strategy requires technology X, which you currently don't have and is rather obvious you need to acquire.
2. **Latent gaps.** These are gaps that you could have identified upfront, but that you haven't. They were already present, but you just didn't see them. An example is that you thought you had the competences to enter a new market but find out that in practice you don't have them.
3. **New gaps.** These gaps weren't there at the time you generated your strategy, and they are a result of unforeseen changes within or outside of the organization. Examples

are the unexpected resignation of key people or a sudden steep increase in the price of the materials you need.

At the start of the strategy execution process, you are only aware of the first type of gap. Throughout the strategy generation process, you must keep abreast of changes and take into account the possibility that latent and new gaps could emerge. The strategy process outlined in this book is designed to support you in this.

"Strategy making is like driving a car in fog.
You have an idea where to go,
but you can only see a few car lengths ahead."

STRATEGY AS A NINE-STEP PROCESS

Having seen some of the key characteristics of strategy generation and strategy execution, we can now move on to a more detailed look at the steps of the strategy process. From the literature and interactions with entrepreneurs, managers, and executives, I have extracted five key steps that cover the strategy generation process and four steps covering strategy execution.

Step 1. Activating key stakeholders. *Making key persons in the organization receptive to new strategy and mobilizing the resources needed for strategy generation.*
At this first step, you make your organization ready for new strategy so that the strategy generation process is not doomed to fail before it actually starts. An important reason for strategic failure is that organizations don't pay sufficient attention to strategy. They are so invested in strategy execution or in their day-to-day work that they fail to engage in strategy generation on time or with sufficient drive and ambition. In this case, strategy generation needs to start with making the organization strategically active and getting it from strategy execution mode into a strategy generation mode. Obviously, if your "organization" is just you, or if people are already convinced, you can skip this step. In all other cases, though, it's crucial. This step is discussed in Chapter 3.

Step 2. Mapping strategy. *Identifying the organization's current strategy by describing it on the basis of its ten core elements.*

At this step you develop an understanding of the organization's current strategy by mapping it onto all ten elements of the Strategy Sketch. This is not so much about mapping the formal strategy that has been written down, but rather the actual and more detailed strategy as lived by the organization–what it currently does. This step is pertinently *not* meant to restrict strategy generation to what is already there or to small incremental changes. However, without a proper understanding of the organization's status quo, it's hard to really innovate or improve it. This step is discussed in Chapter 4.

Step 3. Assessing strategy. *Judging and testing the quality of the organization's strategy against relevant criteria.*

At this step, you assess your strategy in order to diagnose its quality and to identify its strengths and weaknesses. You judge and test how good your strategy is and where it can or should be improved. This step serves two roles. First, it can be an assessment of your current strategy. As such, it's a good starting point for revealing how your strategy could be improved at the next step. Second, it can also be an assessment of your newly generated strategy. As such, it serves as a judgment of the quality of the new strategy and its chances for success. This step is discussed in Chapter 5.

Step 4. Innovating strategy. *Renewing and redesigning the organization's strategy through incremental or radical innovation.*

At this fourth step you start the actual generation of new strategy. Based on the existing strategy, explicitly deviating from it, or starting from scratch, this step focuses on generating new, better, different, or innovative ideas for your strategy. As such, it's the most creative step of the strategy generation process. Next to developing new ideas, this step also explicitly looks at what parts of your existing strategy should be kept and what parts should be left behind. The result of this step is a second complete Strategy Sketch that describes your future strategy along all its ten elements. This step is discussed in Chapter 6.

Step 5. Formulating strategy. *Capturing the organization's strategy in words and pictures that can be understood by the target audience.*
At this last step of strategy generation you turn your strategy into a form that can be communicated to others. This is an essential step, as a strategy can only be really effective when formulated in a clear and comprehensible manner. This last step forms a temporary closure of the strategy generation process. As explained above, strategy generation and execution are ongoing processes that are inextricably linked. However, at some point in time, you need to stop generating new ideas and focus on their execution. This step is discussed in Chapter 7.

Step 6. Bridging gaps. *Identifying the gaps between your current and your aspired strategy and defining projects and tasks to bridge them.*
The first step of strategy execution is identifying the differences between your current and your new strategy. If you have followed the five steps for strategy generation, this is a straightforward step. You compare the Strategy Sketches for both situations (steps 2 and 4) and identify the gaps between them along all ten elements. Subsequently, you define what you can do to bridge the gaps. The result of this step is a *Strategy Backlog*–a list of projects and tasks to be executed. This step is discussed in Chapter 8.

Step 7. Organizing strategy. *Identifying the most important organizational deficiencies and defining projects and tasks to solve them.*
Executing a strategy often requires substantial changes in the organization. Therefore, the second step of strategy execution is to evaluate your organization and its fitness for executing the strategy. Using a framework comparable to the Strategy Sketch– the Organizational Map–you assess your organization to identify those areas where changes are necessary. Similar to step 6, you define projects and tasks, which you add to your Strategy Backlog. This step is discussed in Chapter 9.

Step 8. Planning strategy. *Developing and committing to a dynamic, prioritized course of action and a way of working for closing the gap between the actual and the aspired strategy.*
In this eighth step, the Strategy Backlog from steps 6 and 7 is turned into an action plan that contains the most important

projects and tasks for the short and medium-term and to which the organization commits. This step includes completing your Strategy Backlog, prioritizing actions, creating a "realization rhythm," establishing the execution team, and setting up a way of communicating. This step is discussed in Chapter 10.

Step 9. Realizing strategy. *Effecting the aspired strategy by putting the execution plan into action and managing relevance, progress, and emotions over time.*

In this last step, based on your prioritization, you turn your strategy into action, starting with those tasks that have the highest priority. To manage the process and keep it up to date, you actively track whether the strategy that was generated is still the right strategy to execute, whether you are making sufficient progress, and whether people are still on board. This step is discussed in Chapter 11.

This nine-step process is depicted in the figure below. It shows the interconnectedness of strategy generation and strategy execution.

The Strategy Process

DELIBERATION AND EMERGENCE: A THREE-CYCLE VIEW OF STRATEGY

I mentioned several times that strategy is an iterative, emergent process of constant adjustment. The circles in the figure above illustrate this point. At the same time though, strategy is also a deliberate and stepwise process, which is illustrated by splitting up the process into two phases and nine steps with a logical order. So, strategy is both deliberate and emergent, but how does this work in practice? To understand the answer, it's helpful to see strategy as a "deliberately emergent" process consisting of three interrelated cycles.

> *"Strategy is a deliberately emergent process consisting of three interrelated cycles."*

The first cycle is the five-step strategy generation cycle. It starts deliberately with the activation step triggering the organization to think about strategy and the possibility to change or renew it. The next three steps form an iterative process in which new strategy emerges through a procedure of mapping, assessing, and innovating. This process is emergent because it's designed to benefit from unexpected events or unanticipated ideas. This first cycle is reflected in the upper half of the figure above.

The second cycle is formed by the four steps of strategy execution presented above. It also starts deliberately with the formulated strategy that results from the strategy generation stage. After that, it's a highly iterative process of bridging, organizing, planning, and realizing the strategy. Through this process, strategy is executed in a step-by-step incremental manner. This cycle is presented in the lower half of the figure above.

Finally, we have the overall cycle in which strategy generation and strategy execution come together. This cycle is deliberate since it starts with strategy generation and then moves on to strategy execution. It's also emergent since strategy execution feeds into strategy generation as well; this indicates that during execution you may need to change the strategy in ways that were originally unintended. Or you may develop or stumble upon ideas that make an even better strategy possible.

Maybe you wonder why we need three cycles and why just one would not be enough. You might, for example, be familiar with the Plan-Do-Check-Act process, the lean startup approach to entrepreneurship, the scrum approach to project management, or the rapid prototyping approach to innovation. These approaches are mostly based on a single cycle in which a goal, idea, or product feature is quickly implemented and tested in practice. The insights of these iterative approaches are useful. However, generating and executing a strategy involves much more than pivoting around a goal, idea, or product.

If you were just focusing on the value proposition, such approaches could work. You would come up with a new value proposition and test and adjust it in practice. However, there are nine additional elements of strategy that you need to consider as well and an organization that needs to be changed. This would make it a costly exercise if you were to try immediately to execute the strategy and test it, rather than first putting a little more thought into it. It would mean, for example, that you would make investments before you were confident your strategy was worth executing. Iterating during strategy generation is usually much cheaper in terms of effort, time, and money because you are still only changing an idea. This makes a three-cycle approach favorable over a one-cycle approach.

THE RIGHT MINDSET: TEN MOTTOS

To generate and execute strategy successfully, it's not only important to follow the right steps, as that could too easily result in following the approach dogmatically. It's at least as important to have the right mindset. Only with the right mindset can you truly appreciate the approach. It can be described along the following ten key mottos.

MOTTO 1. JUST DO IT

For years, Nike's tagline has been "Just Do It." This captures exactly the kind of mindset needed for strategy: a focus on action rather than on endless deliberation. Management gurus such as Robert Waterman, Tom Peters, Jim Collins, and Rosabeth Moss Kanter have all found in their research that organizations with this "just do it" mentality perform much better than others. Accordingly, they argue that there is nothing worse than an organization that suffers "paralysis by analysis"–that is, stagnating because any decision is postponed until "all" necessary information is available to make the decision. This view applies to strategy as well: it's better to do *something* rather than wait and do *nothing* because you don't know what to do.

MOTTO 2. PERFECT IS THE ENEMY OF GOOD

In his bestselling book *Good to Great*, Jim Collins argues that "good is the enemy of great." He says that many organizations tend to settle for something that is good enough or okay rather than trying to achieve something really great. In that way, *good* gets in the way of *great*. The opposite, however, is true as well. Aiming for something great–especially if it's the "perfect" strategy–can get in the way of executing good strategy. Striving for perfection is like trying to find the pot of gold at the end of the rainbow; it will absorb a lot of effort, but it won't happen. Therefore, it's useful to keep the "Pareto principle," better known as the 80/20 rule, in mind: 80% of the outcomes can be achieved by 20% of the effort. The exact percentages don't matter, but there is much wisdom in this rule. Focusing on achieving 80% rather than 100% can save you a lot of time, money, and effort that can be spent on other things, while still getting good results.

"Striving for perfection is like trying to find the pot of gold at the end of the rainbow."

MOTTO 3. YOU CAN'T HAVE IT BOTH WAYS

In his other bestselling book *Built to Last*, Collins, together with Jerry Porras, tells us that you shouldn't focus on making choices between A and B, but on realizing both. Thus, you should focus on the long term *and* the short term, change *and* stability, and purpose *and* profit. Kim and Mauborgne, in their work on "blue ocean strategy," argue the same: create products that have the best price *and* the highest added value. That's all nice, but in practice, you'll need to make trade-offs all the time. Of course it's good to try to achieve as much as possible. At any given point in time though, you most likely don't have the luxury (time, money, people) to get everything you want. Instead, you have to set priorities and make tough decisions about what to do and what not to do.

MOTTO 4. THERE ARE MANY WAYS TO SKIN A CAT

A fourth thing to keep in mind is that there is no single best strategy or approach that works universally. There is no golden recipe for successful strategy generation or execution and thus your creativity is needed. This is exactly why this book doesn't offer a simple recipe or best practices that will lead you to "guaranteed" success. There is *no such thing*. Instead, the main approach of this book is to show you all relevant aspects of strategy and provide you with ideas and tools for using them. In this way, you can use the book as a rich source for choosing ideas, solutions, and mechanisms for making strategy that works in your specific context. This enables you to think of alternative solutions and helps you develop your own, personal approach to strategy.

MOTTO 5. FIND 10,000 WAYS THAT WON'T WORK

Strategy requires an open mind and eagerness to learn and experiment; not only should you avoid striving for the single best and perfect strategy, but you should also actively try out new things you may not be so certain about. Thomas Edison (the inventor of the light bulb and about 1,000 other things) had a nice way of saying this: "I have not failed. I've just found 10,000 ways that won't work." This is exactly the kind of mindset needed for strategy in today's dynamic world, with no fear of failure and even a willingness to fail deliberately, albeit quickly and cheaply. Rather than sitting behind your desk or discussing things in a meeting room, successful strategy today requires that you put things to the test, learn from it, and adjust.

MOTTO 6. PERSIST BY PULLING OUT

Most strategy literature assumes that organizations and the world in general are rather malleable. This implies that organizations and environments can be designed and changed to your liking so that they are exactly as you need them to be for your successful strategy. Consequently, the advice is to persist and make it happen and "don't accept no for an answer." While I am strongly in favor of persistence and would definitely encourage you to challenge the "not possibles" you may face, you should also be realistic and flexible. Be prepared to pull out or change the strategy you're pursuing once you determine it's not feasible. You might perceive this as weak. But expert entrepreneurs also work in this way: they would rather change their goals than chase ones they can't achieve. So you're in good company! And keep in mind that giving up a particular line of action doesn't mean you're quitting. On the contrary, it means that you persist, but challenge your initial assumptions and look for alternative ways for unique and sustainable value creation.

MOTTO 7. SPEED UP BY TAKING IT SLOW

There is a paradox in many strategy efforts: managers' anxiety to quickly move to strategy execution leads to the actual execution taking much longer than needed. Often managers move directly from a rather abstract, newly-formulated strategic direction to detailed project planning. This doesn't work, and this is exactly the reason why I focused so much on generating *executable* strategy along the ten elements of the Strategy Sketch. Rather than rushing into execution, you should have a concrete idea of your strategy–otherwise, how do you know what to execute? You might think this is a bit at odds with the previous mottos, which emphasize action rather than deliberation. The thing I'm highlighting here, however, is that any action is more likely to be productive if it's clear where it fits into the strategy.

MOTTO 8. THE POWER OF SIMPLICITY

Strategy is complex, in both its generation and its execution. As seen at the beginning of this chapter, strategy includes no less than ten core elements which all need to be in place and mostly aligned for daily success. As you'll see in Chapter 9, strategy execution involves another ten organizational elements to take into account. Strategy is indeed complex, and it makes no sense to pretend it isn't. But over-complexity is also a problem. Strategy is often turned into complicated projects or programs that are hard to manage, monitor, and execute. Such complexity results from trying to develop a complete strategy and an execution plan upfront before one actually starts executing. The approach in this book is to keep it simple and focus on the most important things and simple action plans. You should execute these first, and only then make new ones.

MOTTO 9. WE'RE IN THIS TOGETHER

Traditionally, strategy is a top-down activity: it's generated at the top and executed further down in the organization. However, good strategy affects the entire organization, and it requires contributions from all over the organization. Obviously, people from all over the organization should be involved. This does not mean that strategy should be made from the bottom up, as that would suggest a democratic approach to strategy that misses the point. It does mean, though, that strategy is a collaborative process in which people from different levels and roles and with different views and experience contribute from their own particular perspective. This implies that the "bottom" of the organization is also involved in strategy generation and that the "top" is also included in strategy execution. As research shows, such a collaborative approach leads to strategy that is better in terms of quality and easier to execute because people want it.

MOTTO 10. NO PLACE FOR HIPPOS

The final motto concerns the kind of leadership required. As referred to above, the approach of this book doesn't align well with a traditional top-down view on leadership. What is required is a modest, serving kind of leadership in which the leaders' primary task is to do whatever it takes to get the best out of the organization. Of course, you have to pursue your views and make tough decisions if necessary, or else you are not a leader. However, you should also acknowledge and embrace the possibility that others *might know better* and get out of their way if that helps make progress. There is no place for HiPPOs. A *HiPPO* is someone who believes that the Highest Paid Person's Opinion is all that counts. HiPPOs are leaders who are so self-assured that they think their ideas and instincts are superior to anyone else's and any counterevidence. If you are one, you need to urge yourself to adopt a different leadership mindset. I am pleased to refer you to page 329 of the "Conclusion" for this.

IN SUM: A PHILOSOPHY OF PRAGMATISM

The mindset captured in these ten mottos can be best summarized as a *pragmatic* mindset. It focuses on results and getting things done, rather than finding and aiming for the best possible strategy. Pragmatism is not just a mindset. It's an entire philosophy, a relatively young one that developed in the late nineteenth century in the United States. It's mainly a response to overly rationalistic "truth"-seeking philosophies that are dominant in Western thinking. It's also an attempt to bridge the gap between thinking and doing, between ideas and actions.

> *"By its focus on getting things done and on reconnecting thinking and doing, pragmatism provides a productive way out."*

By its focus on information gathering, analysis, and planning, the dominant approach to strategy is rather rationalistic and truth-seeking. And, as argued above, one of the key problems in strategy is exactly the disconnect between thinking and doing. By its focus on getting things done and on reconnecting thinking and doing, pragmatism provides a productive way out of this conundrum and is a useful stream of philosophy to serve as a basis for this handbook.

STRATEGY AS A PARTICIPATIVE PROCESS

At its heart, strategy is a *people* process. Even though the emphasis is often on the analytical side, at the end of the day it's *people* who drive the process, interpret how things are, come up with ideas for the future, and execute the strategy. I favor a participative approach to strategy making, in which a wide range of people is involved throughout the process. I will explain why and describe with whom and how it can be done.

WHY? THE IMPORTANCE OF PARTICIPATION

The fact that strategy is traditionally generated at the top of the organization suggests that the more complex and important a decision is, the fewer people should be involved. If you think about it, this doesn't make sense. Wouldn't it be far more logical that, the more complex and important something is, the *more* people should be involved? Strategy, especially in today's dynamic times, is complex and important. Furthermore, with the fast changes around us, people's expertise is often the only available source that we can rely on because "hard" data is lacking. I can only conclude that strategy making needs to be participative to be successful because you simply need all the expertise available.

Research supports this conclusion. Both in practice and in the literature, there is much dispute about the advantages and disadvantages of participation in strategy making. Participation, it's argued, can lead to better strategies and more commitment, but also to delays, political games, and unproductive compromises. Empirical research, however, is clear about it: the advantages are real, while the disadvantages are not. As it turns out, if done well, participation even results in faster, less political, and less compromised strategy making.

> *"Empirical research is clear about participation: the advantages are real; the disadvantages are not."*

Participation enables strategy making to be more successful in three important ways: better strategy, smoother execution, and competence development.

1. **Better strategy.** The more people who participate, the bigger the knowledge base to tap and the more different perspectives can be taken into account. Especially if people have different types of expertise and experience, involving them in strategy making leads to

more and better ideas. It also reduces the likelihood of narrow-minded groupthink. And, by having people from different parts of the organization collaborate, participation also creates more coherent and cohesive strategy.

2. **Smoother execution.** For effective execution, it's crucial that people *want* to execute a strategy; because people have had their say in the process, participation significantly increases the chances that they will. This is especially the case if they agree with the strategy and feel a bit of co-ownership: it is *their* strategy too. But even if they disagree with the outcome, they'll at least feel that the strategy process has been fair by involving people throughout the organization.

3. **Competence development.** Through participating in the strategy process, people develop their strategic competences. They "learn by doing" and on the way they become better at generating and executing strategy. Furthermore, the organization itself enhances its strategic competence by going through the strategy process collectively. In a world full of changes and uncertainties, such strategic competence can be a significant source of competitive advantages.

WHO? PARTICIPANTS IN THE STRATEGY PROCESS

As a starting point for deciding who should be involved in the strategy process, it's important that both people from the top and people from other parts of the organization participate in strategy generation and execution. This means that people from throughout the organization are involved in strategy generation so that their expertise and needs are taken into account. It also means that people from the top are involved in strategy execution. It's their responsibility to show the organization's commitment to the strategy and take the lead in the transformation. Simply delegating execution to a process or project manager does not work.

The approach outlined in this book works best if strategy generation and strategy execution are guided by a heterogeneous team of different people from within (and sometimes outside) the organization. Having experimented with various team sizes and compositions, I came to the following rules of thumb.

- **Team size.** A team size of about ten (plus or minus five) was found to be most appropriate. With a team size of ten people, a good balance was found between efficiency and quality. With a substantially lower number, quality decreases because there are too few perspectives and too limited a knowledge base. With a substantially higher number, the process becomes inefficient. If you really need to include more people, it makes more sense to split them into separate teams to involve them in selective parts of the process.

- **Member requirements.** In deciding who should be on the team, it's useful to include people who are both *vocal* and *influential* in the organization. They need to be vocal because they need to be able to express their views and actively contribute to discussions. They need to be influential–formally or informally–because they will have to take the lead in executing the strategy.

- **Team heterogeneity.** Teams should be heterogeneous. Ideally, they consist of a mix of disciplines, levels, experience, and attitudes.
    - *Disciplines.* All relevant disciplines in the organization, such as sales, production, and engineering are needed.
    - *Levels.* Representatives of all relevant management levels should join since all are needed for realizing the strategy.
    - *Experience.* You need people with different backgrounds and levels of experience who can bring in different perspectives.
    - *Attitudes.* A mix of enthusiasts and critics is desired to generate the necessary sharpness and help create a strategy that is both analytically sound and socially feasible.

Next to internal team members, external people can play an important role. Three roles are particularly relevant: facilitators, experts, and stakeholders.

- **Facilitators.** To effectively lead the process, you need external facilitators or internal dedicated strategy facilitators with no other role in the organization. Ideally, you should have two of them to make sure process, content, and group dynamics are managed.
- **Experts.** It can be beneficial to include one or a few experts in the process. Typically, these are knowledgeable about a specific topic that can inspire the organization to think beyond their current way of working. Generally, they only need to participate in the specific sessions where their expertise makes a difference.
- **Stakeholders.** It can be fruitful to involve stakeholders, such as customers and suppliers, in selected stages of the process. They have their own specific expertise and perspective on the situation. Furthermore, since they will be affected by a change in strategy, fruitful collaboration will increase the probability of success for everyone involved.

HOW? STRATEGY MAKING AS JOINT PROBLEM SOLVING

My preferred and recommended way of working is through team-based interactive sessions. With the team suggested above, you go through a series of half-day or full-day sessions in which together you map, assess, innovate, formulate, bridge, organize, and plan strategy. These sessions should be followed by shorter follow-up meetings during realization. Thus, the strategy is not generated by the board, management team, or external consultants, but by the various members of the team together. Also, strategy execution is not delegated to a project manager but led by a strategy team with strong involvement of the leaders in the organization.

When engaging in such a series of sessions, it's key to have people participate in an effective way. Let me first summarize what this *does not* mean.

- Participation does not mean democratic strategy making, where the people who participate also decide the strategy. This could be the case, but this is not needed and often not recommended. It's still mostly leaders who make key decisions.
- Participation does not mean talking with everybody about the strategy as a whole. Because everyone has their specific role in the organization, most people don't have the information necessary to do that. Having everyone talk about the strategy as a whole would just lead to an ill-informed, overly-generic discussion.
- Participation does not mean turning strategy into a battle in which everyone fights for themselves. Of course, everyone has their own interest, needs, and wants. This is good because it means that people will be engaged. However, the energy this creates needs to be channeled towards collaboration, not towards fights.

Flipping these descriptions of what participation is not shows what it should be: a productive dialogue focused on joint problem solving. A productive dialogue is a conversation in which the team collaborates on generating and executing strategy with the organization's interest in mind; it's a dialogue in the sense that people listen to each other and focus on commonalities rather than differences. This dialogue becomes productive if everyone brings in their specific expertise and views. Rather than having people talk about the strategy in general, they talk about what it means for them in their role in the organization, and how they see the ten elements of strategy and organization from their perspective.

> *"Strategy making should be a productive dialogue focused on joint problem solving."*

The focus on joint problem solving is key. To avoid people taking positions, it's crucial that the dialogue focuses on existing problems, on the improvements that can be made, and on how to realize these improvements together. An effective way to achieve this is to clearly separate ideas from decisions throughout the strategy process. As long as people know that what they talk about is still just ideas, they'll be quite willing to contribute productively. Once decisions are being made, though, their own interests start interfering. This is one of the main reasons why the first two steps of strategy execution (bridging and organizing) focus on suggesting possible projects and tasks, and the last two steps (planning and realizing) on making decisions and commitments. This takes the politics out of the first two steps.

Making strategy in this way asks for an atmosphere of trust and transparency. You want people to be honest, and you want all issues and challenges on the table–especially the tough and nasty ones. This approach requires a particular type of leadership. Not the traditional directive leadership or charismatic visionary leadership, but a more servant type of leadership. At the end of the book, I return to this point. But let's first go through the steps of the strategy process in the next nine chapters.

INTRODUCING THE FOUR EXAMPLES

Throughout the book I turn to four example organizations to illustrate all the elements and steps of strategy generation and execution. In order to anonymize them, all four are based on a mix of real organizations plus a bit of fantasy to fill in the details. Together, they cover a broad variety of organizations: large and small, young and old, product-based and service-based, and for-profit and non-profit. In this way, there should always be one or two that you can relate to.

I've chosen four "normal" organizations as examples. It might well be inspirational to use exceptional examples such as Apple, Tesla, Google, or Starbucks. However, examples that are closer to the everyday practice of most organizations are easier to translate into your own situation and as such are more helpful. The following four organizations will be our companions for the rest of the book.

Macman–the solid machine manufacturer
Size: 223 people   **Turnover:** € 26 million   **Age:** 52 years
Main product: Steel processing machines (2 large customers)
Led by: Director Ivo and a management team of 4

Strategic challenge: What could be our next big idea? Macman has done well with its current line of steel bending and cutting machines. The market is shrinking though, and the company needs an alternative core product to rely on.

Hospicare–the businesslike general hospital
Size: 4412 people **Turnover:** € 358 million **Age:** 31 years
Main product: General health care (1109 beds)
Led by: A 4-person board of directors with Ingrid as chairman
Strategic challenge: How to compete in a changing market? Hospicare has long provided general health care, just like other general hospitals. Changes in regulations and increasing competition ask for specialization and choices.

GoforIT–the fast growing IT new venture
Size: 21 people   **Turnover:** € 2.3 million **Age:** 4 years
Main product: Online financial software and apps
Led by: Frank (commercial) and Liu (technology)
Strategic challenge: How to grow in a sustainable manner? GoforIT has so far mainly relied on enthusiasm and creativity. Things are going very well now but to grow further they need more structure in everything they do.

Comcom–the freelance communication advisor
Size: 1   **Turnover:** € 50 thousand   **Age:** 13 years
Main product: Communication plans, PR, and text writing
Led by: Anisha
Strategic challenge: How to grow and at the same time enjoy work more? Anisha wants to remain on her own and faces two strategic challenges: how to distinguish herself from others and how to increase revenue and impact without simply working more.

PART II

STRATEGY GENERATION

3

STEP 1: ACTIVATING KEY STAKEHOLDERS

T his chapter presents the first step of the strategy generation
process: activating key stakeholders. It explains what
this step entails and why it's needed. It also presents six
activation tactics that you can use to successfully perform it.

> **Activating Key Stakeholders** = Making key persons in the
> organization receptive to new strategy and mobilizing the
> resources needed for strategy generation.

THE ACTIVATION CHALLENGE

The first step of the strategy process is activating key stakeholders in
the organization. Key stakeholders are people in the organization
that have a big say in whether a new strategy will be adopted or not,
and whether the organization will engage in strategy generation in
the first place. You can think of the owners, the CEO, the (rest
of the) board, the management team, or anyone else who makes
key decisions for the organization or has an influential role in the
process. At this step you try to convince these people to remain
open-minded and motivated during a process of new strategy
generation. As such, this step helps you make them receptive

to new strategy and mobilize the resources needed for strategy generation.

In most organizations this step is necessary initially because the development of new strategy is far from automatic. There is often a tendency not to pay sufficient attention to strategy generation, or to start too late. If in your organization the key stakeholders are already convinced (or if you're just on your own), you could probably skip this step. In all other cases though, it's essential as a start of the strategy generation process.

What you are trying to do at this step is to turn an organization that is strategically inactive and primarily concerned with strategy execution into one that is strategically active and also engaged in strategy generation. In other words, it helps break out of the strategy execution cycle into a strategy generation cycle.

The Activation Challenge: Breaking Out of the Strategy Execution Cycle

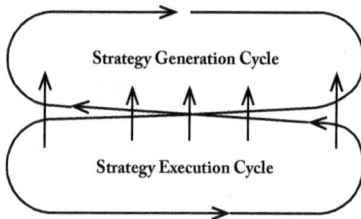

The strategy execution cycle is characterized by a focus on the short term and by being primarily concerned with running the organization and performing its day-to-day activities. It also includes efforts to make these activities more efficient (or "lean"), faultless (through quality management initiatives and continuous improvement), and cheaper (by cost-cutting, automation, standardization, and so forth). All these activities are important for an organization since they enable it to perform and improve its primary activities.

However, there is a limit to what can be done in terms of efficiency, quality, and costs. At some point in time further improvement along this line can only be marginal or close to zero. It's often at that point that organizations start realizing they need to try something new and change their strategy. And often this is too late since there is no time or money left and there are no suitable people available to engage in a strategy generation process. Activation is needed to avoid these situations and to make sure that the organization starts thinking about new strategy on time and with sufficient drive and ambition.

"Make sure the organization starts thinking about new strategy on time and with sufficient drive and ambition."

EXCUSES AND CAUSES FOR STRATEGIC INACTIVITY

To understand how you can activate your organization so that it starts engaging in strategy generation, it's useful to first get a sense of the reasons why organizations are strategically inactive. We can divide them into common but invalid excuses, and genuine but avoidable causes.

COMMON (BUT INVALID) EXCUSES FOR STRATEGY INACTIVITY

It's quite easy to find excuses to avoid engaging in strategy generation. Over the past years I've heard many of them from CEOs, managers, and entrepreneurs that show how they resist. The following ten are my favorites.

1. **No time. Too busy with running the business.**
   Invalid because this simply means setting the wrong priorities. Of course it's attractive to focus on the short term only, but if there's anything that research shows, it's that organizations that also give priority to strategic innovation perform better.

2. **No money. We have a crisis and must cut costs first.**
   Invalid for the same reason. It just shows that the organization has set the wrong priorities in the past and is now stuck in day-to-

day work. Usually, the crisis itself is a result of this and, although attractive, it cannot be attributed to external forces. Of course times may be difficult, but at the end only the organization itself can do something about it, so blaming others is of no use.

3. **No use. We're at the mercy of what happens around us.**
   Invalid because it victimizes the organization and underestimates its power and autonomy. Of course you depend on your environment. But you can influence it as well, even in highly regulated industries such as health care or banking. You always have some freedom in choosing your environment and in doing things differently from others.

4. **Not allowed. Headquarters or my boss doesn't allow us.**
   Invalid because this victimizes the person saying it. Of course, some organizations provide little room for creativity and strategic thinking through strict rules and regulations. However, usually this excuse exaggerates the strictness of the rules and regulations. We can assume that they were set for the benefit of the organization. But if breaking them helps more, there is a good chance you will get more room.

5. **No need. We are doing fine without strategy.**
   Invalid because it isn't true. Every organization has a strategy. Whether you are aware of it, though, is another question. The organization's strategy might not have been written down, but if you look at what the organization does today and what kind of decisions were made in the past, you can extract what its factual strategy is. This is why the next step (mapping strategy) is so important, as it gives insight into the current, actual strategy of the organization.

6. **Too small. Strategy is for big firms, not for us.**
   Invalid because it's nonsense. Strategy is for every organization, including one-person businesses and startups. It's true that most strategy models and theories have been developed with large firms in mind. This, though, does not mean strategy is not relevant for small organizations. It

doesn't even mean these models are not applicable; the large majority of them are.

7. **Not applicable. We are a non-profit organization.**
Invalid for a similar reason. Whether an organization is profit-oriented or not doesn't say anything about the relevance of strategy. In order to be successful, non-profits must also earn money and think about all ten elements of the Strategy Sketch. Only if there is no competition at all and customers are forced to buy your products and services is your organization in a position where strategy is not relevant. These cases are rare, though.

8. **Done that. We tried it, but it didn't work.**
Invalid because it says more about the strategic capabilities of the organization than about the importance or applicability of strategy itself. It also signals a lack of perseverance. Okay, things might not have worked out well the first, second, or third time, but failure is unavoidable, and rather than giving up it should be taken as a learning experience.

9. **Too abstract. Strategy is too much blah blah.**
Invalid because it only says something about how strategy is perceived, not about what strategy is actually about. I understand this excuse, for strategy is often mystified and made bigger than it is and many strategy tools and approaches are rather abstract. However, this should not distract you from the fact that strategy is essential. I hope to show in this book that it can be very practical and concrete too.

10. **No benefit. We don't need extensive plans.**
Invalid because this only concerns a particular way of dealing with strategy, not strategy in general. I certainly agree that meticulous plans are mostly not very useful, but this doesn't mean strategy itself is not useful. It just means that we need to find an effective way of strategy generation that doesn't rely on extensive plans.

Most of these excuses are either reasons not to engage in *bad* strategy or just faulty reasons overall. As I hope to have shown though, they are *not* reasons to not engage in *good* strategy.

> *"Both the excuses for strategic inactivity and its causes can be overcome."*

GENUINE (BUT AVOIDABLE) CAUSES OF STRATEGIC INACTIVITY

That we find so many excuses for not engaging in strategy is not surprising. There are strong forces at play that are in favor of keeping things as they are. Generally, people and organizations have a tendency to go "back to normal" and stay there as long as possible. Like an object that you throw in one direction, people and organizations tend to stay on the course they are on as long as there are no active impulses to change that course. In strategy there are many organizational and psychological factors that cause this tendency. Key organizational ones include path dependence, success trap, and performance delay.

- *Path dependence.* Past strategies have led to the organization's current processes, technology, culture, and so forth. These cannot be easily changed.
- *Success trap.* Once things go well, there seems no reason to change. Success even fosters investing more in what the organization already does.
- *Performance delay.* Today's performance is a result of yesterday's strategy. Signals that things may go worse come with a delay.

While these organizational causes of strategic inactivity may be strong, they can be overcome with a reasonable dose of common sense. Just being aware of them might already be sufficient because you can then take them into account. Psychological causes of inactivity, though, are harder to deal with, as they relate directly to the way people think. Rationally, the odds are obvious: strategy is key to every organization's long-term health.

So, if we were all rational, organizations would do much more about strategy and this step would not be necessary. However, as decades of research in cognitive psychology show, we have all kinds of nonrational biases that influence our decisions—and that means strategy often does not get the attention it deserves. Some of the important psychological causes of inactivity are uncertainty avoidance, confirmation bias, personal loss, hubris and losing face, conformation, and escalation of commitment.

- *Uncertainty avoidance.* People generally have a fear of the unknown and naturally prefer to keep things as they are.
- *Confirmation bias.* People generally see what they like to see. They might be overoptimistic about the success and potential of the organization's current strategy.
- *Personal loss.* People have obtained particular positions that they like to keep. New strategy might harm those positions; they may resist if they lose more than they gain.
- *Hubris and losing face.* Admitting that new strategy is needed may feel like admitting you were wrong—especially if you're late in initiating new strategy or the creator of the current strategy.
- *Conformation.* People generally like to do what others do—within the organization or in the industry. If this is the way things are apparently done, why change?
- *Escalation of commitment.* People like to be consistent. Once on a particular track, they are inclined to keep on investing in it—despite evidence that change is better.

Together, these organizational and psychological causes of inactivity make strategy a rather unlikely phenomenon to happen automatically in the average organization. But the good news is that there are several things you can do to overcome this. In the following pages you will find six activation tactics that you can use for this.

Activation tactic	What it does
1. Open people's minds	Making new strategy *imaginable*
2. Reveal the urgency	Making new strategy *unavoidable*
3. Sell the benefits	Making new strategy *advantageous*
4. Take away risks	Making new strategy *feasible*
5. Just start	Making new strategy *happen*
6. Enforce action	Making new strategy *mandatory*

ACTIVATION TACTIC 1. OPEN PEOPLE'S MINDS

The first activation tactic is making strategy *imaginable* by opening people's minds. The aim of this tactic is to take away the main barriers to imagination by challenging people's taken-for-granted ideas and assumptions. What you are trying to do with this tactic is to create awareness that things could be different from what they are. This is especially relevant if people have worked for a long time in one industry, for one organization, or in one function. There are several ways to do this.

> *"Take away the main barriers to imagination by challenging people's taken-for-granted ideas and assumptions."*

1. Ask why the organization does what it does

You want to show people that it's not self-evident or even logical that the organization does what it does. One way is looking back at the past and asking *why* things are done the way they are. Often, there are no rational reasons why a particular strategy is followed or why the organization is organized as it is. Instead, this may be a result of certain people working for the organization that left long ago (such as a previous director), or of certain technologies that were used. If you can make people realize that things are largely a result of circumstantial factors, this may help them to realize that things could easily have been different.

2. Show what has changed around you

Another useful tactic to open people's minds is to have them look at changes in the industry or in the broader society. Just look back ten years (or five) and look, for example, how new technologies (especially IT) have influenced the kind of products and services offered and the way of doing business today. You can show them these changes, but it's more powerful if they reveal the changes themselves. A simple exercise can be to ask them the five most important changes in the industry over the past ten years and have them rate the likelihood that similar significant changes will happen in the next ten years.

3. Let them draft a new organization

Often people find it very hard to look beyond the current organization. When you try to get them involved in strategy generation, they might tell you that nothing is possible, because the organization (structure, culture, size, etc.) simply is what it is. One way to trigger their imagination is asking them what the organization and strategy should look like if they could start completely from scratch with a new organization (including a new legal entity) next to the existing one. Once they start thinking about that, there is a good chance that they will become enthusiastic and start realizing that what they are sketching could also work with the current organization–or that it's actually possible to start a completely new legal entity.

4. Give examples of organizations that have changed radically

A fourth way to make new strategy imaginable is giving examples of organizations or industries that have gone through rather dramatic changes. The most powerful examples are those that the people in your organization can easily relate to. It's preferable that you seek examples of organizations within your own industry, or of industries close to your own. If you can't come up with these examples, you can also use examples of well-known organizations that redefined their strategies. Some inspirational ones are:

a. *Nokia*: from paper mill to telecom giant.
b. *LEGO*: from relying on a patent to relying on user interaction.

    c.   *Xerox*: from photographic paper to copiers and printers.
    d.   *Philips*: from consumer electronics to health care.
    e.   *3M*: from mining and sandpaper to tape and Post-it Notes.

If you don't know these examples well enough, just search them on the Internet. Wikipedia in particular is useful for this as it often gives a detailed account of the history of organizations.

ACTIVATION TACTIC 2. REVEAL THE URGENCY

A second tactic for activating strategy generation is showing that new strategy is *unavoidable*. This includes creating the well-known "sense of urgency" that is emphasized in change management approaches. The core of this tactic is signaling the problems associated with giving too limited attention to strategy generation before they turn into real problems. The following four tactics can be used for this.

1.   **Ask whether the organization will still exist in five years**
A simple tactic to reveal the need for new strategy is asking your key stakeholders whether the organization will still exist in five years if it just continues doing what it does today. This makes them think about ongoing developments in the organization's surroundings and whether the current strategy is appropriate for that. If their answer is no, you probably have them on board. Otherwise, you can continue with the next tactic.

2.   **Reveal internal signs of a need for new strategy**
Another way to show that strategy generation is needed is letting people face facts. You want to show them signs indicating that the organization's current strategy is reaching its expiration date or signs that reveal a lack of attention to strategy. These are ten key internal signs.

    a.   Over 80% of revenue comes from existing products.
    b.   There is a strong dependence on a few large customers.
    c.   No significant new customers were attracted over the past year.

d. No significant new products/services were sold over the past year.

e. There is an increasing focus on cost reduction and efficiency.

f. Margins and prices are decreasing or too low.

g. There is a defensive attitude towards the current business.

h. No significant changes in staff happened over the past year.

i. There is no strategy process or systematic attention to strategy.

j. The economy or others are blamed for bad results.

If you recognize three or more of these signs in your organization, it's a signal that your strategy requires more attention.

"Signal the problems associated with too limited attention to strategy generation before they turn into real problems."

3. Reveal external signs of a need for new strategy

Also in the organization's environment are signs indicating a need for new strategy. Ten important ones that you can use to convince key stakeholders to engage in new strategy generation are noted below.

a. The demand for the kind of products you offer is shrinking.

b. The number of jobs in the industry is decreasing.

c. An increasing standardization of products/services is taking place.

d. Price competition is increasing or is already fierce.

e. Old competitors exit, are taken over, or go bankrupt.

f. New competitors come and do things differently.

g. New technologies enter the industry.

h. Industry boundaries are increasingly blurred.

i. Predictions are unreliable due to growing uncertainty.

j. The media are questioning the industry's viability.

The larger the number of signs you recognize here, the more urgently a new strategy is needed.

4. **Give examples**

Examples work here too, especially of industries or companies that died or failed otherwise because of insufficient changes to their strategy. Like with the first activation tactic, examples close to your own organization are the most powerful. Otherwise, consider the following.

- *Record industry*: redefined through digital music.
- *Newspaper and printing industry*: having problems due to online content.
- *Kodak*: failed to switch to digital photography.
- *Nokia*: no timely switch to smartphones.

Like with the examples mentioned earlier, you could just search the Internet for more information or consult Wikipedia. Also helpful are lists of declining industries or of jobs that will disappear in the not-so-distant future, mostly because of developments in IT. Search, for example, "declining industries" or "disappearing jobs" for inspiration.

ACTIVATION TACTIC 3. SELL THE BENEFITS

The next tactic to get the strategy generation process going is to show skeptics that new strategy is *advantageous* for the organization or for them personally. Whereas the previous tactic emphasized the perils of not engaging in strategy generation, this tactic emphasizes the possible gains of doing so.

1. **Emphasize organizational gains**

The first thing you can do is to stress the organizational benefits of being engaged in new strategy generation. These include the following ten reasons.

a. It motivates people and gives the organization new energy.
b. It avoids always focusing on costs and inefficiencies.

c.   It leads to a more productive usage of the organization's potential.
d.   It helps find new or better sources of income.
e.   It creates opportunities to make happier customers.
f.   It helps to do things better and differently than your competitors.
g.   It creates oversight and insight into the organization.
h.   It fosters coherence and alignment of what the organization does.
i.   It provides a good reason to get rid of unwanted things.
j.   At some point you'll have to do it anyway, so why not now?

You probably have a good idea who will be sensitive to what arguments. So, instead of simply listing all of these advantages, it's better to emphasize those that will appeal most to your audience.

2.   Emphasize personal gains

If showing organizational benefits is not enough, you can also stress the personal gains of new strategy. Obviously what these gains are precisely depends on the particular position and personality of your skeptic. So, here it would also be best if you know who is sensitive to what arguments. Generally, though, you can think of the following reasons.

1.   It provides an opportunity to realize personal ideas or ambitions.
2.   It offers a possibility for getting rid of things they don't like.
3.   It gives them influence on the organization's direction.
4.   It helps safeguard or improve their position in the organization.
5.   It provides an opportunity for showing what they are capable of.
6.   It encourages learning new skills and gathering new experiences.
7.   It gives a sense of pride if they are successful.
8.   It makes it more likely that they can hire people rather than fire them.

9.   It's fun–certainly more fun than cost cutting.
10. At some point they'll have to do it anyway, so why not now?

"Show skeptics that new strategy is advantageous for the organization and for them personally."

3.   Ask for people's dreams and ambitions

You could also turn it around. Rather than selling the organizational and individual benefits above, you can also ask people what they would like to achieve. They might have ideas, dreams, or ambitions that they would like to realize for the organization or personally. These may be hidden, because people have already concluded it would be impossible and have given up. However, if you insist and ask what they would really like to achieve if everything were possible and if they had all the resources they needed, I bet you would get some interesting answers. Then, your next question to them is when would it be more likely that they can realize their ambitions. Is this when the organization continues as it does, or when it starts working on a new strategy? Assuming their answer is the latter, you have sold them the benefits of engaging in new strategy generation.

4.   Give examples

For this third tactic, giving examples also works well. It also works best here if these are examples that people can easily relate to. For illustrating the organizational gains of a renewed strategy you should ideally use examples of organizations that are similar to yours and that have successfully changed their strategy. For illustrating the personal gains it helps to give examples of people that have personally gained from new strategy and that hold similar positions to the ones you are trying to convince. For both types of examples you can think of:

- A good competitor that has renewed its strategy.
- A customer or supplier which has reinvented itself.
- A similar-sized organization in another industry.
- An old organization that was unlikely to change but did.

If you can't find any good examples, you could also think of the usual suspects: organizations and people that have been very successful as a result of constant improvement and innovation of their strategies and that are often used as examples. This includes Apple, Tesla, Google, Starbucks, and their leaders, or any other organization that has followed a successful strategy–Ikea, Coca-Cola, Ryanair, 3M, Samsung, BMW, and so on.

ACTIVATION TACTIC 4. TAKE AWAY RISKS

A fourth activation tactic is making new strategy *feasible* for the organization and for your key stakeholders. After the previous tactics everyone might be convinced that a new strategy is needed. However, if major hurdles are seen, it still doesn't happen. The purpose of this fourth tactic is to take these hurdles away by reducing the risk of failure.

1. **Limit organizational risks**

For limiting the organizational risks associated with new strategy we can draw from a variety of tactics used in entrepreneurship. Since there will always be some failure, the core idea is to do it quickly and cheaply. To achieve this you could do one or more of the following.

   a. Invest time, resources, and money based on what you can afford to lose without harming the organization. In this way you decide upfront what your maximum investment will be and thereby control your risks.
   b. Isolate the actions and resources that are needed for the new strategy from the rest of the organization to ensure that the strategy generation process doesn't disturb the ongoing business.
   c. Install a step-by-step strategy process that requires a go/no-go decision before each step. This ensures that you can stop the process at any time before big investments are made.
   d. Postpone the "point of no return" as far as possible. First focus on everything that can still be undone. This

keeps you flexible and helps you avoid agreeing on commitments that you later regret.

e. When going live, start with a real-life pilot with customers that tells you whether the strategy works in practice. This ensures that if you fail, you fail cheaply and quickly.

f. Share risks with customers, partners, or suppliers by involving them early on in the process. Make their success dependent on your success. This creates commitment and aligns interests.

g. Sell before you actually make something. Try getting commitments before you make significant investments. This makes you depend less on sales estimates since you are already certain of some sales.

> *"Since there will always be some failure, the core idea is to do it quickly and cheaply."*

2. Limit personal risks

To convince people to engage in strategy generation, you also want to limit their personal risks. They might have a lot to lose from a new strategy–or at least they may think so. The following tactics help to limit this.

a. Do all of the above to limit organizational risks. If the organizational risks are lower, people's personal risks are reduced as well, especially since your key stakeholders are usually the ones that are held accountable.

b. Ask about their concerns and how these concerns could be taken away. Thus, instead of doing it yourself, let them provide the solutions. This tactic works well in sales, and it works equally well in strategy.

c. Take responsibility. Make sure that you are to blame, not them, if the new strategy fails. Of course this implies some risk on your side, but if you are convinced of the need for new strategy, why not take it?

d. Share responsibility. If strategy generation is a collaborative process in which many people are involved and the risks are shared, make sure that everyone shares blame if the new strategy fails.

3. Get the affordable loss on the table

An important reason why organizations are not sufficiently strategically active is that people fear losing time, money, or face due to an unsuccessful new strategy. Arguing against this or trying to reassure them doesn't really work because why would you know better than them? You probably don't. And even if you know better, this still doesn't take away their uncertainty. What does work, though, is helping them specify their "affordable loss"–this is what people are willing to lose if things don't work out. Setting their affordable loss gives them control over the worst thing that could happen, and by giving control you reduce the uncertainty. So, what you want to do is ask people what time, money, or other resources they would be willing to invest in the generation of new strategy even if there is a substantial chance of losing it. This provides you with some sort of budget that can be used for strategy generation.

4. Give examples

Examples work here too, particularly if people can relate to them. In this case you want to give examples of unlikely successes or of organizations or people that started with little and managed to grow it into a successful strategy without running major risks. If you don't have examples that are close to your organization, you can consider using the following.

a. *eBay*. Pierre Omidyar started eBay in 1995 as a hobby project next to his fulltime job. He argues that precisely because time and money were limited, eBay has become so successful because it led to a simple product and organization without unnecessary features and staff.

b. *Amazon*. Jeff Bezos started Amazon in 1994 with an investment by his parents and–how clichéd–in his own garage. Although he told his parents that there would be a 70% chance they would lose their money, they invested anyway.

    c.   *Chipotle Mexican Grill.* Steve Ells started Chipotle in 1993 with the idea that it would be a cash cow from which he could later start a fancier restaurant. It started very low profile with just burritos and tacos and was put together very simply with plywood. The relatively small amount of money needed came from Ells' dad.

ACTIVATION TACTIC 5. JUST START

A fifth activation tactic is to simply start making new strategy *happen*. Instead of trying to convince people and waiting until they get moving, you can also be entrepreneurial and just start. Sometimes this is the best and easiest way to get the strategy generation process going. In this way you basically first skip the whole strategy generation process and immediately jump to execution–on a small scale. Once people see that your actions work out, you've set an example that might convince them to engage in strategy generation.

> *"Do something that clearly deviates from the current strategy or that exemplifies the new strategic direction."*

You want to do something that clearly deviates from the current strategy or that exemplifies the new strategic direction that you have in mind. It's also quite powerful if you can do something that your key stakeholders consider infeasible or too risky. If you cannot come up with something yourself, you might want to consider doing some of the following.

1.   *Get a quick win.* There might be low-hanging fruit that reflects the strategic direction you're anticipating, that is easy to realize, and that immediately has a positive impact. By taking these actions, you show that change is possible and that there are benefits to the new strategy

2.   *Get a new customer.* If the new strategy implies entering or creating a new market it may be fairly convincing if you can tell people you already have a first (potential) customer.

3. *Find a new source of income.* One way to renew your strategy is to innovate the revenue model by finding new sources of income. So, what you can do is just try to arrange this on a small scale. If, for example, your current revenue model is based on hourly rates for a service, you could just try and sell the same service for a fixed price. If this works, you have some evidence that change is possible.

4. *Break a rule.* There might be some rules, habits, or structures in the organization that impede progress and cause new strategy not to get off the ground. To break out of this stalemate, you can do something that intentionally deviates from the norm. You can, for example, deliver a small project on your own instead of with the usual team to show that things could be done faster and more efficient.

5. *Find an ally.* Instead of trying to convince key decision makers you can also try to find someone in the organization that sympathizes with your ideas and who is also ready to act. By acting together, you can make more impact. And if he or she does the same, your impact might gradually spread throughout the organization.

6. *Fail quickly and cheaply.* If the organization is risk-avoiding or if there is some fear of failure, you might want to deliberately fail. If you do this in such a way that the consequences are minor, this can show others in the organization that failure isn't as bad as they thought. This can be a bit risky, though, since your failure might also make people even less willing to engage in strategy generation.

ACTIVATION TACTIC 6. ENFORCE ACTION

The first five activation tactics are all meant to help people in one way or the other get in a strategy generation mode. They are friendly tactics, assuming people are generally willing to engage in strategy making. These are the preferred activation tactics to use, which is why they have been presented in this order.

However, in some cases, a friendly approach is not enough. Whatever you do to make strategy imaginable, unavoidable, advantageous, feasible, and happen, sometimes people may still resist or not see the point of engaging in strategy generation. In that case you can do one of two things: give up or enforce. Since we're at the beginning of the strategy process, you don't want to give up. So, this leaves enforcement as your last resort. When adopting this final activation technique, it's important to keep the following five principles into account.

1. *Be realistic.* Only use this activation tactic if you *can* use it. That is, if you have the power to enforce the threat—to replace people, demote them, cut their wages, etc. If you don't have the power and still use threat as a means, you run the risk that people will simply smile at you or ignore you. Trivial as it may sound, you can only use power if you have power. So, before using this activation tactic, make sure you have the power, or have it used by someone that does have that power.

2. *Be clear.* If you want to make people do something, it should be crystal clear what it is. This is always the case, but especially when people have shown no interest and no response to any of the previous five activation tactics. So, be sure that whatever you tell them is 100% clear and concrete so that there can be no misunderstanding. If it can be misunderstood, it will be misunderstood.

3. *Be consistent.* Don't confuse people by saying conflicting things, or by saying one thing and doing another thing. One of the pitfalls of leaders is that their behavior signals something else than what they say—like cancelling a strategy meeting just after you have announced how important strategy is for the organization. Walk the talk, no matter how small the deviating behavior seems to be. Small things matter a great deal, also in strategy.

4. *Be persistent.* Generating and executing strategy requires persistence. This is always the case, but especially if you have to use enforcement. You can't let things go for a day, or let some people get away with not complying to

what they have been told to do. Harsh as this sounds, this is the only way to make this activation tactic work. Exceptions undermine its power in the same way as inconsistencies.

5. *Be careful.* Don't overdo it. Using too much coercion too early is ineffective for two reasons. First, it may trigger a strong response and increased resistance along the line "if you play it hard, we play it hard." Second, once you have already used all your power in the beginning, there's nothing left as a next option. Therefore, it's best to start carefully and limit the amount of force used to what is strictly necessary.

THE FOUR EXAMPLES

STRATEGY ACTIVATION AT MACMAN

It was evident to Director Ivo and his management team that new strategy was unavoidable and advantageous. They were well aware change was needed. The main bottlenecks to actually starting were that they didn't really see how and just saw problems ahead. This meant their strategy needed to be made imaginable and feasible.

- *Making new strategy imaginable.* Macman's leadership was stuck in the mindset of "we are a machine manufacturer." What helped was looking back at their history–they were a producer of semi-finished steel products before they actually started making their own machines. Realizing this opened up their minds a bit. What worked even better was asking them "Why?" and "Why not?" numerous times until they realized that their minds were mainly shaped by assumptions than by unbreakable truths.

- *Making new strategy feasible.* They assumed new strategy meant hiring expensive consultants, spending a lot of time on analyzing, and writing extensive plans. They blew up strategy generation into something big. What helped was showing them they could start small and work iteratively, relying in the first instance mostly on the resources and competences the firm already had.

STRATEGY ACTIVATION AT HOSPICARE

At Hospicare the main bottlenecks were convincing the board of directors that new strategy was unavoidable and advantageous. Although Chairman Ingrid–through her previous jobs in business–was convinced they needed to look beyond the "normal" health care business, the other members were more traditional and optimistic about the current strategy. They argued that "things have gone well, go well, and will keep on going well the way we do it."

Given the hospital's fact-based mentality, Ingrid figured she needed to give them "hard" evidence that change was needed. She asked her staff to compile a report with a) the performance of the hospital over the past ten years in terms of margins, innovation, and revenue, and b) an overview of developments in the hospital's environment in terms of competitors and demand for care. This worked. As it turned out, things hadn't gone so well and weren't going well at all. This convinced the rest of the board that things certainly would not go well if they didn't change their strategy. Furthermore, Ingrid managed to show the personal benefits of strategic change. The board members were all quite proud and sensitive about their positions and achievements. She used this by reminding them how a successful change would be good for their careers.

STRATEGY ACTIVATION AT GOFORIT

At GoforIT strategy activation was not needed. They clearly didn't lack imagination and saw plenty of opportunities to grow, expand, or even redefine the company. Also, feasibility was not an issue since they were convinced of their own abilities. They were also aware that they needed to do something given their fast growth over the past three years. There were increasing internal problems and a lack of structure and focus in their activities. So it was evident that actually having a strategy was unavoidable and advantageous.

STRATEGY ACTIVATION AT COMCOM

For Anisha it was clear that she should change her strategy. Change was not so much unavoidable–she could go on like before for many years without any real problems–but she really wanted it because she saw a lot of advantages (more fun, more money, more time). Like Macman, her main bottlenecks were related to the imaginability and feasibility of new strategy. She had secretly imagined how to redefine her business (she dreamt of becoming a famous food blog writer) but could not see how she could do that. What worked well in her case was looking at inspirational examples of some well-known blog writers and journalists and just telling her to start now alongside her current job. The risks and costs of this were minor and if it didn't work out she could still rely on her current business.

4

STEP 2: MAPPING STRATEGY

This fourth chapter presents step 2 of the strategy process: mapping strategy. It explains how the Strategy Sketch can be used to map an organization's strategy along with its ten core elements. It also provides various questions, exercises, checklists, and examples for doing this. Because we need to discuss all ten elements, the chapter is a bit lengthy. You can, of course, just pick those elements you want to read or use.

Mapping Strategy = Identifying the organization's strategy by describing it on the basis of the ten core elements of the Strategy Sketch.

THE MEANING AND ROLE OF MAPPING STRATEGY

As a second step of the strategy process, mapping strategy is about identifying the organization's strategy by describing it on the basis of the ten elements of the Strategy Sketch. At this step you make the organization's current strategy explicit. As noted earlier, I don't mean the organization's formal strategy. If there is one, it's usually written down and relatively easy to identify. What I mean, though, is the organization's actual strategy as is reflected in what the organization does, its status quo. This step plays four important roles in the strategy process:

1. *Understanding.* By making all ten elements of the current strategy explicit, this step reveals what is underneath the strategy as formulated. As such, this step creates an in-depth understanding of the organization's current strategy.
2. *Communication.* Mapping the organization's strategy also provides a means to talk about strategy in a coherent manner. With the Strategy Sketch as a basis, this step makes sure that everybody talks about the same things when they use the word "strategy."
3. *Revealing ambiguity.* Mapping also helps find blind spots and ambiguities in the organization's strategy. While you are mapping all ten elements you may find out that you need more information about some, or that there is substantial disagreement.
4. *Stepping-stone.* As part of the strategy generation process, mapping strategy is an important stepping-stone to the next steps. The mere act of mapping out your strategy might already reveal points for improvement and directions for new strategy. In some cases you might even be able to immediately move on to execution.

"Tip: print or draw an empty Strategy Sketch and start filling it in while you read further."

HOW TO USE THE TOOLS

Chapter 2 introduced you to the Strategy Sketch and its core elements. Based on that chapter you have a sense of what the ten elements mean and why they are important for strategy. In this chapter you find further information and tools that help you actually map out your strategy along these ten elements. For each element, you find the following tools:

- *Questions to ask.* Two sets of questions that help you a) assess what the element currently looks like in your organization, and b) come up with new directions.

- *Beyond-the-obvious exercise.* A simple exercise that helps you look beyond what first comes to the mind. With this exercise you can ensure that the mapping of your strategy has sufficient depth.
- *Inspirational checklist.* A list of ideas that can help you check whether you considered enough options for a particular element or maybe some you have overlooked. This also helps you to think about new directions.

While going through the following pages it can be useful to immediately start mapping your strategy. For this it's handy if you draw the Strategy Sketch (see page 16) on an empty DIN A3/Tabloid format paper or download and print it from thestrategyhandbook.com. While reading about each element below, you can then already start filling in your Strategy Sketch with the first ideas that come to mind.

THE TEN ELEMENTS OF STRATEGY

1. Resources & competences

Although you could start by mapping any element of the Strategy Sketch, I personally prefer to start with your resources and competences. This makes you first look at the organization itself and understand what you have, what you are good at, and what makes you unique. In this way you start close to home with what you already have at your disposal. When you start mapping this, it's useful to take the following into account:

- Don't make long or complete lists of resources and competences. Focus on the most important ones; those that are most valuable or that your competitors don't have.
- Your most valuable and unique resources or competences can be unexpected. They need not even be related to your core products or services. They can, for instance, be your selection and hiring process. Therefore, look broadly.
- Look also at combinations of resources and competences. The reason you're good at something is usually a combination of factors. For example, it may be because

of your particular knowledge, equipment, people, *and* location that you outperform others.

- Dig deeper by asking "why" a couple of times to find out which competences lie beneath a particular resource or competence.
- Also evaluate what you don't have, what you miss, what your weaknesses are compared to others. Which resources or competences should you have or develop?

QUESTIONS TO ASK

For assessing your *current* resources and competences:	For using or developing *new* resources and competences:
• Which means do you have that others don't? • What are you really good at that others can't do or find difficult? • What slack resources or unused capacity do you have access to? • What would you miss most when it's gone? • What competences allowed you to get or develop your current resources and competences?	• What else can you do with your resources andccompetences? • How can you make them more unique or valuable? • How can you protect them better against imitation? • What means can you easily obtain, but others not or with difficulty? • What resources or competences should you let go, outsource, or sell to others?

BEYOND-THE-OBVIOUS EXERCISE

When asking someone about their most important resources and competences it's common to get responses such as "our people," "our knowledge," or "our culture." These general responses are not the most useful ones for strategy generation. To get more in-depth responses, you can do the following simple exercise. Let people imagine there has been a big fire or another disaster and that the whole organization has been destroyed. Then you ask them one of the following two questions: "What would be the thing that you miss most and that can only with difficulty be replaced or rebuilt?" or "What would be the minimum that you need to restart the organization and that you cannot buy elsewhere?" In this way you get the really essential and unique resources and competences on the table.

INSPIRATIONAL CHECKLIST

To identify your best resources and competences, consider whether compared to others you perhaps have the...

- ...most efficient way of working.
- ...cheapest or fastest way of producing or delivering.
- ...best location for suppliers or customers.
- ...best access to people or resources.
- ...most advanced or smartest technology.
- ...best skilled, creative, or intelligent people.
- ...friendliest and most loved staff or representatives.
- ...most loyal customers or employees.
- ...most effective selection, hiring, or development program.
- ...largest or best network of partners.
- ...largest or most complete facilities.
- ...biggest pockets or best financial situation.
- ...strongest or most trustworthy brand.
- ...best ability to involve customers or suppliers.
- ...best domain name or online findability.
- ...best design skills in terms of esthetics or usability.
- ...

2. **Partners**

After identifying your resources and competences, a natural next step is to map key partners. These are the people and organizations that you work with and that make your products or services more valuable. While identifying them, take the following into account.

- Your network could be unique and hard to copy. If so, it could give you a competitive advantage next to resources and competences. Therefore, look for partners that others don't have.

- Look carefully at what is your unique value compared to your partners' unique value. You might depend too much on their strengths rather than on your own. This makes you vulnerable and over-dependent.
- Take some time to look at all your personal offline and online contacts. Which of them could you use in your organization?
- Also think about unusual partnerships that you have or could make–this helps you to think outside the box and to come up with innovative strategies.
- Look at what they can bring, but also at your relationship with them. Do they share the same values, are they dependable, do they have an interest in working with you?

QUESTIONS TO ASK

For identifying your *current* partners:	For finding *new* partners or using them better:
<ul><li>With which organizations are there formal contracts?</li><li>Who does the organization depend on or frequently work with?</li><li>Which organizations support or help you most?</li><li>Who do you know? Who is in your own network or that of colleagues?</li><li>What useful contacts do your partners have?</li></ul>	<ul><li>What can your partners do more for you than they currently do? What unused means do they have?</li><li>Who benefits from your organization or has similar interests but doesn't work with you yet?</li><li>What organizations would you find attractive to work with? And which ones would like to work with you?</li><li>Which partners are not beneficial for you and you are better off without?</li></ul>

BEYOND-THE-OBVIOUS EXERCISE

When you map your partners there is a risk of just listing the obvious organizations that you work closely with. A useful exercise, giving a different view on who your (potential) partners are, is to draw a customer-centered stakeholder map. A stakeholder map contains the people and organizations relevant to your organization. Rather than putting your organization itself at the center, though, you put the customer at the center. Around that draw two circles. The inner circle contains those people and organizations that directly influence your customer; the outer circle contains the ones with an indirect influence. Once you finish the picture, you should ask yourself how many of them you already work or collaborate with. The rest are your potential partners.

Example of a Customer-Centered Stakeholder Map

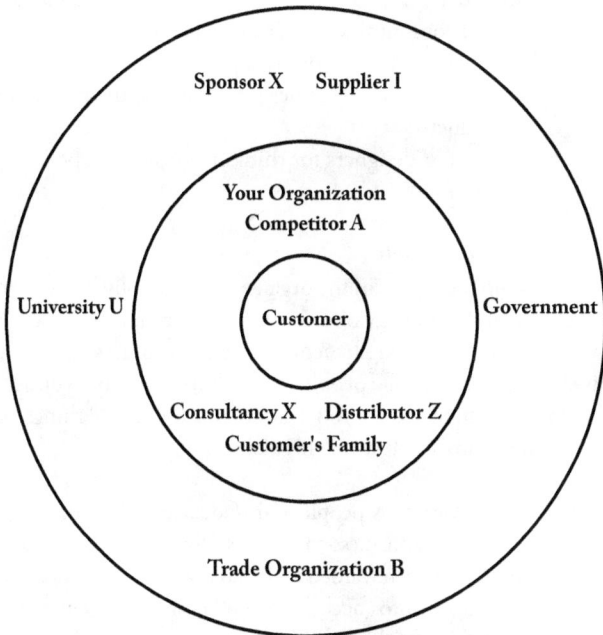

INSPIRATIONAL CHECKLIST

To identify your partners and the reasons they are important, consider whether these include or could include particular…

- …customers, for co-creating your products/services.
- …suppliers, for innovating your products/services.
- …competitors, for joining forces against others.
- …universities, for gaining advanced knowledge.
- …schools, for hiring well-educated employees.
- …accountancy firms, for accessing new customers.
- …local or regional governments, for obtaining funding.
- …distributors, for getting your products to customers.
- …interest groups, for working for the same purpose.
- …trade or industry associations, for representing you.
- …investors for obtaining funding, contacts, or advice.
- …complementors (offering products that are complementary to yours) for better serving the market.
- …local communities for creating goodwill.
- …media for creating positive publicity.
- …influencers or celebrities for increasing the desirability of products.
- …artists or designers for thinking outside the box.
- …

3. **Customers & needs**

After mapping the means of the organization I usually move to the market side of the Strategy Sketch; to customers and needs and to competitors. So, the next element in line is customers and needs. This element concerns the people and organizations that you serve and which of their needs you fulfill. The following things are useful to take into account for this element.

- See customers as people and understand their needs and concerns. In business-to-business, for example, know how purchasers are rewarded and who makes the final decision.
- Also take into account your customers' customers. Look at what their needs are and how this affects your customer. And think about which of them is most important.

- Decide whether you want to target a large and broad market or a specific niche. Usually the latter is more realistic to start with. Make choices and avoid naïve reasoning such as "Our product is for everyone" or "There are 7 billion people, if only 0.001% would buy our product."
- Understand the difference between what people need and what they want. Needs are driven by problems, wants by desires. These are two very different things.
- Be aware that customers may not be aware of what they want and need. Rather than asking them, find out what they are trying to achieve, their "job-to-be-done," and what blocks them to achieve that. Then you discover what they really want and need.

QUESTIONS TO ASK

For understanding your *current* customers:	For finding *new* customers or serving customers better:
• What common characteristics do your customers have? • What people use or pay for the product/ service and who makes or influences the buying decisions? • What are these people's needs so that they can do what they need to do? • Which of their problems can or do you solve? • What are they willing to pay for?	• Can you make your customers more loyal or buy more? • Do your customers have needs that you could also fulfill? • Who could your customers recommend you to or who else is within reach of your network? • Who is currently not yet served but would benefit from your product? • Which customers are you better off without? Who costs you more than you benefit?

BEYOND-THE-OBVIOUS EXERCISE

An exercise borrowed from the business model guys: make an empathy map. An empathy map is a sheet of paper divided into six blocks with six questions helping you to place yourself in the position of a customer (see the picture below). This helps you get a more advanced understanding of their needs and concerns. The simplest way to do this exercise is to keep a specific customer in mind and answer the questions for that customer. You can repeat this for various customers.

Empathy Map

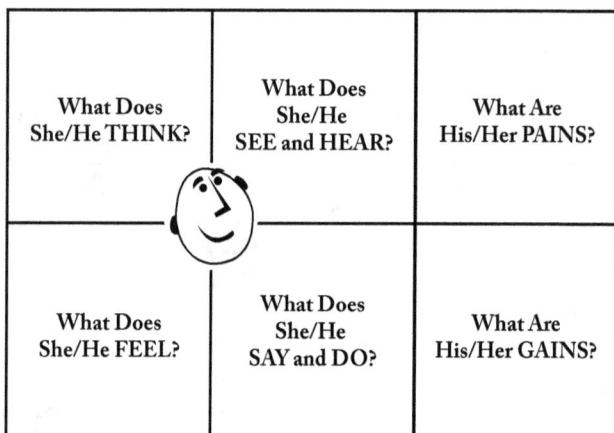

| What Does She/He THINK? | What Does She/He SEE and HEAR? | What Are His/Her PAINS? |
| What Does She/He FEEL? | What Does She/He SAY and DO? | What Are His/Her GAINS? |

INSPIRATIONAL CHECKLIST

To identify the needs of the persons or organizations that use or pay for your product/service, or who make or influence the buying decisions, consider for example whether they have the need to…

- …save time or speed up.
- …save money or get a reduction.
- …reduce the risks that they bear.
- …feel more secure or appreciated.

- …focus on what they like or are good at.
- …get a particular job done.
- …have fun or be entertained.
- …boost or maintain their status.
- …express their identity.
- …connect with other people.
- …improve their physical condition.
- …improve their mental or emotional condition.
- …enjoy convenience.
- …try something new.
- …improve themselves or achieve something.
- …act in good conscience or ease their mind.
- …make a difference or have a positive impact.
- …experience something beautiful.
- …

4. **Competitors**

To complete the market side of the Strategy Sketch, the next element in line is competitors. Mapping them gives you a good understanding of who they are, how strong they are, and how you are different from them. When you do this, you should take the following into account.

- Think broadly about who your competitors might be. Substitutes can be broad and unexpected. Jewelry and expensive cars, for example, are very different products, but are substitutes for expressing status and identity.
- Take your customer's perspective. At the end, any alternative that the customer may consider when deciding whether or not to buy from you is a competitor. This includes doing nothing, or doing it themselves.
- You need competitors, if only to compare yourself to when positioning yourself for your customers. Having good competitors can even be beneficial, as they help establish a healthy market.
- Although you should generally try to do things differently from your competitors, being too unique can also be dangerous. This is especially the case if your customer wants dual sourcing (at least one other organization that can offer the same products/services as you).

- Take into account that being a competitor is a *role* that people and organizations can take. At another point, they may also be partners or customers.

QUESTIONS TO ASK

For understanding *current and potential* competitors:	For finding ways to *avoid or benefit* from competitors:
• What organizations offer similar products or services than you? • Who could easily start offering something similar? • Who offers products that substitute yours? • With whom or what will customers compare you? • Who makes your life most difficult and vice versa?	• Can you use your competitors' strengths to your advantage? • Who do you want your customers to compare you to? • How could you make your competitors irrelevant? • Where in or outside the industry is there less competition? • What competitors are beneficial for you? Can you join forces?

BEYOND-THE-OBVIOUS EXERCISES

I assume you have a good sense of who your most important direct competitors are. But you also want to map those that are off your current radar. There are two short exercises that you can do to identify them. For the first exercise make a list of 5-7 keywords that describe your unique products or services and some of their unique features. Then start searching the Internet using these keywords. You'll be surprised about the organizations that show up. Given that they are found using "your" keywords makes it likely that they are important competitors. Thus, this first exercise helps to identify competitors offering similar products to you.

The second exercise helps you to think more in terms of substitutes. For this exercise ask two questions: "If your company never existed, how would customers satisfy their needs?" and "If your industry never existed, what alternatives might satisfy your customers' needs?"

INSPIRATIONAL CHECKLIST

To identify ways in which you could be hindered less by competitors or even benefit from them, consider for example whether and how you can...

- ...collaborate, merge, or form an alliance with them.
- ...share information or other resources with them.
- ...license your technology to them so that you benefit from every product they sell.
- ...convince them or make it attractive for them to sell your products or services.
- ...serve customers that they cannot serve.
- ...move to a different niche or region.
- ...learn from what they do wrong and do better.
- ...find out what they do and make sure you do what they don't.
- ...make them irrelevant by creating a new market.
- ...offer your products to a new type of customer.
- ...add or increase particular features of your products.
- ...reduce or omit particular features from your products.
- ...exploit your unique resources and competences and thus focus on what you can do better than them.
- ...do something that they would not expect from you.
- ...

5. **Value proposition**
The core of your strategy is your value proposition. It reflects what products, services, and added value you offer and how you offer this to your customers. When you map this element of your strategy, it's useful to take the following into account.

- Don't try to be complete when describing the value of your products or services. Focus on the essence. What features are most valuable and unique?

- When you think about the value of your product or service to the customer, ask yourself *why* the customer buys your product and not another product, or a product from someone else.
- It can help to think about your value proposition in terms of *form* and *function*. The product, service, and way of offering are about the *form* of your offer (for example a book). The value is about the *function* (or "use value") that your offer has for the customer (such as creating an understanding of strategy).
- Remember the difference between needs and wants. The main value of your products and services could relate to tangible needs (problems, something functional) but also to less tangible wants (aspirations, desires, something emotional).
- It can be useful to make a systematic comparison of your products and services to those of competitors. Make a list of features and compare them. Where do you stand out?

QUESTIONS TO ASK

For understanding your *current* value proposition(s):	For developing *new* value proposition(s):
<ul><li>What products or services do you offer?</li><li>What makes them different from those of others?</li><li>What value do they have for customers?</li><li>Why do people buy them?</li><li>What is special about them?</li></ul>	<ul><li>How can your products or services be made more valuable?</li><li>What features can you improve, expand, or add?</li><li>What products, services, or features can be downgraded, simplified, or dropped?</li><li>What related or complementary products or services can you offer that your customers also need?</li><li>How can they be made more accessible?</li></ul>

BEYOND-THE-OBVIOUS EXERCISE

You have your own idea about what is valuable about your products or services, but this is not necessarily the same as what your customers think. To increase your chances of seeing it their way, you can do a small role-playing exercise. Start by simply asking people to describe the value of the products or services they're selling. Then you ask them, "So this is what you're selling. But what is your customer buying?" Tell them to take on the role of customer and then describe the value of your products or services again. The more realistic you make this, the better the description will be. Encourage them to imitate a particular customer and literally use their voice or way of saying things. You'll be amazed how people start seeing things differently in this way. Of course you can also do the exercise yourself instead of asking others.

INSPIRATIONAL CHECKLIST

To identify the value of your products and services, consider why people buy them or should buy them. For example, your (current or future) customers buy your products or services because they are...

- ...low-priced, cheap to buy, or good value for money.
- ...cheapest in terms of total cost of ownership or life-cycle costs.
- ...easy to understand and use, convenient.
- ...frequently offered, available everywhere.
- ...fun, enjoyable to use or experience.
- ...technologically sophisticated, using new technology.
- ...well designed, beautiful, esthetic.
- ...status enriching, making people feel better.
- ...exclusive, available nowhere else, expensive.
- ...used by many or important others, popular, trendy.
- ...personalized, flexible, custom-made, tailored.
- ...based on a good personal relationship, friendly.
- ...simple, to the point, without frills, effort-reducing.
- ...complete, advanced, thorough.
- ...reliable, fault-free, solid, robust, risk-reducing.

- …modern, fashionable, up to date.
- …long-lasting, sustainable, durable.
- …environmentally friendly, efficient, green.
- …

6. Revenue model

With the first five elements we've covered those parts of your strategy that reveal how your organization creates value. This sixth element reflects what you get in return for this, from whom, and in what form. When you map out your revenue model you should take the following into account.

- Although your customers might be the first you think of when it concerns payment, look at others as well. Basically, anyone who benefits from what you are offering is a possible candidate for paying you.
- Your revenue model needs to match your value proposition. This means that if you offer low value, you can't ask for a high price. But it also means that if you create high value, you should set a price consistent with that. By asking for too low a price, you confuse your customers.
- Don't easily reduce your price or rate. There is no way back. If necessary, offer temporary reductions. Also, understand price sensitivity: can you raise prices without a significant reduction in demand?
- Look at margin and volume. Both high-margin low-volume and low-margin high-volume strategies work.
- Think about more than money alone. Maybe someone cannot pay, but what else can they help you with? Information, access, resources, time, advice; anything with a value can be considered. In the end, others might want to pay for these.

QUESTIONS TO ASK

For capturing your *current* revenue model:	For developing or finding *new* revenue models:
• Where does your revenue come from? • Which people or organizations pay? • For what do they pay? • How much do they pay? • How, or in what form do they pay?	• Can you change how customers pay, when, or for what? • Who benefits but doesn't pay yet or not enough? Can you let them pay? • Can you make your revenue less dependent on your efforts? • Can you turn products into services and vice versa? • What revenue streams should be dropped? Which ones are too complicated or don't bring enough?

BEYOND-THE-OBVIOUS EXERCISE

It's usually not very difficult to map out your current revenue model. There is a big chance that most of your revenue comes from customers and that you rely, for example, on a "p times q" model (number of hours/items times the price per hour/item). A useful exercise for revealing other revenue generating options is drawing a *value network*. This is a picture showing how money and other resources flow between key players. Start by drawing all the important stakeholders on a sheet of paper. Next, using arrows, draw what value exchanges there are between them. Next to each arrow write what each player offers and what they get in return. In a balanced value network, all the players contribute *and* receive. The latter may be indirectly, though, through other players—as illustrated in the example here: customers pay you for delivery services that a distributor offers. Once completed, the value network might reveal players that benefit more than they contribute. These are your potential sources of untapped revenue.

Example of a Value Network

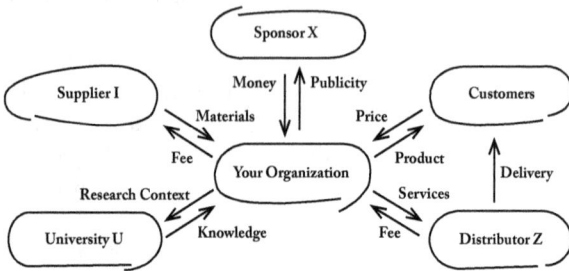

INSPIRATIONAL CHECKLIST

To find new ways in which customers or others can pay, consider whether your revenue model could be based on…

- …selling the product/service. The default for most products.
- …bundled pricing. Sell products/services as a package deal.
- …disaggregated pricing. Let people only pay for what they want or use.
- …usage fees. Fee per click, minute, day, etc.
- …renting or leasing. Fee for using a product/service for a given period.
- …subscriptions. Receive a fixed fee per month or so.
- …memberships. Fee for being a member plus getting free extras.
- …content vault. Unlimited access to content, materials, or tools.
- …vouchers and gift cards. Pay in advance, use the product/service later.
- …freemium. Offer free and paid versions of the product.

- …open source. Free product, revenues come from ancillary services.
- …advertising. Free product, but advertisements to look at.
- …licensing. Fee for using copyrights, patents, or brands.
- …shares or crowd funding. Invest in potential future revenue.
- …donors and sponsors. Voluntary payments with little return in favor.
- …subsidies. Governments pay for jobs, sustainability, or innovation.
- …brokerage. Fee per successful transaction.
- …auctioning or reverse-auctioning. Let people bid.
- …flexible pricing. Vary prices based on demand.
- …open pricing. Leave it to the customer what to pay.
- …barter. In kind payment or swapping goods.
- …no-cure-no-pay (or less-pay). Customers only pay if satisfied.
- …affiliation. Fee per new customer that is brought in.
- …dropshipping. Sell products without handling them yourself.
- …platform. Bringing together supply and demand for a fee.
- …interest. Fee for loans or other forms of financing.
- …bait-and-hook. Offer a cheap product plus sell expensive supplies.
- …

7. **Risks & costs**

Your strategy doesn't only come with revenue–it also involves risks and costs. So, when mapping your strategy, you also want to identify the financial, social, and other risks and costs your bear. When mapping this, you want to take the following into account.

- There often is a trade-off between costs and risks. Hiring freelancers, for example, reduces risks, but it can also increase variable costs. The best advice is to look for ways to reduce both.

- To understand costs, identify your main categories of expenditures. In doing so, think about fixed vs. variable costs and direct vs. indirect costs. This will give you a high-level, strategic understanding of your organization's cost structure.
- To understand risks, try and identify their likelihood, possible impact, and detectability. The larger their likelihood and impact, and the harder they are to detect, the greater the risk.
- Make a distinction between internal risks (the risks that you can avoid, like safety risks), external risks (the risks that are caused by factors out of your control, like hazards) and strategic risks (the risks that you deliberately take on to better serve your customers, like in a guarantee).
- Look at the relation with your revenue model and value proposition to check whether things that involve risks and costs add sufficient value. So, for each activity or element of your strategy compare how much value they add and how much costs and risks are involved.

QUESTIONS TO ASK

For assessing your *current* costs and risks:	For *diminishing* your costs and risks in the future:
<ul><li>For each other element: what risks and costs are associated with it?</li><li>How large are these risks and costs and who bears them?</li><li>Which ones are necessary and which ones can be avoided?</li><li>What can you afford to invest or lose?</li><li>Is this more or less than you currently do?</li></ul>	<ul><li>Can you eliminate, reduce, or share some costs or risks?</li><li>Can you hedge or neutralize them by other elements of your strategy?</li><li>Can you transfer or outsource them to someone else?</li><li>Can you postpone costs, or make them variable instead of fixed?</li><li>Can you benefit from increasing some of the risks or costs you bear?</li></ul>

BEYOND-THE-OBVIOUS EXERCISES

It's relatively easy to see *what* costs and revenue you have. It's harder to see, though, *when* and *where* they occur. There are two exercises you can do to gain these insights. The simplest one is drawing a line chart of how your overall revenues and overall costs have developed over the past years. Depending on the kind of organization you have, it might be most useful to do this by year, quartile, or month. This chart gives you an insight into the level of your revenue and costs and *when* they occur.

If you want more in-depth insights into *where* costs and revenues are made, you should link them to the key activities of your organization. This will show you whether the activities on which you spend most time or money are also the ones which have the most added value for the customer. You can do this through the following three steps.

1. Make a list of the key primary and secondary activities of your organization. Primary activities are those that contribute directly to your products/services, such as production, logistics, or sales. Secondary activities are your overheads. Examples are finances, human resource management, and marketing. The more refined you make your list of activities, the more refined your insight will be.
2. Map out the percentage of your total number of hours spent or of the total costs each activity is responsible for. This shows you where you spend your time and money.
3. Judge how much added value each activity has for your customer. Judge whether the time or money you spend on a particular activity is in balance with the added value it has for the customer.

This exercise may show you, for example, that you spend 20% of your time or budget on refining the looks of your webpage or on optimizing the performance of your product, whereas these activities have only little value for the customer. As such, it shows you where unnecessary costs are made.

INSPIRATIONAL CHECKLIST

To diminish the costs or mitigate the risks that the organization bears, consider whether and how you can...

- ...make customers pay all or part in advance.
- ...delay payments to suppliers so that you keep your cash.
- ...do the opposite: pay suppliers early if you can get discounts.
- ...sell something before actually making it.
- ...share risks and costs by making others co-owners.
- ...outsource activities or hire freelancers.
- ...focus on what you really need, not more.
- ...ask others for access to their resources rather than buying them.
- ...make others commit before you take action.
- ...standardize or simplify products or services.
- ...share capacity or capabilities with others.
- ...reduce or reuse waste, materials, space, and energy.
- ...fail small and quickly through trial and error.
- ...make things mobile, e.g., through telecommuting.
- ...buy second hand or barter goods and services.
- ...clean up unnecessary assets and paperwork.
- ...keep things flexible and keep actions reversible as much as possible.
- ...stage projects and abandon them when needed.
- ...invest only what you can afford to lose.
- ...work on alternative products/services in parallel.
- ...

8. **Values & goals**

After mapping out the first seven elements you have a good sense of how your organization creates value and what it gets in return. The eighth element that is crucial in any strategy are your values and goals. These reflect what is important for the organization and where it should go in the future. When mapping this element you should take the following into account.

- Without values or goals an organization might easily drift, meander, or stagnate. On the other hand, too strict goals and values might make it dogmatic and blind. Balance is needed.
- Values and goals might be noble, such as solving poverty in the world. They can also be more mundane, such as a 5% yearly growth. Good goals are just out of reach: you think you can achieve them, but don't know exactly how. In that way, they create the creative energy that you want in your organization.
- Financial goals easily suppress other goals. Beware and regularly check which ones take the lead so that the organization keeps on track toward what it's really aiming for.
- Values and goals need not always be SMART (specific, measurable, achievable, relevant, and time-bound). They might be more open and uncrystallized, as long as they are functional for the organization.
- The organization's formal and written values and goals might be different from the informal, factual values and goals that appear in decision-making and in what the organization actually does.

QUESTIONS TO ASK

For explicating *actual* values and goals as they appear in actions and decisions:	For explicating *desired* values and goals for the future:
<ul><li>What criteria have been most decisive in key decisions so far?</li><li>What has been achieved in the past three years?</li><li>If the organization continues what it is doing, where will it end up?</li></ul>	<ul><li>What is really important for the organization? Why was it founded?</li><li>Who are the organization's main stakeholders? What should the organization do for them?</li></ul>

• How would employees or outsiders describe the organization's values and goals? • Are official values and goals shared throughout the organization?	• What long-term goals or ambitions would create excitement? • What is the right thing to do for the organization? How can it make a better impact? • What values or goals are hindering progress and should be adjusted?

BEYOND-THE-OBVIOUS EXERCISE

In many organizations it's quite clear what the official values and goals are. They are often written down in statements or reports and you often find them on the organization's webpage. The organization's *actual* values and goals as they appear in people's decisions and actions, though, are much harder to identify. Since these show what actually drives the organization you want to understand these too. There is a simple exercise to do this. The basic idea is that you look at a number of important or recent decisions or actions and identify the implicit or explicit criteria that were used there. More specifically you could look at the criteria used…

- …in the three most recent or largest investments.
- …in the three most recent or important strategic decisions.
- …to assess the performance of people or departments.

This exercise might reveal, for example, that the most important criterion used is cost reduction. And this might be substantially different to what the organization's official values and goals say.

INSPIRATIONAL CHECKLIST

To identify the organization's values and goals, consider whether it's important that the organization…

- ...grows fast and becomes large.
- ...remains small and personal.
- ...has a strong international presence.
- ...is profitable or makes a lot of money.
- ...makes your shareholders or owners happy.
- ...serves a particular group of customers.
- ...solves an important and pressing problem.
- ...is a fun and energizing place to work.
- ...makes a difference to this world.
- ...is known for its ... (fill in yourself).
- ...is the most innovative of its kind.
- ...has the most satisfied customers.
- ...is bought by another organization.
- ...is there to stay in the long run.
- ...has the best reputation in the industry.
- ...changes the world or makes it a better place.
- ...is efficient and sustainable.
- ...

9. **Organizational climate**

Next, to identifying the values and goals that drive the organization, we also need to understand the organization itself. Therefore, the next step is to map out the organizational climate–the structure and culture that are characteristic for the organization. When doing so, you should take notice of the following.

- Culture and structure are strongly related. They both reflect the organizational climate and there is no point in spending a lot of time in trying to separate them.
- Look both at the formal and the informal structure and culture. If these are very different, this can be a problem. If so, decide which one needs to be changed.
- There is no one best organizational climate that works in all organizations. What is important, though, is that it matches your strategy. Therefore, carefully look at what culture and structure suit your strategy–and vice versa.
- Ask newcomers and people from outside your organization how they would characterize its culture.

These people might see this differently (and better) from you.

- Assess what is good and bad about your organizational climate and how easy or difficult it is to change. This gives you a sense of where you stand and how your organizational climate will facilitate or hinder the execution of your strategy.

QUESTIONS TO ASK

For assessing the *current* organizational climate:	For *changing and improving* the organizational climate:
<ul><li>How precisely and rigidly are tasks defined and how are they divided?</li><li>How is power divided and used and who is the most powerful?</li><li>How does communication take place? Who communicates with whom and about what?</li><li>What is characteristic of the organization?</li><li>What kind of symbols, rituals, or stories are frequently used?</li></ul>	<ul><li>What is the main thing that needs to be improved in terms of the questions in the left column?</li><li>What would the ideal culture or structure look like if you could build the organization from scratch?</li><li>What organization is a role model for yours?</li><li>What would be the first thing to drop or change about the organization's structure or culture?</li></ul>

BEYOND-THE-OBVIOUS EXERCISE

There might be all kinds of assumptions about your organization's climate. Employees might say, for example, that the organization is particularly innovative, or that it's like a big family. But is this really so? To break out of these assumptions, you can do the following exercise. The core idea of this exercise is that you make people look at their organization in an unusual manner by using metaphors. To get a good sense of the organizational climate, ask them one or more of the following questions.

- If our organization were an animal, it would be a … because …
- If our organization were a food, it would be … because …
- If our organization were a sport, it would be … because …
- If our organization were a TV show, it would be … because …
- If our organization were a color, it would be … because …

You can also use other metaphors such as a season, a plant, type of building, car model, toy, type of furniture, and so on. Make sure that people do not just name the animal, food, etc., but also explain why.

INSPIRATIONAL CHECKLIST

To identify ways to improve the organizational climate, consider whether and how you can…

- …give people more autonomy and responsibility.
- …make people work and think more entrepreneurially.
- …create an atmosphere in which failure is allowed.
- …rely less on analysis and more on action.
- …encourage people to accept and act under uncertainty.
- …allocate time and resources for exploration.
- …combine the short term with the long term.
- …do only what is urgent and/or important.
- …understand and focus on what customers really want.
- …create a flexible and learning organization.
- …foster a sense of reality among all the people.
- …keep procedures, forms, and spreadsheets simple.
- …avoid complex structures with many layers.
- …create small units in which people know each other.
- …foster collaboration within and between units.
- …realize a large extent of transparency and openness.

- …motivate people to give everything they can.
- …work towards goals and values that matter to people.
- …challenge people to go beyond the status quo.
- …get rid of disturbing or underperforming people.
- …clean up the entire organization at least once a year.
- …

10. Trends & uncertainties

So far we've looked at the organization and its immediate surroundings–its partners, customers, and competitors. But the broader environment is also important for strategy. As a last step, you should also pay attention to the trends and uncertainties in the organization's environment. When you map these, take the following into account.

- Think local, regional, national, and global. There may be relevant trends and uncertainties at each of these levels.
- Don't aim for long lists of factors, trends, events, etc. Rather, focus on the most essential ones. Also, rather than just mentioning them, make explicit what they mean for your organization.
- Be aware that any trend or uncertainty in your environment also affects your competitors. Therefore, a trend that looks like an opportunity could be a threat if competitors can better handle it. The same applies to threats; if you can handle them better than competitors, they are opportunities.
- Any trend or uncertainty that you can observe and name reflects what Peter Drucker (a famous management guru) has called "the future that already happened." Don't fall into the trap where you start thinking that you can actually predict the future.
- Mind gradual changes. They are easily overlooked because you get used to them; they require deliberate and careful observation.

QUESTIONS TO ASK

For assessing *current* trends and uncertainties:	For finding ways to *respond* to them:
• What important trends are going on in the industry and society? • Which ones can you better deal with than competitors? And vice versa? • What will definitely change in the next few years? • Which are the biggest uncertainties the organization faces? • How uncertain is the environment of your organization? How dynamic and complex is it?	• Can you find a way to benefit more from what goes on? • Can you move to a more favorable environment? • Can you make the organization less dependent on the trends and uncertainties it faces? • Can you exploit opportunities or turn a threat into an opportunity? • What does it take to exploit the opportunity? Do you have it or can you easily develop it?

BEYOND-THE-OBVIOUS EXERCISE

There is a good chance that mapping out trends and uncertainties just leads to general trends such as aging or globalization. These may be important, but you also want to go more in depth. One way to do this was already partially mentioned in Chapter 3. The first tactic to reveal the urgency of new strategy ("Ask whether the organization still exists in five years") is also a good starting point for revealing trends and uncertainties. So, for this exercise you start by asking whether the organization will still exist in five years if it just continues doing what it does today. If the answer to this question is "no," your follow-up questions are "Why not?" and "What are the important factors in your environment that cause you to remain unchanged?"

INSPIRATIONAL CHECKLIST

To identify the relevant trends and uncertainties for the organization, consider the positive and negative consequences of triggers such as...

- ...entry, exit, mergers, splitting, acquisitions, and alliances of competitors, suppliers, or customers.
- ...changes in people's habits, needs, or preferences.
- ...changes in the composition of the population.
- ...one technology taking over another technology.
- ...developments in adjacent industries.
- ...political events, taxes, subsidies, laws, or regulations that change the rules of the game.
- ...the economy going up and down.
- ...local or global disasters or other crises.
- ..."megatrends" such as globalization, power redistribution, urbanization, climate change, aging, increased interconnectivity, and mobility.
- ...changes in the norms about what is right and wrong.
- ...maturation and commoditization of current markets.
- ...opinions of opinion leaders, media, or the public.
- ...availability and distribution of money, materials, skilled people, information, or other resources.
- ...changing online or offline infrastructure.
- ...

THE FOUR EXAMPLES

Below you will find the completed Strategy Sketches of our four examples. I am not saying these are perfect examples, or even particularly good ones. They just show you the kind of information that is typically mentioned in this second step of the strategy generation process. When you have a look at these four sketches, you'll obtain a good sense of what the strategies of these four organizations look like. You might also see inconsistencies, questions, or problems, but that is also quite common–if the sketches were perfect, there would be no reason to engage in strategy generation in the first place!

MACMAN

Risks & Costs

Our main costs (and risks) come from the materials needed to produce our machines and from the long time we have them in stock. Also personnel costs are relatively high compared to competitors. We have ran an extensive 'lean' program the past two years, meaning that most inefficiencies and waste have been eliminated.

Revenue Model

We earn most of our income through selling our machines and through offering services and maintenance. We have experimented with leasing out our machines, but that has not worked so far.

Partners

Our main partners are:

Two universities for keeping our technology up-to-date and for hiring new engineers.

Suppliers of steel: our own machines can be so precise because of the quality of material we receive.

For the rest we are pretty independent and we are proud of that.

Resources & Competences

Our main resources are our engineers. They are highly qualified, hard to get, and without them the company could not exist. Competitors offer higher wages, but they like working for us.

We have two main competences:

1.) translating vague customer needs into precise machine specifications and

2.) providing a fun and challenging working place for our engineers.

For the rest we still have about 20% unused capacity.

Value Proposition

We design, produce, install, and service high-precision custom-made steel bending and cutting machines that can accurately process very large steel sheets.

Our machines provide the customer with the lowest total cost of ownership in terms of money.

Values & Goals

There are a couple of things we really find important:

-Although we could very well, we don't serve the weapon industry

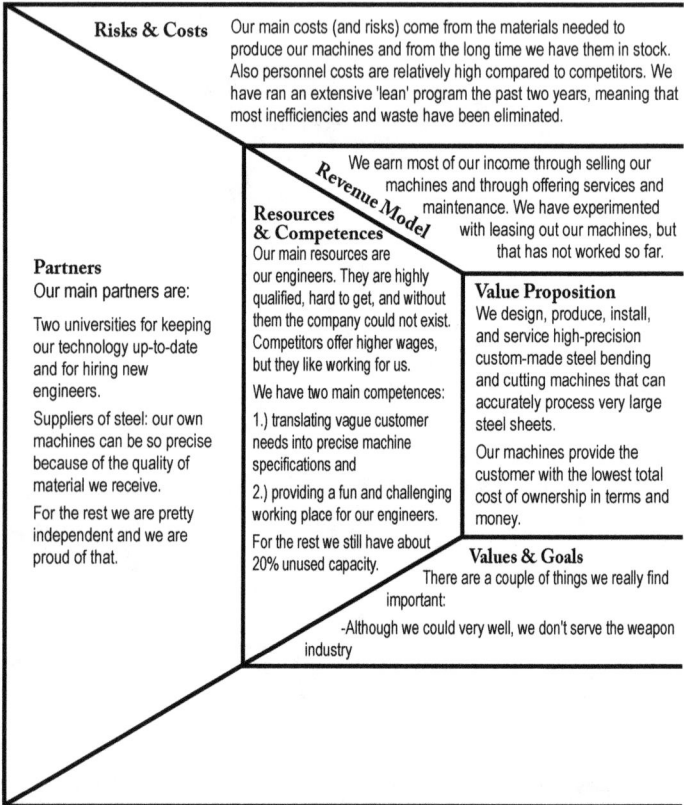

Trends A main threat comes from China, where they are increasingly able to produce with high accuracy - at low cost. Increasing steel prices are worrisome too. Weapons industry is attractive and growing, but we say we don't want this...

Uncertainties
Plastics seems to grow but it is unclear whether we are able to produce machines for that.
Not so many uncertainties it seems; we are in a pretty stable industry. At least so far.

Competitors
We have plenty of competitors.

Three in Europe, offering a similar quality level. Our main advantage is the personal relationship we have with customers, but we're too expensive.

Competition mainly came from the US so far, but three new Chinese competitors have entered the market recently.

We mostly compete with Company X for new orders. To be honest, they are just as good as we but offer lower prices.

Customers & Needs
Our main customers are 2 large high-precision machine manufacturers in Europe that require steel cutting and bending machines.

Few irregular other customers.

The customers of our customers are manufacturers of medical precision instruments. They need extremely reliable and accurate equipment.

-Our employees should be modest, like their work, and listen to customers

-We don't need to grow, but we do want to keep our current size

Organizational Climate
The climate of our organization can be best characterized as hard-working, loyal, high-tech, and fun. We lack an entrepreneurial sprit though, which is why we are not good at coming up with new ideas.

HOSPICARE

Risks & Costs
Exploring 'low-cost' options: cheaper 'beds' (suitable for simple care)
workflow has been optimized - saved costs but customers not happy.

Revenue Model
The usual way: through
insurance; getting less and less
attractive.

Partners

We have: Insurance
firms-they are customers,
but we also need to work
with them.

Suppliers of equipment:
Firms A,B,C,and D.

Six sigma company: helped
improving efficiency &
workflow.

We need: Marketing
partner to better 'sell' our
care.

Academic hospital to team
up with.

**Resources
& Competences**

Location: in a densely
populated area with no other
hospital nearby.

Surgeons: the best skilled.
Expensive though.

Competences: fast and
reliable operations - shortest
time in hospital for patients.

Value Proposition
General health care - as legally
defined.

Overall highest certainty that an
operation succeeds (compared
to competitors)

Patients say service and
'human touch' could be
improved.

Trends Upcoming commercial health providers, operating outside the normal circuit.
Increased specialization.

Uncertainties
Regulation, regulation, regulation - changes all the time
Acceptance of invoices by insurance firms - do we get everything paid?

Experimenting with selling directly to
patients - in a separate business.

Customers & Needs
Two types with conflicting needs:

1. **Patients:** mostly from the region.
Need general healthcare.

1a. **Patients** from the whole country
for treatment X & Y
(our specialization).

2. All **health insurance firms** in the
country. Need: offering their
customers the lowest fee.

2a. **Insurance firms E and M** at which
the majority of our patients is insured.
Also want lowest insurance fee.

Competitors
1. Other **general hospitals,**
particularly Hospital W (nearby)

2. Also **academic hospitals,**
particularly for the parts we're
specialized in.

3. Increasingly: **commercial
firm** outside the conventional
circuit.

Values & Goals
Grow, we have to, in order to compete.
1500 beds at least.

Do more with our specializations. We're good at them,
but don't use them. Create a commercial spin-off.

Organizational Climate
Professional, no-nonsense, & business like. Pretty tough and individualistic culture.
Career-oriented. Could be more people minded.

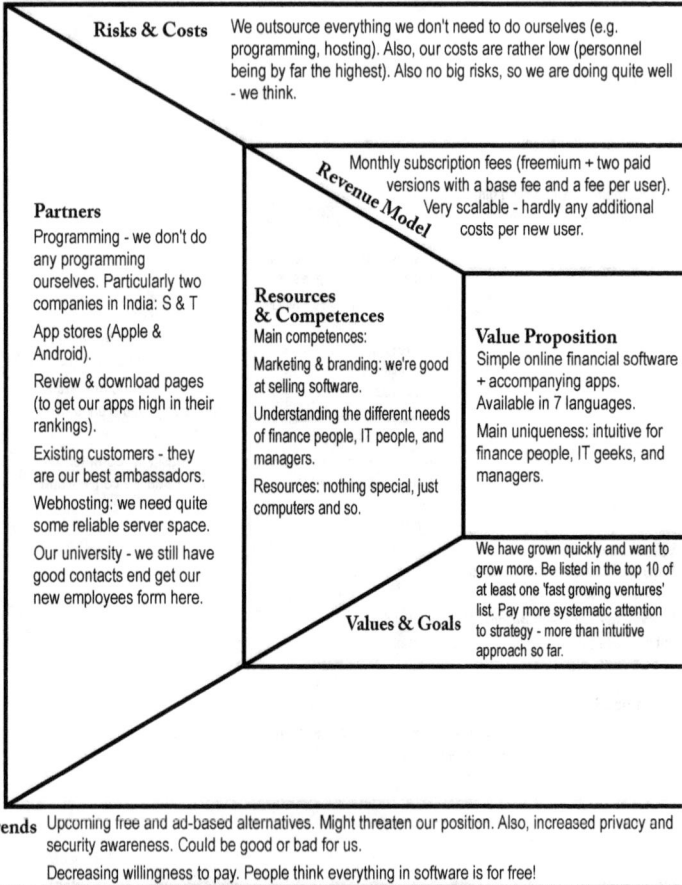

GOFORIT

Risks & Costs
We outsource everything we don't need to do ourselves (e.g. programming, hosting). Also, our costs are rather low (personnel being by far the highest). Also no big risks, so we are doing quite well - we think.

Revenue Model
Monthly subscription fees (freemium + two paid versions with a base fee and a fee per user). Very scalable - hardly any additional costs per new user.

Partners
Programming - we don't do any programming ourselves. Particularly two companies in India: S & T

App stores (Apple & Android).

Review & download pages (to get our apps high in their rankings).

Existing customers - they are our best ambassadors.

Webhosting: we need quite some reliable server space.

Our university - we still have good contacts end get our new employees form here.

Resources & Competences
Main competences:

Marketing & branding: we're good at selling software.

Understanding the different needs of finance people, IT people, and managers.

Resources: nothing special, just computers and so.

Value Proposition
Simple online financial software + accompanying apps. Available in 7 languages.

Main uniqueness: intuitive for finance people, IT geeks, and managers.

We have grown quickly and want to grow more. Be listed in the top 10 of at least one 'fast growing ventures' list. Pay more systematic attention to strategy - more than intuitive approach so far.

Values & Goals

Trends Upcoming free and ad-based alternatives. Might threaten our position. Also, increased privacy and security awareness. Could be good or bad for us.

Decreasing willingness to pay. People think everything in software is for free!

Uncertainties
How long can we still rely on our technology? It can be easily copied by others. We're relying on our brand, but that is a bit shaky.

Competitors
Plenty.

Providers of free financial software. (not really good, but customers consider this first).

Providers of paid financial software. (more threatening, but they are still quite conventional).

Closest to what we do: Companies R, T, and Z. Customers choose for them too, and their software is a bit comparable.

Customers & Needs
Small business across the globe (5-50 employees).

So far mainly in Latin America, Southern Europe, and Australia.

Within these companies:

Users: financial departments

Decision-makers: owner/CEO

Key influencer: IT department

Get a foothold in Germany - a challenge since our software deviates from the 'normal'

Organizational Climate
Very entrepreneurial and creative - but also messy. We are bunch of enthusiasts, but we probably need more structure if we want to grow further.

COMCOM

Risks & Costs
Costs are very low: working from home and outsource printing etc. I have standardized my way of working-and am pretty efficient now, I must say.

Revenue Model
Hourly rate, but I don't what that anymore. Maybe fixed rate for standard product?

Partners
Strategy consultant who works a lot with accountancy firm. My services are complementary and I get a lot of leads through him.

Printer who prints brochures, reports, etc.

2 other communication advisors (if we're too busy, we recommend each other)

Resources & Competences
Writing skills
Knowledge of accounting (through my customer-base)
Big network in health-care (related to my previous job: I was internal communication advisor)

Value Proposition
Services: Communication plans, PR & text writing.

Main value for customers: getting better & more attention from prospective clients.

How: Interaction with customers is completely digital (mail, Skype, chat, etc.)

Values & Goals
I want to stay independent as a freelancer. I want (and need) more income: increase revenues with at least 20% (soon).

Trends
Price competition - freelance competitors ruin the market by asking ridiculously low rates.

Uncertainties
Can I keep my current customers?? They are asking me to reduce prices all the time...
What will be a profitable niche? I have contacts in the restaurant business, but will this fly?

Customers & Needs
For some reason mainly small to medium-sized accountancy firms (60-70% of turnover).

They need to show how they are different from their competitors (exactly what I need myself as well...)

Competitors
Many many other communication advisors. They do more of less the same (in the same country).

Marketing companies: can offer more than just communication (also strategy, not my strong point).

I don't want to work more. 50 hours is enough. It would be cool if I could write about things I am really interested in (food!)

Dream: a blog or website read by thousands of people.

Organizational Climate
Not much of an organization - just on my own. I want to work digitally (keeps things flexible)
Need a better work-life balance-the job is starting to be no fun anymore.

least for now. If you choose to do this, you should have a look at the fast and frugal approach to strategy generation noted below.

A FAST AND FRUGAL STRATEGY GENERATION FORMAT

While I certainly recommend following the remaining steps as well, you now have the basic ingredients for strategy generation. If you just want to stick to the basics for now, this can be a productive way to proceed.

1. Get a handful of people together who are quite different and relevant for your strategy. You could also do this on your own, but variety usually helps.
2. Print or draw the Strategy Sketch on a large sheet of paper, at least DIN A3/Tabloid format, but bigger is better. Put it on a table or wall so that everyone can see it.
3. Map out your current strategy using the first set of "Questions to ask" for each element. Write down short statements directly on the paper or using sticky notes.
4. Gather new ideas using the other questions, examples, beyond-the-obvious exercises, and inspirational checklists. Write these ideas down too, preferably using another color.
5. Pick the three best ideas and develop them further on a clean Strategy Sketch. Build a complete Strategy Sketch that shows a coherent picture around these ideas. This works particularly well if you take different value propositions or customer groups as a starting point.
6. Go away and test your ideas in practice with customers, suppliers, employees, and others.
7. Come back, evaluate, and repeat until you're done.

Instead of using paper and Post-its, you could also do all of this in a digital format. There are various digital workspace tools or online collaborative whiteboard platforms that you can use for this. They simulate the traditional paper-based approach and add additional features such as remote working. Or, like I do, you can also opt for a low-tech digital solution, creating your own digital "paper and Post-its" in PowerPoint or Keynote.

5

STEP 3: ASSESSING STRATEGY

This chapter presents step 3 of the strategy process: assessing strategy. It presents ten Strategy Checks that can be used to assess your current or new strategy, or to compare strategic options. You don't always need all of them, but together these checks form an extensive assessment toolbox that should give detailed insights into the quality of your strategy. It also includes a short version on page 132–the Strategy Checklist.

> **Assessing Strategy** = Judging and testing the quality of the organization's strategy against relevant criteria.

WHY AND WHEN TO ASSESS YOUR STRATEGY

There is one obvious reason why you want to assess your strategy: to know whether it's good enough. While mapping it, you might already have some idea about the quality of your strategy. You might have encountered inconsistencies, problems, or possible ways to improve it. On top of this, it pays off if you do your assessment in a more systematic way. Therefore, the third step of the strategy process is *assessing* strategy.

There are two logical points where you may want to assess your strategy. The first is *before* you start thinking about new strategy. After you have mapped your strategy in the previous step, assessing it gives you a lot of information about whether it requires improvement and where it can be improved. This is valuable input for the next step–innovating strategy. In some cases, the insights you get might be so good that you can even skip this whole step: once you know the problems, the solution might be obvious.

The second point when you want to assess your strategy is *after* you have come up with a new strategy. In this case you do your assessment after step 4 (Chapter 6, "Innovating Strategy"). The main reason at this point is that you want to get an idea of the quality of your newly developed strategy. So, before you are going to spend a lot of money and energy on executing it, you want to check whether it's likely to succeed or not. At this point you might also have generated a number of strategic options or possible directions rather than just one. In that case, assessment helps you choose between these options.

TEN STRATEGY CHECKS

While there is an endless number of criteria that you can use to assess your strategy, I have found the following ten particularly useful.

1. *Coherence check.* Do the elements match? Do they add up to a coherent strategy or not?
2. *Efficiency check.* Are all elements used up to their maximum potential? Can they be better exploited?
3. *Effectiveness check.* Does the strategy work? Are you achieving what you want and getting an adequate performance?
4. *Uniqueness check.* Is the strategy unique enough? Is it sufficiently different from what competitors are doing?
5. *Flexibility check.* Is the strategy sufficiently flexible? Can it easily be adapted to changes if necessary?
6. *Robustness check.* Can the strategy sustain long enough? Can it withstand internal and external changes, crises, and disruptions?
7. *Scalability check.* Is the strategy scalable? Can it grow or shrink easily without too much effort and investment?

8. *Responsibility check.* Does the strategy comply with ethical and moral standards? Is it right what is being done?
9. *Actionability check.* Is the strategy clear, concrete, and focused so that people can understand it? Is it realistic?
10. *Energy check.* Does the strategy motivate and inspire? Does it cover things that you and your people really care about?

Each of these strategy checks is further explained in the following pages. You will also find a brief Strategy Checklist on page 132 that helps you to check your strategy in a fast and frugal way.

STRATEGY CHECK 1. COHERENCE CHECK

Good strategy is coherent and without too many contradictions. Therefore, a first check that you want to do is to assess whether your strategy is sufficiently coherent. This is done by looking at the relationships between the ten elements and assessing whether they make sense in combination. With ten elements, the number of possible combinations is virtually unlimited and it makes no sense to look at all of them. If there are particular combinations that are especially important for your organization, you should definitely look at those. If, on the other hand, you don't have any upfront idea which relationships are most important, I suggest checking the following eight combinations. These are the ones I find myself regularly referring to in my own work.

1. **Resources & competences + Organizational climate + Values & goals.** *Does what you want and aspire to match with what you actually have or can do with the organization?* To check this you can start with your values and goals and ask whether it's realistic to obtain the required means and organizational climate. You can also start with your means and organizational climate and check whether your values and goals are challenging enough but also not out of reach for your organization.

2. **Resources & competences + Partners.** *Who has the most important resources and competences: you or your partners?* While it's good to have strong partners, your value proposition should not depend more on them than on your own strengths. Also check whether there is not too much overlap between your own resources and competences and theirs.

3. **Customers & needs + Value proposition + Competitors.** *Does your value proposition really match what your customers need and is it sufficiently different from what competitors offer?* When customers compare your offer to that of competitors, they should have sufficient reason to choose you. Therefore, you want to check whether you are actually creating the kind of value your customers are looking for.

4. **Customers & needs + Value proposition + Values & goals.** *Is what you offer and who you offer it to in line with your values and goals?* There might be a tendency to be opportunistic and to say yes to whatever customer that comes your way— especially in difficult times. But if this dilutes your strategy or keeps you away from what you actually say you want to focus on, it might be better to say no to some customers.

5. **Revenue model + Risk & costs.** *Is your revenue sufficient relative to the risks and costs you bear?* Your strategy can both start with the intention to maximize returns as well as to minimize and control the risks and costs you are willing to bear. Whatever starting point you choose, though, you want to make sure that your risks and costs are not disproportionally high compared to your revenue model.

6. **Values & goals + Risks & costs.** *Are the risks and costs associated with your strategy acceptable for the organization?* Any strategy comes with a particular level of risks and costs. Whether these are acceptable depends on the values and goals that are important for the organization. If, for example, trust, reliability, and certainty are key values, you probably want to bear less risks and costs than if entrepreneurship, fast growth,

and boldness are emphasized. Therefore, you need to assess whether the risks and costs of your strategy are in line with the organization's values and goals.

7. **Values & goals + Partners.** *Do you work with partners that match you own values and goals?* The best partners are partners that have similar values and goals as you. This facilitates the collaboration, and makes it more likely that you realize your values and goals. You want to know whether your partners find the same things important as you or whether there are mismatches that can hinder fruitful cooperation. For the latter you need to decide what to do. Do you adjust your values and goals, stop collaborating, try to reach an agreement, or do you just go on?

8. **Trends & uncertainties + Values & goals.** *Do you effectively combine seizing opportunities happening in your environment and sticking to your goals?* Seizing opportunities might help you, but it might also lead you to drift away from your goals. When sticking to your values and goals you actually follow your strategy, but you also might miss out on opportunities. Since both have their advantages and disadvantages choices need to be made.

STRATEGY CHECK 2. EFFICIENCY CHECK

The second check that you can do to assess your strategy is an efficiency check. This check answers the question as to whether you are using the ten elements to their full potential, or whether there is room for improvement. As such, with this check you look for untapped potential in any of the ten elements of the Strategy Sketch.

1. *Resources & competences.* Do you use all your resources and competences and do you use them in the best possible way? Or is there still capacity, information, skills, knowledge, etc., that could be better exploited?
2. *Partners.* Do you have all the partners you need and do you have the best partners you can find? Do you use all

the relevant strengths of your partners? Do you benefit at least as much as they do from the partnership?

3. *Customers & needs.* Do you serve the best possible customers and do you serve as many of their needs as you realistically can? Or are there still better customers or needs that you could serve as well?

4. *Competitors.* Do you do all you can to outperform, avoid, or benefit from your competitors? Do you focus on the competitors that are best for you? Do you benefit at least as much from them as they do from you?

5. *Value proposition.* Do you offer the best value proposition that you can offer with your organization? Do you create as much value as you can with your strategy, or are there ways to increase this?

6. *Revenue model.* Do you use all the revenue-generating options there are? Does everyone that benefits from your strategy also sufficiently pay in one way or another? Or can they pay more?

7. *Risk & costs.* Do you minimize the costs and risks you bear, or are there still unnecessary ones that you can avoid?

8. *Values & goals.* Are all the relevant values and goals made explicit and do you really focus on them? Do you use them sufficiently as drivers and motivators for the organization?

9. *Organizational climate.* Do you have the best organizational climate that you can imagine? Does it sufficiently foster the execution of your strategy? Do you use it sufficiently to your advantage?

10. *Trends & uncertainties.* Have you identified the most relevant trends and uncertainties? Do you use them to your advantage in the best possible way?

STRATEGY CHECK 3. EFFECTIVENESS CHECK

A third strategy check that you want to do is an effectiveness check. Basically, with this check you assess whether your strategy works or not. Two dimensions of this check are important: what criteria you use (what do you measure?), and what you use as a yardstick (what do you compare your performance to so that you know whether it's good or bad?).

EFFECTIVENESS CRITERIA

With respect to the criteria we can distinguish between a *basic*, overall effectiveness check and a *refined*, element-based effectiveness check. To do a basic effectiveness check you could use the popular "Triple Bottom Line" (or 3Ps), which is widely adopted by organizations all over the world. Following this framework, you should assess your strategy in terms of profit, people, and planet.

- *Profit*, or economic impact. For this criterion, numerous financial ratios can be used such as ROI (return on investment), EBITDA (earnings before interest, tax, depreciation, and amortization), or EPS (earnings per share), to name just a few.
- *People*, or social impact. This concerns the positive and negative impact of the strategy on its employees, communities, or other type of stakeholder. Instruments to measure social impact include SROI (social return on investment) and SIA (social impact assessment).
- *Planet*, or ecological impact. This concerns the positive or negative environmental impact of the strategy. The Ecological Footprint or Trucost approach are examples of instruments to measure against this criterion.

If you don't know all these assessment instruments–which is likely since not all of them are widely used yet–you can look them up on the Internet by just typing in their name, or by searching more broadly using terms such as "financial ratios" and "social impact measurement."

"You should be picky and select only those criteria that you find especially relevant for your organization."

For a more *refined* effectiveness check, assess each element of the Strategy Sketch separately. While a basic effectiveness check gives you a good impression of the overall effectiveness of your strategy, a refined check provides you with more actionable information. Once you find out that a particular element of the strategy doesn't meet your standards, it's clear that that element needs to be improved. The following criteria can be used for a refined effectiveness check.

Element	Example Criteria
Resources & Competences	Capacity utilization level; Brand value; % of sales spent on R&D; Number of training hours per employee; Number of patents; Projected future earnings; Return on investment.
Partners	Number of partners; Partner satisfaction level; Diversity of partners; Number of complaints per partner; Time spent on negations per partner.
Customers & Needs	Number of customers; Customer satisfaction level; Customer loyalty; Order quantity; Number of repeat orders; Profitability per customer; Number of new customers through customers.
Competitors	Number of competitors; Market share; Growth rate of the market; Concentration ratio; Average margin in the industry; Herfindahl index; Number of new competitors.
Value Proposition	Design, usefulness, quality, and reliability of product/service; Punctuality of delivery; Value-for-money.
Revenue Model	Sales revenues; Discounted cash flow; EBITDA; Profitability per product; Earnings per share; Growth rate.
Risk & Costs	Number of defects, delays, and injuries; Potential loss x probably of risk; Annual loss expectancy; Liquidity; Solvency; Fixed/variable costs; Inventory conversion period.
Values & Goals	Clarity of values and goals; Awareness level; Compliance with legal and ethical standards; Clarity of performance indicators; Degree of monitoring and control against values and goals.
Organizational Climate	Employee satisfaction; Employee turnover; Absenteeism rate; Degree of formalization; Degree of employee initiative; Openness of communication; Risk tolerance.
Trends & Uncertainties	Degree of uncertainty; Speed of change; Complexity of the environment; Ratio of positive and negative trends; Dependency on particular trends or uncertainties.

Together, these ten types of effectiveness criteria form a comprehensive measurement system for measuring how effective your strategy is. Compared to the current most-used approach–the Balanced Scorecard–this set of criteria is much richer and more complete. Generally, this is an advantage, because it allows you to develop more detailed and relevant insights into the strategic performance of your organization. However, you should make sure that you don't use all of them. This will be way too much and it will complicate your strategy process or even let it stagnate. You should be picky and select only those criteria that you find especially relevant for your organization. A handful or two should be enough.

YARDSTICKS

Assessing your strategy against these criteria gives you a lot of information about the effectiveness of your strategy. However, to judge whether your scores are good or bad, you also need to compare them to some sort of standard–you need a yardstick. There are four types of yardsticks you can use, including goal-based, stakeholder, relative, and absolute.

- *Goal-based yardstick.* First, you can use your own goals as a main yardstick for assessing your strategy against the criteria above. The main question then is whether or not you achieve what you want with these various criteria. If, for example, your aim was to achieve a revenue increase of 10%, you can measure your performance against this aim.
- *Stakeholder yardstick.* A second yardstick that you can use is relevant stakeholders' expectations. These could be your customers, suppliers, employees, financiers, or any other type of stakeholder that is important to your organization. The key question with this yardstick is whether you do what your main stakeholders expect or ask from you.
- *Relative yardstick.* You can also compare yourself to others and thus take a relative point of comparison. Think, for example, of an industry average, or a comparison with your most important competitors. Along those lines you can assess, for example, whether your employee turnover is below, on, or above your industry's average.
- *Absolute yardstick.* Finally, for some criteria there are commonly adopted threshold values that can be used as a yardstick. Examples are the "quick ratio" which generally should be 1 or higher, or "zero waste"–which should be zero.

STRATEGY CHECK 4. UNIQUENESS CHECK

As the definition of strategy indicates, good strategy aims at developing a unique and sustainable way of value creation. Accordingly, a fourth criterion to assess your strategy is its uniqueness. Three aspects of uniqueness are important: the sources of uniqueness, the degree of uniqueness, and the sustainability of uniqueness.

SOURCES OF UNIQUENESS

Strategies can be unique in many ways. In fact, uniqueness can be found in all ten elements of the Strategy Sketch. So, to assess the uniqueness of your strategy, you can compare your strategy to others and judge whether you...

- ...possess unique resources or competences that others don't have.
- ...have access to unique partners in your network.
- ...offer a value proposition with one or more unique features.
- ...serve a unique group of customers or a unique need they have.
- ...have a unique relationship with one or more competitors.
- ...use a unique revenue model, a way of making money.
- ...have a unique risk or cost advantage or way of managing these.
- ...have unique values or goals that drive the organization.
- ...have a unique organizational culture or structure.
- ...are exposed to unique trends or uncertainties.

If one or more of these elements is indeed unique, this is a good basis for building your strategy. This applies even if this uniqueness may look bad initially (such as high fixed costs, a negative organizational climate, or customers that systematically complain and pay late). Although perhaps bad in your current strategy, they reflect what you currently have. Try seeing them as strengths and find a way to use them. You might, for example, have costs that are relatively high but also largely variable, have employees that complain because they care, or have customers that want to tell you something through their annoying behavior. Of course, not all uniquely "bad" characteristics can be turned into advantages. However, it's still useful to at least have a look at them in this way.

DEGREE OF UNIQUENESS

Your strategy need not be 100% unique. That would be impossible and even if it were feasible you would have such an exotic or obscure organization that it would be very unlikely that it would attract many customers. On the other hand, your strategy is never completely identical to your competitors' strategy, if only because your organization's name, people, location, or customers are different. In between these extremes, it makes a lot of sense to assess the degree to which your strategy is unique. When you do this, it's useful to identify which of the following five degrees of uniqueness apply to your strategy.

1. **Unique to the organization.** Your strategy is new for you but is already used by your competitors. This is usually not so good since it means you're not unique anymore.

2. **Unique to the region**. Your strategy is similar to strategies used in other regions (another continent, country, city, and so on) but is not used yet in your region.
    Example: Ryanair's low-cost strategy, which was already used by Southwest Airlines in the United States.

3. **Unique to the market segment**. Your strategy has been used to serve particular groups of customers, but not the ones you are addressing.
    Example: car manufacturers offering features for cars in the lower segments which were previously only available to higher segments.

4. **Unique to the industry.** Your strategy looks like strategies used in other industries, but has not been used in your industry so far.
    Example: Airbnb's home-sharing strategy which looks like car-sharing strategies.

5. **Unique to the world.** As far as you know, no one else has done anything similar. This can be really good and groundbreaking but also risky.
    Example: Cirque du Soleil's unique combination of theatre and circus.

Generally, the more unique your strategy is, the more potential it has. However, the risks also increase, so you always should assess whether the level of uniqueness is suitable for you.

> *"It's nice to be unique today, but what if others see what you do and copy it as soon as they can?"*

SUSTAINABILITY OF UNIQUENESS

A third aspect of uniqueness that you need in order to assess your strategy is the sustainability of that uniqueness. It's nice to be unique today, but what if others see what you do and copy it as soon as they can? Where does that leave you with all your efforts? To assess the sustainability of your uniqueness, you can ask the following four questions.

1. Can (parts of) your strategy be legally protected by patents, copyrights, trademarks, or other legal forms? *Example:* Nike's "swoosh" logo or Adidas's three stripes.
2. Can (parts of) your strategy be monopolized so that you are the only one able to use it? *Example:* Facebook's user base.
3. Can (parts of) your strategy be kept secret or hidden for competitors so that they don't know enough to copy? *Example:* DuPont's trade secret for producing Kevlar.
4. Can (parts of) your strategy be made so complex that they are virtually impossible for others to understand or imitate? *Example:* CERN's large hadron collider.

If you want your strategy to be sustainable and imitation-proof, the answer to at least one of these questions should be yes. If this is not the case, these four questions show you the various ways in which you could make it harder to imitate.

STRATEGY CHECK 5. FLEXIBILITY CHECK

Given that change happens everywhere and a crisis may happen at any time, you also want your strategy to be sufficiently flexible so that you can quickly respond, innovate, and adjust. A strategy should not be changed all the time, but not being *able* to change it when necessary is a problem that you want to avoid. As with the previous checks, this strategy check is also relevant for all the elements of your strategy. To assess the flexibility of your strategy, you should ask the following questions.

1. *Resources & competences*. Are you able to keep your resources and competences up to date? Do you renew them enough? Can you get rid of them if necessary?

2. *Partners*. Can you switch to other partners if necessary? Are you not too dependent on some of them? Can you easily get new partners or let existing partners go? Can they change with you?

3. *Customers & needs*. Are you sufficiently aware of the changing needs or habits of your customers? Can you quickly adjust your offer to new customers or to new customer needs?

4. *Competitors*. Are you sufficiently aware of your competitors and their strategies? Can you respond quickly enough to their actions?

5. *Value proposition*. Can you improve or change your products or services easily? Can you offer new or additional products or services if required?

6. *Revenue model*. Can you easily change the way you make money? Can you increase prices without losing too many customers?

7. *Risk & costs*. Can you easily change your risk profile? Can you change your cost structure when circumstances ask for it?

8. *Values & goals*. Are your goals and plans sufficiently flexible? Do you change them enough when circumstances ask for it?

9. *Organizational climate*. Is the culture or structure of your organization sufficiently flexible? Are people able to change their habits, jobs, or ways of working?

10. *Trends & uncertainties*. Are you sufficiently sensitive to changes in your environment? Can you respond quickly enough to unexpected events and crises?

Not all the elements of your strategy should necessarily be flexible. If they are, there is a great chance that your organization will drift and lack a clear and recognizable profile. Furthermore, there are no clear rules that tell you how flexible you need to be. That depends very much on the dynamics and complexity of your industry and on whether your strategy is built around being flexible or not. This means that it's largely up to your own judgment whether you think your strategy is sufficiently flexible or not. You do want to make sure, though, that none of the elements of your strategy really lock you in and form a barrier against change and innovation.

"Compared to a flexible strategy, a robust strategy has the advantage that it gives the organization stability."

STRATEGY CHECK 6. ROBUSTNESS CHECK

Ensuring that your strategy is flexible is one way of dealing with changes and unexpected events. Another way is to make your strategy more robust. A robust strategy is a strategy that, as a whole, can remain largely unchanged even when there are changes, crises, or disruptions in some of its elements or in the environment. Compared to a flexible strategy, a robust strategy has the advantage that it gives the organization stability, rather than requiring continuous adaptations.

The most comprehensive way of assessing the robustness of your strategy is to come up with a number of scenarios–including unlikely but disruptive ones–and judge whether your strategy is capable of dealing with the majority of them. If this is indeed the case, it indicates that your strategy is not affected by changes in your environment–and is therefore robust. This gives you some degree of certainty that your strategy works out, even if things might turn out differently than you expected, for example in the face of an internal or external crisis.

Another way to assess the robustness of your strategy is to ask yourself what happens to the other elements if one element of your strategy changes significantly. Thus, for example, if your most important people were to leave the organization (reflecting a change in resources and competences), could you still offer the same value proposition to the same customers? Or, if your biggest customer suddenly left, would your revenue model still be profitable? To put it a bit more systematically, you can ask the following three questions for each element of the Strategy Sketch.

- If something *disappears* in this element, can the other elements and the strategy as a whole remain unchanged?
- If something is *added* to this element, can the other elements and the strategy as a whole remain unchanged?
- If something *changes* in this element, can the other elements and the strategy as a whole remain unchanged?

STRATEGY CHECK 7. SCALABILITY CHECK

As a seventh check you may also want to assess whether your strategy is scalable enough. Traditionally, a *scalable* strategy is a strategy that is suitable for growth. This means that you can increase your revenue or impact relatively easily compared to the extra effort this would require and that there are no substantial barriers against growth. Scalability seems unimportant for some organizations. After all, if you don't want to grow, you probably don't care too much about scalability. However, even then it might still be useful to assess your strategy's scalability. This will show you whether you could achieve the same revenue or impact with less effort. And who doesn't want that? There can be growth barriers related to each of the ten elements of the Strategy Sketch. To identify them, you can use the following questions.

1. *Resources & competences.* Are there enough resources available? Can you get the people you need? Do you have the capacity and skills to produce on a larger scale?
2. *Partners*: Can you get sufficient and suitable suppliers? Can they deliver everything you would need?
3. *Customers & needs.* Are there enough potential customers? Is the overall market large enough?
4. *Competitors.* Can you grow without increasing the level of competition? Will competitors not respond with countermoves?

5. *Value proposition.* Do your products and services appeal to a large market? Are they not limited to a particular niche?

6. *Revenue model.* Would the revenue model still work if sales increased substantially? What about the pricing strategy?

7. *Risk & costs.* Would your risks and costs rise less than your revenue? Or at least not more than your revenue?

8. *Values & goals.* Do people in the organization want to grow? Is growth in line with the organization's values and goals?

9. *Organizational climate.* Is the organizational structure suitable for growth? What about the organizational culture?

10. *Trends & uncertainties.* Are you still able to respond to ongoing trends? Are you facing important new uncertainties?

Scalability works the other way around too: a truly scalable strategy can also be easily *downscaled*. This may be needed, for example, when the demand for your product or service decreases, when it's impossible to hire and retain sufficient staff, or when there are shortages in the supply chain. To check whether your strategy can be sufficiently downscaled, you can again look at all ten elements and reverse the questions that were formulated above.

STRATEGY CHECK 8. RESPONSIBILITY CHECK

Good strategy is not only good in terms of benefits for the organization, but also in terms of legal, ethical, and societal norms and values. Views on what is good, though, can differ quite radically.

- On the one extreme, there is the "shareholder view." This argues that it's good for the organization and for society if the organization aims exclusively at generating revenue or profits for its shareholders. The reason is that organizations will try to make the best of their resources in this way. And if everyone does this, society as a whole is better off. Thus, in this view a strategy is good if it maximizes shareholder value.

- On the other extreme there is the "stakeholder view." This argues the other way around: It's good for the organization and its stakeholders if the organization is good for other stakeholders as well. The reason is that organizations depend on their stakeholders. Only by satisfying them can the organization sustain its position over time. Thus, from this point of view strategy should do well for others too.

In practice, you probably combine these two views. Often the interest of the organization itself takes priority over the interests of others, although others are also taken into account.

In this eighth strategy check, you assess whether the strategy sufficiently accounts for the interests of various stakeholders. There are two versions of this check: a simple one and an elaborate one.

A SIMPLE RESPONSIBILITY CHECK

For a simple approach to assess whether your strategy is responsible or not, you can use Texas Instruments' guidelines for ethical decision-making. It consists of the following six questions.

- Is everything that needs to be done to realize the strategy legal? If not, change it.
- Does your strategy comply with organizational and societal values? If not, change it.
- Does your strategy require you to do anything that would make you feel bad? If so, change it.
- How would it look if news media reported about your strategy? Bad? Change it.
- Do you know whether the things you need to do to realize your strategy are right or wrong? If wrong, change it.
- You aren't sure? Ask until you get an answer.

A MORE ELABORATE RESPONSIBILITY CHECK

If you want to know more specifically whether your strategy is responsible and whether it makes the organization do the right thing, you can carry out a more elaborate responsibility check. This check includes two sets of questions. The first is about whether you sufficiently avoid causing negative effects and the second about whether you sufficiently generate positive effects.

Questions for assessing whether you sufficiently *avoid negative* effects:	Questions for assessing whether you sufficiently *generate positive* effects:
• Are any people mistreated? Think of employees, suppliers, customers, neighbors, communities, etc.	• Do you make peoples' lives better? Think of employees, suppliers, customers, neighbors, communities, etc.
• Are any resources depleted? Think specifically about natural resources with limited availability.	• Do you create or upgrade resources so that they can be used in a better way? Think of the treatment of materials or energy as byproduct.
• Is there any waste or pollution that could be avoided? Think of energy and unrecyclable materials.	• Do you add something valuable to the world? Is it better off with your organization than without?
• Do you use or get more than you actually need? Think of revenue, luxuries, bonuses, etc.	• Do you let others benefit from what you don't really need? Think about philanthropy, charities, etc.

• Do you create or increase social problems? Think of reduced standards of living or wellbeing, inequality, injustice, reduced freedom, etc.	• Do you solve or reduce social problems? Think of improving the standard of living, wellbeing, equality, justice, freedom, etc.
• Do you, intentionally or unintentionally, encourage others to make a negative impact? Think about setting a bad example, promoting unethical behavior, etc.	• Do you, intentionally or unintentionally, stimulate others to make a positive contribution to the world? Think about lecturing, foundations, role model, etc.

The more affirmative answers you have in the left column, the more room there is for improvement. And the more affirmative answers you have in the right column, the more your strategy is responsible.

STRATEGY CHECK 9. ACTIONABILITY CHECK

In the end, a strategy is only as good as its execution. This is the reason that the entire strategy generation process focuses on generating *executable* strategy. This makes actionability an important ninth criterion to assess your strategy. Actionability has two main parts: can people understand the strategy and can it be attained.

An understandable strategy is a strategy that is clear and concrete and that has a certain focus. Strategies that are all over the place or that are hardly recognizable are hard to execute. This applies most certainly to formal strategies. If they are written down in vague and abstract terms, they are not actionable. It is for this reason that strategy formulation is included as a separate step in the strategy process (step 5). But it applies to unwritten, informal strategies too. If it's not clear what an organization does today, or what it is supposed to do, it's very hard to know what is expected from people. To assess this, you can ask the following questions.

1. Is the strategy focused enough and does it reflect choices about what to do and what not to do?
2. Is the strategy simple enough so that people can grasp it as a whole?
3. Is the strategy concrete and tangible enough to understand what executing it means?

To be really actionable, a strategy also needs to be attainable. It should be reasonably realistic and match the organization's capacities and capabilities. A strategy can be great in every other respect, but if it's not attainable, it's not going to be executed. As the next chapter shows in more detail, what is attainable depends to a large extent on one's willingness and ability to innovate and invest. This check is not an invitation for lowering your ambitions. However, decades of research has shown that unrealistic expectations are amongst the key drivers of failure in strategy execution. To assess the attainability of your strategy, you can ask the following three questions.

1. Do we have the time, money, and other resources required to execute this strategy?
2. Do we have the right skills and competences to execute this strategy?
3. Do people believe in and support the strategy so that they are willing to execute it?

"The point of doing all these assessments is not to arrive at some perfect utopian strategy. Looking for that will paralyze you rather than help you move on."

STRATEGY CHECK 10. ENERGY CHECK

No matter how well a strategy meets the other nine criteria, it will be laborious to execute if people don't really like it or don't see the point of it. In such cases it will drain their energy and they might execute it, but only because they have to, or because they are loyal to the organization. A strategy that energizes people, on the other hand, is a strategy that is hardly stoppable. Even if it is far from perfect regarding many of the other criteria, an energizing strategy can be so powerful that it brings your organization success no matter what.

There are two levels at which you can assess whether your strategy is energizing: general and specific. At the *general* level, you assess whether your strategy fulfills the general criteria of an energizing strategy. Decades of research have revealed what energizes, or motivates, people in their work. It is not their wage or other financial incentives. Of course, if they are truly underpaid, a raise that results from a new strategy may motivate people to execute that strategy. The effect of such incentives, though, are very limited and very temporary.

As Daniel Pink explains in his various books and videos, there are primarily three things that motivate people: *autonomy*, *mastery*, and *purpose*. Autonomy reflects our desire to be self-directed, to direct our own lives rather than being dictated by others. Mastery reflects our urge to get better at stuff, to get challenged, learn, and develop. And purpose reflects our urge to contribute, to make a difference, have a positive impact on others and the world. Given that these three are universal characteristics, we can use them to assess strategy. To do this, you can ask the following three questions.

1. Does the strategy give people enough autonomy to do things the way they like?
2. Does the strategy challenge people enough so that they can learn and get better?
3. Does the strategy reflect a higher, non-financial purpose to which people can contribute?

A strategy that fulfills these three criteria has all the potential to be an energizing strategy. But there is one more thing that you need to assess. The fact that a strategy can be energizing in general does not mean yet that it is also energizing for your specific organization and people. There may be sufficient autonomy, mastery, and purpose, but not the kind that your particular people care about. To be truly energizing, you need a strategy that speaks to people's hearts, that is about the things they personally care about. Therefore, you also need to assess at the *specific* level whether your strategy is energizing. To do this, you can ask the following five questions.

1. Do your people care about the values and goals that your strategy contributes to?
2. Do your people care about the customers and needs that your strategy serves?
3. Do your people care about the products and services offered in your strategy?
4. Do your people care about the resources and competences on which your strategy is based?
5. Do your people care about the culture and structure your strategy implies?

The more confirmative answers you can give to these generic and specific questions, the more energizing your strategy is.

A QUICK STRATEGY CHECKLIST

Doing all ten strategy checks in a comprehensive manner may cost you a lot of time and effort. Sometimes this is necessary, especially if your strategy requires significant investments. However, in case you want a quick insight, you can also use the checklist below. It covers every check with a single question. Keep in mind that it's not the answer itself, but the discussion it triggers that matters most. After all, you want to find out *why* your strategy scores well or not so well on the criteria because that tells you what can be done to improve it.

	YES	MAYBE	NO
Coherence Check: Do all the elements of your strategy fit together?	○	○	○
Efficiency Check: Do you use everything you have to its full potential?	○	○	○
Effectiveness Check: Does your strategy do what it's supposed to do?	○	○	○
Uniqueness Check: Is your strategy sufficiently different from others?	○	○	○
Flexibility Check: Can you change your strategy easily enough?	○	○	○
Robustness Check: Can you maintain your strategy in the face of change or crisis?	○	○	○
Scalability Check: Can you grow without too much extra effort?	○	○	○
Responsibility Check: Are you doing the right thing?	○	○	○
Actionability Check: Can you and your people execute the strategy?	○	○	○
Energy Check: Does the strategy give you and your people energy?	○	○	○

HOW TO USE THE STRATEGY CHECKS

As I pointed out at the beginning of this chapter, there are two points at which assessment is important: a) an assessment of your *current* strategy as a starting point for innovating it, and b) an assessment of your *newly generated* strategy to get a sense of its quality before you actually execute it. In the second case, you might also have developed several strategic options between which you want to choose. In that case, you can use the strategy checks to assess which of the options is preferable.

At whatever point you do the assessment, the ten strategy checks can be used in various ways. You can use them, for example, quickly as a checklist in the back of your mind, but you can also turn them into a formal assessment that requires extensive information gathering and analysis. Roughly you have the following options.

Use them as informal checklist. After reading this chapter you will have a sense of what kind of criteria are important to judge strategy. While moving through the strategy process, you can use this knowledge informally or implicitly when you think about whether your (existing or new) strategy is good enough. If you're with a team, you could judge the strategy or the different strategic options that you have generated during an informal conversation.

133

Peer review. To overcome personal bias or groupthink and to avoid missing important gaps or opportunities, it's recommended to have others in the organization look at the strategy too. You can, for example, ask a group of employees to critically assess what you have come up with, thereby using some or all of the strategy checks. An additional advantage of involving them at this stage is that they might easier commit to the strategy once it has crystalized further.

Customer and supplier testing. Another useful way to assess your strategy is to test it with customers and/or important partners such as suppliers. In the end, customers are the ones who buy your products or services, so their opinions matter very much. Along the same lines, suppliers are also needed to realize the strategy and they might have very good insights that you lack. You probably don't want to use all the strategy checks with them, but for the uniqueness check in particular they are important.

Formal assessment and valuation. A fourth way to assess your strategy is a formal assessment whereby you systematically evaluate the strategy against the criteria of the ten strategy checks. This type of assessment typically requires you to quantify the criteria and to gather as objective data as possible to make sure your conclusions are right. Making an extensive business case is also an example of this type of assessment.

> *"Formal and extensive assessment might help more to reduce* perceived *uncertainty, than that it reduces* actual *uncertainty."*

While all four options can work in practice, their order and priority is in most cases as presented above. The first option is the very least that you should always do. You want to keep at least some of the criteria in the back of your mind while you go through the strategy generation process. Strategy is too important to let personal bias or groupthink play a crucial role.

There is nothing principally against formal and extensive assessments, and especially in cases where substantial investments have to be made, these might be valuable. Generally though, this type of assessment tends to be overused. It costs a lot of time, effort, and money and it might help more to reduce one's *perceived* uncertainty more than it reduces *actual* uncertainty. In other words, you might feel better after a formal assessment, but the actual added value of the information gathered can be questionable. This is especially the case in markets that are very uncertain, such as very new, complex, or dynamic markets. In these kinds of markets, the available information might simply be irrelevant. The best way to assess your strategy there is to go out and test it for real with customers, suppliers, or other stakeholders.

IN CASE YOU NEED TO PRIORITIZE

After carrying out the various checks listed above you might have found many points to improve your strategy. It's unlikely, though, that you can address all of them at the same time. Before moving on to the next step, it can be useful to prioritize the issues that you found and focus your energy on the most important ones.

A simple way to do this is to look at all ten checks and list the ones where you scored a "no" in the Strategy Checklist, or where you found substantial issues. Then you ask yourself which of these issues is the biggest obstacle for making progress, or which of the issues is most urgent and important. Is it the fact that your strategy is incoherent, or that it's inefficient, or that it's ineffective? And so on. Picking the key issue in this way gives you a starting point as to where and how you should innovate your strategy at the next step of the strategy generation process.

THE FOUR EXAMPLES

STRATEGY ASSESSMENT AT MACMAN

Macman's main strategic challenge as they see it themselves is that they cannot come up with the next "big idea" that can replace their reliance on steel cutting and bending machines. While that is important, the strategy assessment reveals two additional issues.

1. Not flexible. Macman is strongly invested in their current technology. Their resources and competences

135

are fully dedicated to producing steel cutting and bending machines. Furthermore, they rely on two large customers, giving them very little room for maneuver.

2. Not efficient. This is rather obvious from the 20% of unused capacity they report. More importantly, perhaps, is that they only serve a small part of their customers' needs. Next to cutting and bending machines they need transportation belts, grinders, drilling machines, and so on. As the customers would prefer to buy these from Macman, there is an unmet demand.

STRATEGY ASSESSMENT AT HOSPICARE

The assessment of Hospicare's current strategy reveals two main bottlenecks.

1. Not effective. Although proud of their performance, they are actually only effective in one indicator: the percentage of successful operations. They do not do so well on other indicators. Patients, for example, are dissatisfied and want more "humane" treatment, and the personnel don't like the businesslike climate of the hospital.

2. Not coherent. Hospicare's ambition to go partly commercial might not fit in with their current poor customer orientation. Currently, patients don't have much choice, but if they were to turn into real customers, they would have to put their customers/patients first and listen to their actual needs.

STRATEGY ASSESSMENT AT GOFORIT

Things are going well at GoforIT, although the assessment shows three issues that require attention.

1. Not unique. GoforIT's products are unique. However, their competences aren't. They acknowledge that their software is rather easy to copy, and they outsource

almost everything they do. This makes their strategy very vulnerable in the medium to long term.

2. Not responsible. GoforIT does very well for its two founders. They have made an incredible amount of money in a few years, but so far no one else has really benefitted. They don't pay their suppliers well and their 19 employees hardly profit from the firm's financial success. GoforIT could do much more to make a positive impact.

3. Not efficient. The efficiency check shows furthermore that GoforIT is not efficient at all. Their technology is not yet fully used, and their market is far from saturated. Given the state of development of the company, though, this lack of efficiency is not an issue—it means there is still plenty of potential for further growth.

STRATEGY ASSESSMENT AT COMCOM

Being a one-person company, the assessment of Comcom's strategy is not very complicated. A quick scan with the strategy checklist confirms what Anisha already knew.

1. Not unique. She doesn't do anything unique compared to her competitors..

2. Not scalable. Her reliance on hourly rates means she cannot increase her income without working more.

6

STEP 4: INNOVATING STRATEGY

This chapter explains step 4 of the strategy process: innovating strategy. It's during this step that new strategy is actually generated. It presents five different approaches to strategic innovation. As the suitability of these approaches depends on the degree to which you should or want to innovative your strategy–your "innovation appetite"–I start with a brief discussion on that.

Innovating Strategy = Renewing and redesigning the organization's strategy through incremental or radical innovation.

DEFINING YOUR STRATEGIC INNOVATION APPETITE

Strategic innovation is rarely completely unbounded. How many organizations are willing and capable of letting their existing business go and doing something completely new? Not so many, and usually that is a good thing. Whether you are involved in a startup or a large mature organization, there are always things that you have built in the past that can be a good basis for new strategy. Think about all the knowledge, experience, and contacts you have. These are probably useful to rely on in your new strategy as well. This means strategy is just as much about changing and improving your existing strategy and about letting things go as about generating new strategy (see also the section on "Strategy generation is emergent" on pp 20-24).

Also, you might face explicit restrictions that cause you to not have complete freedom in redesigning your strategy. Maybe you're part of a bigger organization, or you have clear guidelines, instructions, or regulations that you have to adhere to and which limit your freedom of innovation. Or maybe you already have a clear idea in which direction you want to go, or what the innovation "task" should be that you want people to work on. When you start innovating your strategy, you want to take these boundaries into account.

> *"Once you have specified these boundaries,*
> *it's useful to write them down in an explicit*
> *strategic innovation task."*

On the other hand, strategic innovation would not be strategic innovation if you were to completely stick to business as usual or if you let yourself be too restricted. There is always something in your existing business that you could or should let go, add, or change. And even if there are clear restrictions, or if you might already think you know which direction the new strategy should go, it can still be useful to look further afield. You might be biased, or think too narrowly, and the restrictions you see might be less than you think. It would be too bad if you missed out on promising opportunities just because the innovation step started out as too narrow-minded.

All of this means that, before you start innovating, it's useful to have a good sense of your "innovation appetite"–the degree of innovation that you are able to aspire within the boundaries of your organization. The following three types of boundaries are helpful in judging this: your allowance, your ability, and your willingness to innovate.

ALLOWANCE TO INNOVATE: WHAT ARE YOU ALLOWED TO DO?

A first boundary affecting your innovation appetite comes about through what you are allowed to change. You can think of the following boundaries.

- *Legal regulations and social norms and values* that define what you are allowed to do by law and what society finds acceptable. While these mainly apply to what you currently do, it's likely that they also affect how innovative you can be in changing your strategy.
- *Industry standards and habits* that tell you the "rules of the game." When you ignore these, you risk becoming too much of an outsider that others don't understand anymore. On the other hand, changing the rules of the game or trying to create a whole new game can be a very fruitful strategy too.
- *Policies and financial objectives* by corporate headquarters, the board of directors, or shareholders that tell you what decisions you are allowed to make and what financial objectives should be realized. You might be restricted as to what you can change and what you can't. However, as suggested previously, I wouldn't be too obedient here; try to find out how far you can go.

ABILITY TO INNOVATE: WHAT ARE YOU ABLE TO DO?

Before you start thinking about your new strategy, you should also take the capabilities of the organization into account. Maybe you want to and are allowed to do something radically different, but are you also able to do it? I'm not saying strategy generation should be completely restricted by what is realistic. That will kill most creativity in the process and almost guarantee that you won't come up with any bright ideas. However, you do want some sense of realism and to make sure that you'll actually be able to execute the strategy being generated. Therefore, it's useful to think of the following boundaries.

- *Scope.* Does the innovation sufficiently fit your resources and competences? Can you actually do it? You can come up with the wildest ideas for a new strategy, and let's assume they're great and that there is indeed a market for them. But is your organization best equipped to realize these ideas, or are others much more capable of doing it?

- *Capacity.* Do you have the time, people, and money needed to realize your innovation? You don't need to fully specify this upfront, but some sense of your capacity is useful. Otherwise you might generate great new ideas which simply cannot be realized because the capacity is lacking–think especially about the fact that the normal business will probably have to continue while you're busy with your new strategy.

- *Power.* Do you have the power and influence to make the innovation happen? Are you or your organization in the position to make the required changes or are you dependent on factors that are outside your sphere of influence? If you don't have sufficient power or influence, this doesn't necessarily mean you won't be able to realize your strategy, although it probably means that you need to include others that do have the necessary power or influence.

WILLINGNESS TO INNOVATE: WHAT ARE YOU WILLING TO DO?

A third type of boundary for strategic innovation stems from your own intentions and wishes and those of others in the organization. Maybe you're allowed and able to make a particular strategic innovation, but are you also willing to make it, and does it match the aspirations that you have for the strategy generation process? The following three aspects are relevant here.

- *Readiness.* Are you or others in the organization sufficiently willing to make the required changes? Are people convinced it's a good thing to do? Are you willing to make the required investments? If not, there is a good chance the strategy you come up with won't be properly executed.

- *Preservation.* Are there things in your strategy that you definitely want to preserve? In answering this question it's useful to go systematically through all the elements of the Strategy Sketch. What do you want to keep and what do you want to let go or change?
- *Aspirations.* What do you want to achieve with the new strategy? Maybe there is just the general aspiration that the organization should perform better or survive. However, there might also be more specific aspirations that give a clear direction as to where the strategy generation process should be heading.

Most of these boundaries are not written in stone and between the three categories the latter ones are less restrictive than the first. However, as key determinants of your innovation appetite, they are relevant enough to seriously take into account when innovating your strategy.

> *"Since strategy generation is a creative process with unpredictable outcomes, you want to engage it openly."*

WRITING DOWN THE STRATEGIC INNOVATION TASK

Once you've specified the boundaries of your innovation appetite, it's useful to write them down in an explicit *strategic innovation task*. This will help you make sure that the strategy generation process remains focused and will produce not just wild ideas, but also ideas that are relevant for the organization. You should specify at least the following.

- *Why?* What do you want to achieve through innovating your strategy? Should it lead, for example, to more profits, growth, focus, or scope, or is there a particular problem that should be solved? Also, take into account the outcomes of the assessment step above.
- *When?* What is your strategic horizon–two, five, ten years? What is the timeline, and when should what be ready? Is there, for example, a particular date before

which there should be a clear idea, a proof of concept, or a working strategy?

- *Where?* Which part of the organization is involved? Does it concern the whole organization, or a specific business unit, department, region, or location?

Of course you can specify much more, such as who exactly should be involved at which stage, and how much time and money can be invested. Also, you can make a comprehensive project plan indicating when certain deliverables and milestones should be ready. If possible, though, I would avoid this since it might restrict the strategy generation process too much. Since strategy generation is a creative process with unpredictable outcomes, you want to engage it openly. Once things start to crystalize a bit you can start planning more carefully.

The Strategic Innovation Task

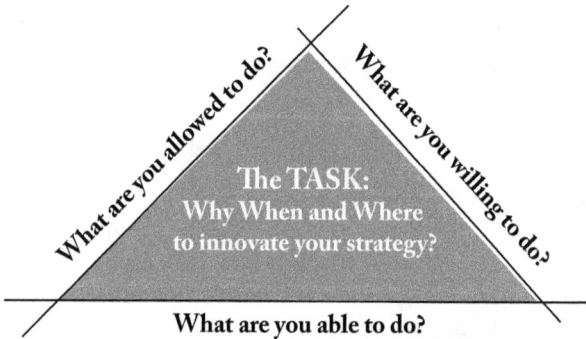

The TASK:
Why When and Where
to innovate your strategy?

What are you allowed to do?

What are you willing to do?

What are you able to do?

FIVE STRATEGIC INNOVATION APPROACHES

You now have everything it takes to get started with innovating your strategy. Your key stakeholders are activated, you know your current strategy and have assessed its strengths and weaknesses, and you have defined your innovation appetite and strategic innovation task. You can now pick one of the following five innovation approaches and use it.

1. *Elementary innovation.* This approach aims for innovations within one or a few of the ten elements of the Strategy Sketch. For example, you are mainly interested in finding a new group of customers, or a new revenue model. As it leaves much of your strategy untouched, this approach is the least radical type of innovation.

2. *Amplifying innovation.* More radical than the first approach, you can also deliberately aim at innovations that make your strategy more scalable. With this approach you stick mostly to the strategy that you already have, but you aim at expanding it to a larger scale so that your impact or revenue increase.

3. *Routed innovation.* Also more radical than the first, with this approach you take one or two elements of your strategy as a starting point and from there on innovate or even redefine the rest of your strategy. So, you start for example with your means (resources and competences and partners) and from there on innovate the rest. As we will see in this chapter, there are six innovation routes that you could follow.

4. *Projective innovation.* Even more radical than the previous approaches, with this approach you take possible future scenarios as a starting point and from there imagine what kind of strategy would fit those scenarios. Start by projecting what the world might look like in five, ten, or even twenty years and then generate strategy that would be appropriate in that world.

5. *Freestyle innovation.* With this most radical type of innovation, you let go of all boundaries and go wild. Obviously, a reality check is needed at some point, but your aim is to start as openly as possible and build attractive castles in the air. With this approach you're really aiming for generating strategy that is new for your organization or even new to the world.

Of course, you don't have to stick to just one approach. You can also use them together, or one after another.

INNOVATION APPROACH 1: ELEMENTARY INNOVATION

I don't need to say very much about this first approach of strategic innovation. As mentioned above, this approach focuses on innovations within one or few of the elements of the Strategy Sketch. Thus, look for examples of your customers and needs and try to find a new group of customers you can serve, or focus on how you can adjust your value proposition, or how you can improve your resources or competences.

In most cases a change in one element of your strategy will also mean some changes in other elements. If you focus on a new group of customers, for example, this most likely also implies some adjustments to your value proposition and to the competitors you're dealing with. Yet, since this approach aims at making small innovations, the overall impact on your strategy usually remains modest; this approach is mostly of an incremental nature.

Chapter 4 on mapping strategy already contained all the information and tools needed to use this first approach. Next to the information helping you to map out your current strategy, the chapter also included information for elementary innovation— the questions to ask, the beyond-the-obvious exercises, and the inspirational checklists. Based on that information, elementary innovation can be done by using:

1. The right columns of the "Questions to ask" tables for each element. While the left column concerns questions about your current strategy, the right column deliberately aims at fostering elementary innovation. Asking yourself these questions can help you think in new directions.
2. The "Beyond-the-obvious exercises." While primarily aimed at providing you with more in-depth insights into your current strategy, these exercises can also provide you with new ideas for each of the ten elements of your strategy.

3. The "Inspirational checklists" that stimulate thinking in new directions by giving examples of what the various elements could look like.

INNOVATION APPROACH 2: AMPLIFYING INNOVATION

Amplifying innovation is particularly relevant if you want or need to grow substantially in the near future. In Chapter 5 ("Assessing Strategy") you already saw a scalability check to assess whether a strategy is sufficiently scalable or not. If the conclusion is that it's not scalable enough, or if your main ambition is growth, amplifying innovation is the type of innovation you are looking for. This section provides you with a variety of scalability tactics that you can use to do this.

While no black-and-white distinction can be made, product and service organizations generally differ substantially in their scalability. The most important reason is that service-based organizations usually rely more on people's personal skills and time than product-based organizations. This often means that service-based organizations are harder to scale and that one has to look for other scalability tactics than for product-based organizations. Along these lines, we can distinguish between two sets of scalability tactics—one for product-based organizations and one for service-based organizations. While your organization might be primarily oriented towards one of the two, I certainly suggest having a look at both sets.

PRODUCT-BASED SCALABILITY TACTICS

Various tactics can be used to scale a product-based strategy so that it generates more revenue or impact without a proportional increase in risks or costs. When thinking about your strategy, consider whether you can do any of the following.

- Increase the price or change the revenue model (like Google, which started with many free products for which they now charge).

- Digitize the product (like Udacity which offers self-paced online courses instead of face-to-face courses, thereby requiring no involvement of lecturers anymore).
- Automate production (like virtually every manufacturing company so that increasing scale does not require more people to do the work).
- Improve capacity utilization (like Amazon, exploiting its server capacity outside its peak hours around Thanksgiving).
- Use economies of scale (like Ford in the early days, which drastically reduced its price per car through a combination of automation and increasing the production volume).
- Use network externalities (like WhatsApp, where each new customer adds value to the product at no cost).
- Simplify and standardize the product (like IKEA, which uses a modular design in the majority of its products).
- Leverage your core competencies (like Yamaha, which applies its refined metal processing skills to engines, musical instruments, and audio equipment).
- Let others do the work (like Apple, which outsources most of its production to other companies).
- "Servicefy" your product (like Dropbox, which sells its software and server space as a service).
- Create "lock in" or "switching costs," thus making it harder for customers to switch (like Spotify, where you have access to music without owning it yourself).
- Give products away for free (like many software companies using freemium models or lower-priced options for specific target groups, thereby increasing their impact).

Please note that quite a few of these tactics can be used by service-based organizations as well.

SERVICE-BASED SCALABILITY TACTICS

There are also various scalability tactics for service-based strategies. When innovating your strategy, consider whether you can do any of the following.

- Increase the price or change the revenue model (like boutique consulting firms who use high pricing as a means to increase the perceived value of their services).
- Digitize the service (like translation services relying heavily on artificial intelligence enabling automated translation).
- Leverage the skills of seniors to juniors (like hospitals or consultancy firms which let juniors perform the simpler tasks while offering services at senior quality level–and price).
- Materialize your service (like me, or other strategy researchers or consultants who write a book or develop a software tool).
- Productize your service (like accountancy firms who charge a fixed price for a predefined service instead of flexible hourly rates).
- Make the service uniform (like McDonalds, which has totally standardized its processes and restaurants).
- Simplify the service to what customers want (like Basic-Fit which strips down gym facilities to the essentials).
- Up-sell to let existing customers buy more (like airlines offering you to upgrade to a better seat).
- Cross-sell between customer groups (like airlines collaborating with car-rental companies and hotel chains allowing the customers of one to also buy from the other).
- Automate parts of the service (like banks offering online banking which can be scaled without significant additional costs).
- Make it mobile (like virtual help desks using chat, Facebook, or other non-personal ways of interaction).

You should also note here that many of these tactics can be used by product-based organizations as well.

INNOVATION APPROACH 3: ROUTED INNOVATION

A third approach to innovate your strategy is taking one or two elements of your strategy as a starting point and from there on innovate the rest of your strategy. This "routed innovation" approach is particularly useful in three situations.

a. If you have no idea where to start once you have mapped out your strategy using the Strategy Sketch. Choosing one clear starting point makes sure you don't get lost in all the possibilities of strategic innovation.

b. If you have a clear idea what you want to keep or find important as part of your new strategy. In that case you can take that element as a starting point for innovation.

c. If you want to deliberately work from different perspectives when innovating your strategy. This would imply you start with one route and switch to another and in the end combine the insights gained as such.

There are six routes that you can follow or combine for this approach to strategic innovation.

1. Market-Driven Strategy

The first and most well-known starting point is to start with an analysis of the market to find out the needs of (potential) customers, and to assess the extent and nature of the competition. This approach is also known as the "outside-in" approach to strategy. Using the Strategy Sketch, it starts with mapping your customers and needs and competitors. From thereon, the rest of the strategy can be sketched by asking questions such as: "What kind of new or additional products, services, or features would customers value?" "How can we differentiate ourselves better from competitors?" and "What kind of resources or competences do we need in order to do that?"

2. Means-Driven Strategy

A second route is to start on the other side of the Strategy Sketch, with the organization's resources and competences and partners. This "means-driven" strategy is also known as the "inside-out" approach to strategy. Means-driven strategy starts with inventorying the current strengths and weaknesses of the organization: what means (money, materials, machines, people, knowledge, etc.) does the organization have and does it have access through its partners. Subsequent questions are: "How unique and valuable are these means compared to competitors?" "What kind of products or services can we develop based on these means?" or "How can we use the available means better?"

3. Identity-Driven Strategy

You can also start innovating your strategy based on the organization's identity; what it stands for and what it aims to achieve. This route starts with making the mission and vision of the organization clear and expressing what goals and values are important. This route is closely linked to the people that work for the organization and the culture that binds them together. In the Strategy Sketch this relates to the elements of values and goals and organizational climate. Typical follow-up questions are "What kind of customers do we find important to serve?" "What kind of business do we want to be?" and "What kind of competences do we need in order to achieve our goals?"

4. Revenue-Driven Strategy

A fourth innovation route is to focus on maximizing revenue and minimizing costs and risks. This "revenue-driven" strategy aims at maximizing the financial returns of a business–making a profit. This route takes the revenue model and risks and cost elements as starting points. From thereon, questions that can be asked are: "What kind of market would enable us to maximize our returns?" "How can we minimize the risks of our business?" or "What portfolio of products and services would we need to obtain a balance between risks and returns?"

5. Context-Driven Strategy

The fifth route is more responsive and opportunistic. It takes the trends and uncertainties that arise in the organization's environment as the main starting point. Organizations following this approach try to make the best of the situation they are in by exploiting trends or avoiding and dealing with the uncertainties they face. Relevant questions for this approach include: "How can we make the best use of the situation we are in now?" "How should we respond to important trends in society?" and "What kind of products or services could we come up with to make use of these trends?"

6. Value Proposition-Driven Strategy

A final route for innovating your strategy is to start directly with your value proposition rather than taking any of the other elements as a starting point. With this route you try to come up with improvements to your value proposition or a completely new one. When you follow this innovation route you take your own value proposition, or the average value proposition as it's offered in the industry, as a starting point. You then look at which features can be created, raised, reduced, or eliminated.

"There are three factors that make one route more logical than another."

Six Strategic Innovation Routes

WHICH INNOVATION ROUTE TO CHOOSE?

I can imagine that you're wondering which of these six innovation routes you should choose. The short and not so helpful answer to this question is: whichever you want. There is some truth in this answer though, as there is no best starting point and in the end it's up to you where you choose to start. Also, you can always start in different places and see what works best for you. You might even want to combine a few or even all of them throughout the strategy generation process.

However, there are at least three factors that make one route more logical than another. In choosing between routes you might want to take the following three factors into account.

1. The outcomes of the previous step–the *assessment* of your strategy. If, for example, the assessment shows inefficiencies in the way you use your resources and competences, reflecting unused potential, it would be

logical to start with a means-driven innovation route here. Or, if your organizational climate or revenue model are not flexible or robust you might want to follow, respectively, the identity-driven or the revenue-driven route.

2. The *uncertainty* of the market or industry you are in. If you are in a very uncertain environment–such as a new or dynamic industry or a complex market–relying on customer needs or on trends can be a bit tricky. If things are so uncertain, you simply cannot know whether the needs and trends that you identify will be true or relevant. The only thing you can rely on in these situations is who you are and what you have. In these situations the means-driven and identity-driven routes are more suitable than a market-driven or context-driven route.

3. The strength of your *values and goals*. If you have a clear idea of what you find important and where you want to go with the organization, the obvious innovation route is the identify-driven route. In this case you may want to start by formulating a clear and compelling vision and mission from which you then derive the other elements of your strategy.

INNOVATION APPROACH 4: PROJECTIVE INNOVATION

All three previous innovation approaches are aimed at improving and innovating your *current* strategy. In one way or the other, they take your existing strategy as a starting point. Projective innovation, on the other hand, starts with projecting one or more possible futures and from thereon deriving what strategy would be suitable for dealing with these futures. This approach can help you look at your strategy in a new way and come up with more radically new and future-proof strategies. Projective innovation consists of the following three steps.

1. Identify Megatrends
Start by identifying the important political, economic, social, technological, legal, and environmental (PESTLE) trends that

are happening. You should focus on what are called "structural developments" or "megatrends"–those trends that are relatively certain and that will probably go on for a while. Think of, for example, important demographic or technological changes that are happening. When you identify these trends, you shouldn't let yourself be too restricted by the PESTLE categories. Use them as a checklist, but don't necessarily stick to them. Also, you can use the websites of the World Future Society (www.wfs.org), the Copenhagen Institute for Future Studies (www.cifs.dk), the World Futures Studies Federation (www.wfsf.org), or other websites like this for insights into the future.

2. Sketch One or More Possible Futures

Once you have a good sense of these megatrends, use them to sketch what your relevant world would look like in five, ten, or twenty years. Try to picture, for instance, what your industry will look like or in what kind of world your future customer will be living ten years from now if the trends continue. For this it can be useful to make an Empathy map (which was introduced in the "Beyond-the-obvious" exercise for customers and needs in Chapter 4 on p 78). Generating this picture (or pictures if you want) should give you a lot of inspiration as to what your future strategy could look like.

3. Derive Implications for Your Strategy

The final step is to identify what the picture you developed means for your strategy. This means you should try to come up with a strategy that would be suitable for the future you have projected. For this you can again use the Strategy Sketch and its ten elements. Thus, you identify what kind of resources and competences you would need, what kind of partners, who your competitors could be, and so on.

With just three steps, this is a simple way to use the projective innovation approach. If you want, you can go much deeper and make your innovation process much more comprehensive. If you choose to do so, I recommend reading more on topics such as futures studies, forecasting, and scenario planning.

"This approach can help you look at your strategy in a new way and come up with more radically new and future-proof strategies."

INNOVATION APPROACH 5: FREESTYLE INNOVATION

Do you want to go even wilder and come up with some crazy ideas for your strategy? In that case, freestyle strategic innovation is a suitable approach. Whereas the other four approaches assume some boundaries to your innovation freedom, you drop these with freestyle innovation. This fifth type of strategic innovation is especially useful in the following three cases.

a.   If you want to come up with a strategy that is really new and could lead to a whole new market. Through freestyle innovation, you might get ideas that you otherwise would not have had.

b.   If you want to depart from your current strategy and do something very different than you currently do. The other approaches might make it too tempting to stay within your comfort zone.

c.   If you want to stimulate creativity within a phase of the strategy generation process. You don't want to actually do something radically new, but some of the crazy ideas might be useful when toned down.

The basic idea of freestyle strategic innovation is that you challenge yourself to take your strategy to extreme situations. This is done by a variety of "What if…" scenarios. The goal is not necessarily to develop complete strategies, but to come up with new ideas.

THIRTY "WHAT IF…" SCENARIOS

Below you'll find thirty very short scenarios that can help you think about your strategy in an unconventional manner. The idea is that you pick one scenario at a time and imagine what your strategy might look like in that scenario. As with other brainstorming techniques, it's important that everything is possible and that no objections are allowed throughout the idea generation process. You can repeat this process multiple times with different scenarios.

What would your strategy look like if…

1. …you started completely from scratch without any limitations or constraints *(Greenfield Scenario)*.
2. …you cut out anything you don't like or which is hindering you in realizing your ambitions (*Weeds Scenario*).
3. …there were a fire and you could only save your single most precious resource *(Fire Scenario)*.
4. …you had to double your revenue without hiring anyone or buying anything for two years *(Multiply Scenario)*.
5. …you had to cut your expenses and staff by half without reducing your revenue *(Diet Scenario)*.
6. …you had to do everything online—or offline if you're a web-based organization *(Online/offline Scenario)*.
7. …you had to run the organization from a bus or camper traveling across the globe *(Mobile Scenario)*.
8. …you had to outsource virtually everything that is done by the organization *(Outsourcing Scenario)*.
9. …you were required to achieve at least 80% of the current results with no more than 20% of the current effort *(80/20 Scenario)*.
10. …your customers had just one tenth to spend of what they normally have *(Poor Man's Scenario)*.
11. …you had to sell your products or services for a price ten times higher than normal *(Rich Man's Scenario)*.
12. …you had to make sure customers queued overnight to buy your product or service *(Wow Scenario)*.
13. …customers asked for something entirely different every year *(Changing Tastes Scenario)*.
14. …you were to win the Nobel Peace Prize, solve world poverty, or stop climate change *(World Peace Scenario)*.
15. …you moved to the most exotic, dangerous, or unique country you know *(Adventurer's Scenario)*.
16. …money didn't exist and you exclusively relied on barter and in-kind payments (payment by goods or services) *(Barter Scenario)*.

17. …your organization were ten or even a hundred times larger *(Explosion Scenario)*.
18. …you copied the best ideas from the best organizations you know *(Aping Scenario)*.
19. …there suddenly appeared an exact copy of your organization *(Copycat Scenario)*.
20. …employees made the decisions instead of managers or directors *(Employee Scenario)*.
21. …your grandma, grandson, or uncle was running the organization *(Family Scenario)*.
22. …your accountant, lawyer, supplier, customer, consultant took over *(Partner Scenario)*.
23. …Richard Branson, Michael O'Leary, Steve Jobs, Walt Disney, Henry Ford, Warren Buffett, or Bill Gates took over *(Star Entrepreneur Scenario)*.
24. …Jesus, Mother Theresa, Martin Luther King, Jr., the Dalai Lama, Mohamed, or Buddha was running the organization *(Compassion Scenario)*.
25. …the Kardashians, The Rock, Cristiano Ronaldo, Taylor Swift, or any other celebrity influencer led your organization *(Celebrity Scenario)*.
26. …you merged with the most unlikely organization you can imagine *(Unlikely Marriage Scenario)*.
27. …you were alive 10, 100, or 1000 years from now or 10, 100, or 1000 years ago *(Time Traveller Scenario)*.
28. …the market grew each year by at least 20% *(Optimist Scenario)*.
29. …the market decreased each year by at least 20% *(Pessimist Scenario)*.
30. …you just followed your intuitions or instincts even though you cannot justify them *(Guts Scenario)*.

Of course you don't need to restrict yourself to these scenarios. Any other scenario that takes you out of the normal is also appropriate.

COMPLETING THE STRATEGY AND SELECTING STRATEGIC OPTIONS

All five innovation approaches aim at finding and developing new ideas for your strategy. New ideas, though, are not complete strategies yet. And you might even have plenty of ideas between which you need to make a choice. This means that some additional work may be needed before you can move on to the last step–Formulating strategy. Two follow-up steps are usually required: turning the idea into a complete strategy and choosing between various options.

1. **Turning an Idea Into a Complete Strategy**

The Strategy Sketch contains all the important elements of a strategy. Therefore, I don't think you will be surprised if I recommend you use the Strategy Sketch to turn your ideas into complete strategies. You can do this as follows. For the ideas that you have come up with, map out the implications for all the elements. In other words, go back to the mapping step and map out an entire strategy around the ideas. Suppose, for example, you have come up with an idea for a new value proposition. You then map out what customers and needs it would serve, who your competitors are, what resources and competences and partners you would need, and so on.

"As a rule of thumb, if you have more than three options, it's useful to first make a quick assessment aimed at filtering out the best three."

2. **Choosing Between Optional Strategies**

There is a big chance that you have come up with multiple options for a new strategy. Since you can't execute all of them, you must somehow choose between them. What you need for this is a way of comparing and assessing the various options you have generated. To do this, go back to the previous step of the strategy generation process–assessing strategy. Instead of assessing a single strategy, assess the various options you have generated and compare them.

There is no strict order for these two follow-up steps. Sometimes you can immediately assess your options before turning them into complete strategies, and sometimes you first want to develop them further before you assess them. As a rule of thumb, if you have more than three options, it's useful to first make a quick assessment aimed at filtering out the best three. Next, turn these options into complete strategies and assess them more systematically.

THE FOUR EXAMPLES

Note: The next few pages describe the strategic innovation approach of the four examples. See the next chapter for the outcomes.

STRATEGIC INNOVATION AT MACMAN

As the assessment showed, Macman's main strategic issues were insufficient flexibility and efficiency. Furthermore, leadership had a hard time imagining feasible alternatives. This makes freestyle innovation suitable, as it encourages generating unconventional ideas. The following two scenarios are particularly appropriate.

- Outsourcing scenario ("What if you had to outsource virtually everything that is done by the organization?"). This scenario helps them think about a more flexible strategy based on collaboration rather than on doing everything in-house.
- Wow scenario ("What if you had to make sure customers queued overnight to buy your product or service?"). This scenario helps them put themselves in their customers' shoes and realize what additional needs they could fulfill.

STRATEGIC INNOVATION AT HOSPICARE

Hospicare's main strategy issues were a lack of effectiveness and coherence. Furthermore, the board needed to be convinced that new strategy was unavoidable and advantageous. In this case a combination of routed and freestyle innovation works well.

- Routed innovation. Hospicare has a strong and distinctive climate and competence; they are very businesslike and focused on successful operations. We use this as a starting point for means-driven and identity-driven innovation. The question here is how these features of Hospicare can be used better.
- Freestyle innovation, using the Wow scenario (see Macman) or the Employee scenario ("What if employees made the decisions instead of managers or directors?"). These scenarios force Hospicare to think about effectiveness from the viewpoint of their customers and employees.

STRATEGIC INNOVATION AT GOFORIT

The assessment of GoforIT's strategy showed that they have no unique resources that hinder competitors from copying them, and that they could do more in terms of responsibility. Because their inefficiency was no issue given the startup stage they are still at, their innovation efforts focused on improving their uniqueness and responsibility.

For the first issue, elementary innovation is suitable. Zooming in on the resources and competence element, the key point is what GoforIT can do to avoid imitation. The questions from the uniqueness check are helpful for this. The copycat scenario ("What if there suddenly appeared an exact copy of your organization?") is also suitable.

With respect to responsibility, GoforIT's founders need to be made aware of the possibility and appropriateness of letting others than themselves benefit from the company's success. The following freestyle innovation scenarios are helpful in achieving this.

- World peace scenario ("What if you were to win the Nobel Peace Prize, solve world poverty, or stop climate change?").
- Compassion scenario ("What if Jesus, Mother Theresa, Martin Luther King, Jr., etc., were running the organization?").

STRATEGIC INNOVATION AT COMCOM

Anisha's problem is that Comcom's strategy is not unique and scalable and that she doesn't see the ways to make it so. At the same time she has a dream of having a famous food blog for which it's unclear whether and when it could generate income.

With respect to the scalability of her current business, amplifying innovation is the obvious choice. In order to make her strategy more scalable she is recommended to apply all the scalability tactics to her company and see which ones she can use.

Once that succeeds, she will be able to spend more time on her dream (a famous food blog) in parallel. If the blog attracts a lot of readers, that will be the time to think about how to generate revenue.

7

STEP 5: FORMULATING STRATEGY

This chapter explains the last step of strategy generation: formulating strategy. In this fifth step you turn your newly developed strategy into a form that can be communicated to others. As such, this step closes the strategy generation process after which you can turn to strategy execution. This chapter starts with an explanation of what strategy formulation entails. It then presents various forms in which you could formulate your strategy using words and pictures, including a strategic plan.

> **Formulating Strategy** = Capturing the organization's strategy in words and pictures that can be understood by the target audience.

THE STRATEGY FORMULATION CHALLENGE

If you were successful in the previous steps, you now have one or more new strategic ideas that you have turned into more or less complete Strategy Sketches. This means you've gathered and produced all the important ingredients of your new strategy. However, it would be a stretch to already call this your strategy. You have a *sketch* of your strategy and its key elements, but this still needs to be turned into something concise, coherent, and convincing that can be communicated to others. Only then can you actually tell people what your strategy is–what your unique way of sustainable value creation is. Thus, the key challenge of strategy formulation is generating an answer to the question of what your strategy is.

This is not a trivial step. Research shows that formulating strategy in a good way is a challenge–to say the least. Common problems are that the formulated strategy is not concrete enough for people to understand what it means, that it doesn't specify clearly enough how it differs from the status quo, that it does not form a coherent and convincing whole that makes sense to people, or that it's not actionable enough for people to actually execute it.

In the first section of Chapter 3, "The activation challenge," we saw that the purpose of the activation step is getting the organization from a strategy execution mode into a strategy generation mode. The purpose of strategy formulation is exactly the opposite: getting the organization back into execution mode. By formulating the strategy the right way, you close the strategy generation process–at least for a while–so that the organization can focus on its execution.

> *"The purpose of strategy formulation is getting the organization back into execution mode."*

ROLES OF STRATEGY FORMULATION

In line with its overall purpose to move back to execution mode, strategy formulation plays six specific roles in the strategy process. Since these roles affect how you should precisely formulate your strategy, it's useful to keep in mind which of them you are focusing on. The roles include refining, fixating, convincing, driving, acting, and signaling.

1. *Refining.* In order to formulate your strategy you need to make it concrete. And as soon as you make it concrete you will also see whether your strategy is as crisp and good as you thought, or whether it still requires refinement.

Thus, a first role of strategy formulation is that it helps refine your strategy.

2. *Fixating.* Centered on the idea of the Strategy Sketch, the previous steps reflect a creative and dynamic process that facilitates idea generation and frequent adjustments to your strategy. This is good for strategy generation, but at some point you will want to fixate your strategy as well. Strategy formulation serves this role.

3. *Convincing.* To get the strategy going, you need to get people involved and committed. This means you may need to convince quite a few people of the strengths and importance of your strategy–such as employees, investors, or the board of directors. Obviously, strategy formulation plays a crucial role in this.

4. *Driving.* As research in cognitive psychology shows, the simple act of making something concrete forms an enormous stimulus to actually doing it–seeing is believing. This applies to strategy as well: formulating it in a concrete manner makes people believe in the feasibility of a strategy. As such, strategy formulation drives the execution of a strategy.

5. *Acting.* Formulating strategy also helps turn the strategy into concrete actions and plans. A well-formulated strategy expresses not only what the strategy is, but also why it works and what it takes. As such, it gives a clear idea of the required actions for the organization.

6. *Signaling.* Strategy formulation can also serve as a subtle (or less subtle) means of communicating to others, such as competitors. It can serve as a warning or an announcement to show them what your plans are or that you are serious. Some bluffing and misleading may be part of this.

YOUR TARGET AUDIENCE

When we look at these six roles, we can immediately see that it also matters for strategy formulation who your target audience is. If you formulate your strategy, for example, to convince investors, you will probably want to emphasize different things than when you formulate it for refining it with the management team, or for driving your employees towards strategy execution. This means that, when formulating your strategy, you should also take into account who you are formulating it for. You should think of at least the following target audiences:

- The management team, strategy officers, business developers, or others involved in strategy generation.
- Employees, middle managers, or others that are involved in the execution of the strategy.
- The board of directors, the CEO, shareholders, or others that have to formally approve the strategy.
- Investors, banks, or others from which you need investments or guarantees.
- Customers, suppliers, partners, or other external parties that are needed for a strategy to become successful.
- Competitors, media, or other external parties that you want to make your strategy known to.

To sum up, the challenge of strategy formulation is to express your strategy in such a way that it fulfills the particular role that you want to a particular target audience.

THE CORE AND STRUCTURE OF YOUR STRATEGY

When I ask people to tell me the strategy of their organization, I get surprisingly different and unsatisfying answers. Some argue that it's "operational excellence" or "customer intimacy" or they provide a description of their core products or of their unique competences. Others give a rather abstract mission or vision statement, or an objective such as growth or consolidation. Still others refer to their strategic plan or they are unable to provide an answer at all.

This variety of answers shows two things: first, that there is no single right aspect to focus on when formulating strategy, and second that there is a lot of room for improvement as to how strategy is formulated. These two refer, respectively, to the core of the formulated strategy (what the key point you are trying to make is) and its structure (how you tell it in a clear and convincing manner).

THE CORE OF THE FORMULATED STRATEGY

The variety of answers described above indicates that people choose to focus on very different aspects of strategy when they formulate it. We could try to harmonize this and suggest a one-size-fits all recipe for how to correctly formulate a strategy. I don't think that's a very fruitful path though, as it limits your ability to express a unique strategy. And why would it be wrong if you focus on your competences, while others focus on their value proposition, goals, or anything else?

> *"When formulating strategy you need to make a choice as to what will be the core of your message."*

Throughout the previous steps we have worked with the ten core elements of strategy. So far, we have treated these ten elements as more or less equal. Whether it's in the mapping, assessing, or innovating step, there was no hierarchy among these elements. I showed you my preferred order of mapping the elements. But that is just my preference, not a law. And it doesn't mean at all that one element should be emphasized more in your strategy than any other. For these three steps it works very well not to prioritize one element over the other. You need to think about all of them and putting one above the others during that stage can already seriously restrict the creativity and openness that you need during strategy generation.

However, when formulating strategy you need to decide what will be the core of your message. Your strategy won't be very appealing if you just list the ten elements without any particular emphasis on any of them. You want to pick one as your core and use the rest to support it.

Maybe not all the elements are equally suited to forming the core of your strategy formulation. The trends and uncertainties, for example, seem less suitable than your value proposition or values and goals because they refer more to the environment you're in than your actual strategy. However, as we'll see in this chapter, each of them can be used as a core.

THE STRUCTURE OF THE FORMULATED STRATEGY

Once you have picked your core element the next step is to build a clear and convincing reasoning that explains why and how your strategy is a good one. Just stating, for example, your value proposition or your values and goals is nice, but it's insufficient to fulfill any of the six roles identified above. Whether you want to refine or fixate your strategy, convince or drive people, make them act, or signal something, you need to say more than that.

"A well-formulated strategy covers all ten elements of the Strategy Sketch."

A well-formulated strategy covers all ten elements of the Strategy Sketch. After all, they are the ten key elements, and if you could do without them in your strategy formulation, they wouldn't be very key, would they? You should use the other nine elements to support the core of your strategy. Thus, if your core is your value proposition, use your customers and needs to explain that there is a market for your value proposition, your competitors for explaining how it's different from what they are doing, your resources and competences for explaining what makes you able to realize it, and so on. The remainder of this chapter shows you how to do this.

FORMULATING STRATEGY IN WORDS

The most obvious way of formulating your strategy is to turn it into words, in some form of written document. The challenge is to find a way of formulating that has the right length, structure, and level of detail. On the one hand a strategy text should be clear and precise enough to express the strategy in sufficient detail to understand it. On the other hand you also want it to be as concise as possible. The next few pages present three steps for doing this.

1. Capture the Core

The first thing you want to do is to pick the core element of your strategy. This can be any of the ten elements; there are no clear rules for making this choice. You might have a personal preference, or the organization might have chosen a particular focus already in formulating the current strategy. Or maybe, during the previous steps, you found that one particular element clearly stood out in terms of importance. In all these cases it might be fairly straightforward as to what the core of your strategy should be. In other cases, though, you might do the following exercise to pick the core of your strategy.

    a.   Let everyone involved in the strategy generation process (or a selection of them) summarize the strategy in one simple sentence. You can let them write this freely, but you could also require them to start the sentence with "Our strategy is ...."

    b.   Share the sentences with everyone, vote, and pick the best. You probably don't want to just use a majority vote, but also discuss the different formulations and come to an agreement.

    c.   Look at which of the ten elements is best captured in the sentence that was chosen. You now have your core.

> *"Try to capture the core element of your strategy in a single sentence."*

Instead of starting with a variety of sentences at the first step, you could also start with one and then iterate. This means that you or someone else writes a first version of the sentence, and others modify it as they like. The risk with this approach, though, is that this leads to endless changes and a less inspiring process. I personally prefer the above exercise.

To support this exercise you can also give examples of how the core of the strategy can be captured in a single sentence. Maybe you know a good example of another organization, but you can also use the following list of ten generic examples.

1. **Resources & competences.** You present your unique strengths that differentiate you from your competitors. *Example format:* our strategy is to build on and further develop these, as well as these means and our ability to do such and such.

2. **Partners.** You present who you work with and the collaborations that give you a unique position. *Example format:* our strategy is to work with these as well as these partners and to use our unique network in such and such way.

3. **Customers & needs.** You define your main customers and thus for whom the organization does what it does. *Example format:* our strategy is to be the supplier of choice for this and this group of customers.

4. **Competitors.** You define who your main competitors are and what you aim to achieve with respect to them. *Example format:* our strategy is to be the best such and such in this as well as this industry or region.

5. **Value proposition.** You point out what you offer in terms of products, services, and their added value. *Example format:* our strategy is to offer such and such products or services that stand out in terms of these and these features.

6. **Revenue model.** You explain what your most important sources of revenue are and where they come from. *Example format:* our strategy is to earn our money in such and such way or to offer our products/services in return for such and such a fee.

7. **Risks & costs.** You explain how you deal with risks and costs and how that makes you stand out compared to others. *Example format:* our strategy is to minimize these risks and costs by dealing with them in such and such ways.

8. **Values & goals.** You state what you want to achieve and/or what is of key importance for the organization. *Example format:* our strategy is to achieve this and this by that and that time, or to serve this and this purpose.

9. **Organizational climate.** You point out what kind of organization you are and what is unique about it. *Example format:* our strategy is to be such and such an organization or an organization characterized by such and such a structure or culture.

10. **Trends & uncertainties.** Your present some key trends or uncertainties in your environment and how you deal with them. *Example format:* our strategy is to jump on these and these trends or to deal with these and these uncertainties in this and this way.

Note: It's not always strictly necessary to pick just one of the ten elements as your core. Maybe you have two that you want to combine. However, I would recommend you stick to one or two because otherwise it's not really a core anymore and your formulation might become diffuse.

2. **Build Up the Reasoning**

After the first step you have captured the essence of your strategy. This is important and it might already give a lot of clarity as to what your strategy is. Next, in order to make it convincing, you also want to explain in more detail why it's a good strategy and what it's based on. For this you must include the other elements of your strategy in your reasoning.

So, what you need to do is to build up a logical chain of reasoning whereby you connect the other nine elements to the core of your strategy. There is no single best order for doing that. On the other hand, with ten elements and ten different starting points there are over three million possible orders (3,628,800 to be precise), which are not equally suitable. Therefore, I will just share with you three templates that have different but equally convincing logics for formulating your strategy.

"Build up a logical chain of reasoning whereby you connect the other nine elements to the core of your strategy."

Example template 1: Means-based template

Our strategy is to…

Build on and further develop these and these means and our ability to do such and such {*Resources & competences*} …

We do this with these and these {*Partners*} …
And an organization that is characterized by {*Organizational climate*} …

These starting points give us an advantage compared to {*Competitors*} …
In an environment which is characterized by {*Trends & uncertainties*} …

Based on this we offer {*Value proposition*} …
To address these and these {*Customers & needs*} …

We make this viable by this and this {*Revenue model*} …
And by dealing in this and this way with our {*Risk & costs*} …

By doing so we reach {*Values & goals*} …

Example template 2: Identity-based template

Our strategy is to…

Achieve this and this by that and that time or to serve this and this purpose {*Values & goals*} …
With an organization that is characterized by {*Organizational climate*} …

We do this by offering {*Value proposition*} …
To address these and these {*Customers & needs*} …

In an environment which is characterized by {*Trends & uncertainties*} …
We can do this better than {*Competitors*} …

Because we have {*Resources & competences*} …
And because we work with {*Partners*} …

This is viable through this and this {*Revenue model*} …
And through this and this way of dealing with {*Risk & costs*} …

Example template 3: Market-based template

Our strategy is to…

Be the preferred supplier of choice for this and this group of customers {*Customers & needs*} …

In an environment that is characterized by these {*Trends & uncertainties*} …
We achieve this by offering this and this {*Value proposition*} …
By which we distinguish ourselves from {*Competitors*} …

By doing so we reach {*Values & goals*} …

> This is viable through {*Revenue model*} …
> And through dealing in such and such a way with {*Risk & costs*} …
>
> We can do this because we have {*Resources & competences*} …
> Because we have {*Organizational climate*} …
> And because we work with {*Partners*} …

If you feel too restricted by these templates, you should adjust them and depart from the suggested wording. These three templates just serve as examples to get you started. As long as you make sure that you cover the ten elements in your reasoning, you should choose whatever structure and way of formulating works best for you.

3. Choose a Format and Length

After you've captured the core of your strategy and built up a convincing reasoning to support it, the last step is to choose an appropriate format and length that serves your purpose. You might want to consider one or more of the following formats.

a. **A one-pager**. A brief summary of your strategy on one side of a single sheet of paper. In this format you use a couple of sentences to capture each element of your strategy along the lines of the templates above. You should try to write densely and thus limit the number of unnecessary and connecting phrases. The additional use of visuals is recommended.

b. **A strategic plan.** This should contain the same message and structure as the one-pager but amended with proof. While the one-pager provides the logic and reasoning for your strategy, a strategic plan adds evidence and further explanations that might be needed to convince people of your strategy.

c. **A single slide.** When you need to pitch your strategy in a couple of minutes, you don't want full sentences and even a one-pager is too long. In that case you might want to prepare a single slide that covers your strategy in 5-7 bullet points.

d. **A short slide deck.** If you have time for a longer presentation, you could prepare a slide deck of about ten slides explaining your strategy. Like in the report above, you also have some room to include evidence to convince your audience.

WRITING A STRONG STRATEGIC PLAN

Traditional as it may sound, the hallmark of good strategy formulation is still a strong strategic plan. Strategic plans have been subject to many critiques, in particular that they are often just gathering dust or are not appropriate anymore in today's fast-changing world. I strongly object to this idea. Correct, a bad strategic plan is not very useful. But a good one is. And for virtually all my clients, the main outcome of the strategy generation phase is that I write a strategic plan with them.

But what makes a strong strategic plan? First, based on my experience over the past decade, I've come to the conclusion that a good strategic plan is about 20-40 pages long. Shorter plans often don't contain enough details and are thereby not concrete, complete, and convincing enough. Longer plans often tend to be not clear and crisp enough and contain too much superfluous text or data.

Second, a strong strategic plan covers all ten elements of strategy, but not necessarily in a recognizable way. Given that a good strategy contains all ten elements, it's obvious that a good strategic plan must cover them too–which is why a good strategic plan cannot be really short. But this does not mean that the plan needs to contain ten chapters or that every element needs its separate section. In my experience that doesn't work. Ten elements are simply too many to create a convincing storyline that people can still follow without getting bored. Along these lines, I often structure my strategic plans as follows.

1. **Introduction:** motivation for the plan + process followed to generate the strategy including who was involved + outline of the plan *(covering none of the ten elements, but*

rather describing why the plan is needed and how it was created).

2. **Context:** internal + external developments (setting the context for the new strategy, covering Trends & Uncertainties and various internal developments concerning, for example, Risks & Costs, Resources & Competences, and Organizational Climate).

3. **Identity and Ambitions:** identity of the organization + core values + sets of ambitions (describing what the organization is, what it stands for, and where it wants to go, covering Values & Goals and the core of the Value Proposition to state what the organization does. It usually also covers goals related to any of the other elements).

4. **Offerings and Positioning:** markets + products and services + difference compared to competitors + revenue model (describing what the organization offers and to whom, covering Customers & Needs, Value Proposition, Competitors, and Revenue Model).

5. **Organization and Realization:** organizational structure required to realize the strategy + means needed + partners needed + change in organizational culture needed (covering Organizational Climate, Resources & Competences, and Partners).

I sometimes use variations of this structure, or add a financial chapter, but the core idea remains the same: five to six chapters that build up a logical and coherent story that together covers all ten elements of strategy and that is progressively concrete and detailed from one chapter to the next. As this works well for my clients and me, I recommend using a similar structure when you write your strategic plan.

THE FOUR EXAMPLES

Based on our four examples, you find four ways of formulating strategy below. You should keep in mind that they are not necessarily good strategies or the best way of formulating them. However, these examples are meant to show you the various ways in which you could formulate your strategy by covering the elements of the Strategy Sketch, without ending up with some mechanical list of those elements.

MACMAN'S STRATEGY

Note: Macman had issues with the flexibility and efficiency of their strategy and were looking for the next big idea. To solve most of these issues, they decided to offer complementary machines and services to the customers of their existing products. They aimed at formulating a brief summary of their strategy that can be shared with all employees so that everybody in the organization understands and knows it. This is their attempt (of course without the elements in brackets).

In a globalizing market in which the number and sophistication of competitors grows and competition is increasingly price-based *{trends & uncertainties}*, our strategy is to distinguish ourselves from other steel cutting and bending manufacturers and particularly from companies X, Y, and Z *{competitors}*, by offering not only steel cutting and bending machines, but also complementary machines and personalized services *{value proposition}* so that our customers–high-precision machine manufacturers in Europe–are relieved of all concerns regarding their machine park *{customers & needs}*.

By doing so we are able to maintain our current size and market share, while increasing our profitability and offering our employees a challenging and comfortable working environment *{values & goals}*. This is viable because our service level and complementary products allow us to charge a premium price above the market average *{revenue model}* and because we have a zero waste policy and outsource the production of complementary products *{risks & costs}*.

We are able to do this primarily because we excel at translating customer needs into machine specifications *{resources & competences}*, because we are the industry's best employer for the past 3 years and are able to attract the most skilled engineers in the world *{organizational climate}*, and because we closely collaborate with companies A, B, and C, which produce all complementary products and with our steel suppliers *{partners}*.

HOSPICARE'S STRATEGY

Note: Hospicare decided to start with a small pilot to commercialize their knowledge of psychiatric problems and their treatment. For this they aim at setting up a new company outside the hospital. They formulate their strategy as follows.

OUR VISION

Ten years from now our hospital will have a hub-and-spoke model with a hospital at the core, surrounded by at least ten private, specialized health centers *{values & goals}*.

OUR MISSION

We offer affordable, reliable, and no-nonsense treatments for people with psychiatric and orthopedic problems and diseases *{values & goals, value proposition, and customers & needs}*.

OUR STRATEGY

Our market is changing. Increasing regulations and decreasing health insurance coverage mean that more and more people need to pay personally for parts of their health care *{trends & uncertainties}*. We respond to this trend by gradually moving away from insurance-based health care to offering low-cost, standardized commercial health care services for patients with psychiatric or orthopedic problems *{revenue model, value proposition, and customers & needs}*.

We aim to do this in the form of a hub-and-spokes model with our current hospital at the core, and small, private health centers as satellites around it. This model provides us with an excellent network of specialized partners that helps us brand our services, share capacity, and mutual learning *{partners}*.

We are able to deliver high quality at low prices because of a) our excellent knowledge of psychiatric and orthopedic problems and disorders *{resources & competences}*; b) our cost-efficient standardized, and lean processes *{resources & competences, risks & costs}*; and c) our professional, business-like and no-nonsense culture and way of working *{organizational climate}*.

No other hospital in our region will be able to mimic our approach in the short or medium-term because none of them have a similar business-like way of working *{competitors}*.

GOFORIT'S STRATEGY

Note: The assessment of GoforIT's strategy showed some issues with respect to the uniqueness of their competences and regarding the sharing of their wealth with employees. However, the founders decided they first want to grow further before addressing those issues. To do so, they want a financial injection from a venture capitalist or a business angel. As a starting point for a presentation, they prepared a single slide. In just five bullet points they cover the essence of their strategy, thereby paying attention to almost all the elements.

GoforIT's strategy for the next two years

- **Our unique product:** financial software and apps that are intuitive for financial people, IT-ers, and managers.
- **Who the competition is:** companies R, T, and Z + other companies offering free or paid financial software.
- **Why we're better than others:** we have employees with these three types of backgrounds (one-third each) + a process in which they work effectively together + our brand.
- **Where the market is going:** a growing number of small businesses, combined with a decreasing willingness to pay → we need to scale up!
- **How we can still make money:** if sales numbers triple, costs increase marginally. Price of products can drop by 50%.

Conclusion: if we can triple our sales in the next two years, we can maintain our position and remain very profitable.

COMCOM'S STRATEGY

Note: Since Anisha is on her own and doesn't need any money from a bank or any other source, she only needs to formulate the strategy for herself so that it's clear for her what her strategy is. She wanted to make her strategy more scalable so that she had to spend less time on her current business while earning the same amount of money.

→ My dream: to write a food blog that is read by thousands of people.

→ The "organization" that I need to realize this dream: just me, having fun while working and with a good work-life balance/mix.

→ My concrete offer that helps me realize the dream:
1. Standardized communication services based on predefined templates. Affordable for the client + easy and low-cost for me.
2. Food blog with interesting news and information about food. First to gain traffic, later on to earn a living.

→ The clients that will buy and use what I offer:
1. Accountancy firms (still the largest group, and I need an income, but I won't make any additional acquisition efforts).
2. Amateur and lower-level professional cooks (target group) + people interested in food (also nice, but a bit broad).

→ Who are my most important competitors:
1. The many other communication services and advisors.
2. Other food blogs and websites, both national and international.

→ Why and with whom I will beat them:
1. Communication services: I will beat them by price through my smart standardized templates!
2. Food blog: Not sure whether I can "beat" the others, but I do have a fun and entertaining way of writing that I know others like. Also, I have quite a good network with chefs of excellent restaurants that are willing to help.

→ How I make my money:

1. Fixed price per service; can be low-priced and still profitable because of the templates I use. Also, it leaves me time to start the food blog.

2. At the start not yet; once I have traffic I will use advertising. I could also sell related products such as recipe books, tools, and so on, but we'll see whether that is going to happen (maybe even a book based on the blogs?). Costs are low (free WordPress site, cheap hosting + my time).

→ What could happen? I have no idea, and to be honest I don't really care too much. Currently people seem to be interested in food, especially healthy food, but I don't know whether this will stay that way. I am just going to make this work and will jump at new opportunities when they arise.

FORMULATING STRATEGY IN PICTURES

Next to formulating your strategy in words, you can also formulate it visually, through images, figures, videos, and the like. Along with the saying that a picture is worth a thousand words, it sometimes may be more effective to formulate strategy in this way than with words. I don't think this can really replace formulating your strategy in words–you'll mostly need to do that anyway–but as a complementary way of formulating it, it can certainly be very valuable.

"Don't let a supposed lack of graphical skills be a barrier against visualizing your strategy."

IT'S ABOUT THE MESSAGE, NOT ABOUT THE LOOKS

It's great if you have the skills to visualize your strategy into an advanced, stylish, or cool image, or if you can hire people who can do this. However, that is not the real point here. Form matters, of course. However, it's far more important *what* you formulate and that people get it, than whether it looks great or not. Don't let a supposed lack of graphical skills be a barrier against visualizing your strategy.

There are unlimited ways to make your strategy visual, and any way is suitable as long as it expresses the strategy in a way that is understood by your target audience. If you already have a form in mind, great; don't let the following few pages restrict your creativity. Skip them and move on. If you need some suggestions, though, you might think of the following four options.

Type of visualization	Great for
Storyboard or whiteboard animation	Expressing the *core* of your strategy
Visual strategy sketch	Expressing the *structure* of your strategy
Causal map or mind map	Expressing the *causal logic* of your strategy
Strategy roadmap	Expressing how strategy unfolds over *time*

STORYBOARD OR WHITEBOARD ANIMATION

When making a storyboard of your strategy you turn it into a visual, cartoon-like story, which shows the core of your strategy. A whiteboard animation does the same, but a recording of the drawing process supported by a voice-over and optional sound effects tells the story. This visualization is great for sharing the essence of your strategy in a simple and energizing way. It helps make your strategy concrete so that you can identify possible problems before actually executing it. There are two basic forms:

- *Freeform.* Just start on a plain whiteboard and build up a picture that tells the story of your strategy. There is also software available for this–just search on the Internet for "whiteboard animation tools."
- *Storyboard.* Divide your whiteboard into four to six boxes and tell a cartoon-like story in simple pictures. Two ways to divide your story between the boxes include, but are certainly not limited to:

- ○ What you offer (*value proposition*), to whom (*customers & needs*), what you get in return (*revenue model*), and who your unhappy competitors are (*competitors*).
- ○ What you want to achieve (*values & goals*), what you need for that (*resources & competences*), with what kind of organization (*organizational climate*), and what kind of partners (*partners*).

Hospicare's Strategy

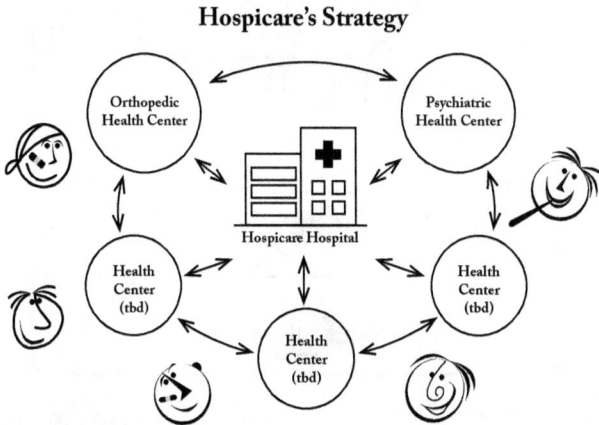

VISUAL STRATEGY SKETCH

Rather than filling the Strategy Sketch with words, you can also draw it in pictures. This visualization shows the overall structure and story of your strategy in a more inspiring and fun way than just in text. This type of visualization is great for stimulating creativity during the strategy generation process and as a visual reminder of the change in strategy.

Comcom's Strategy

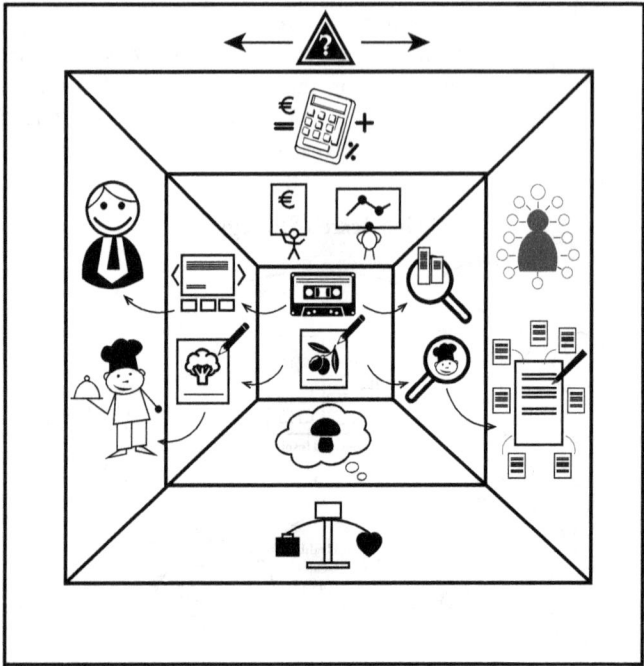

CAUSAL MAP OR MIND MAP

A causal map shows the causal logic of how you achieve your goals and how different parts of your strategy causally link together. At the top of the map draw high-level goals, and below that draw sub-goals and what is needed to achieve them. A mind map is similar, but it puts high-level goals at the center instead of the top. Around that put the sub-goals, etc. This visualization is great for achieving coherence in your strategy and for turning it into actionable plans. To make a causal map or mind map, start with putting the core of your strategy at the top and then connect it to all the other elements in such a way that the causal logic becomes clear.

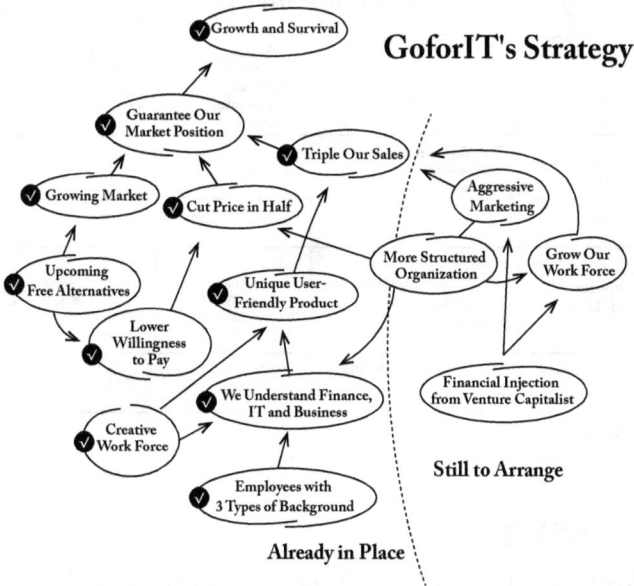

GoforIT's Strategy

STRATEGY ROADMAP

A roadmap visualizes how your strategy unfolds over time. It presents the major developments in the environment and shows how you build up your strategy along with these developments. As a high-level visualization of your strategy over time, a roadmap is a good starting point for making a project plan or a Gantt chart. The most straightforward way to create a roadmap is to divide the "road" towards realizing your new strategy into a couple of phases and plot these horizontally on a sheet of paper. Then, vertically select a number of key factors that change over time. For this you can select a few or even all of the ten elements of the Strategy Sketch. In this way you can show, for example, how you build up your resources and competences over time, which customers and needs you serve over time, and so on.

Macman's Strategy

Element	Year 1	Year 2	Year 3
Value Proposition	Add Personalized Services	Offer Small Complementary Equipment	Start Offering Machine Types X and Z
Resources & Competences	Train Engineers to Sell Additional Services to Customers	Expand Our Plant, Buy Equipment, Hire Additional Engineers	
Partners		Get an Additional Steel Supplier	
Revenue Model	Aim: 80% of Income from Selling Current Machines, 20% from Services.	Aim: 60% from Current Machines, 30% Services, 10% New Machines.	Aim: 40% Current Machines, 30% Services, 30% New Machines
Organizational Climate	Maintain Our Hard-Working and Loyal Culture. Increase the entrepreneurial Spirit and Capabilities.		
And so on	And so on		

PITCHING YOUR STRATEGY

Maybe you have seen the TV program *Dragon's Den*. On this program entrepreneurs have a few minutes to pitch their business ideas to a panel of potential investors. If they can convince one or more investors of the viability of their venture, they can get funding and immediately start negotiating. There's a big chance there will be a point when you also have to pitch your strategy. This is not necessarily a formal pitch to investors. It can also be a quick explanation to a customer or a brief moment when you need to convince someone of your strategy. For those occasions you can use the following steps and guidelines to make sure that you deliver a convincing strategy pitch.

"There's a big chance that there will be a point when you have to pitch your strategy to someone."

STEP 1. CHOOSE THE RIGHT MOMENT TO PITCH

An important decision is when to pitch your strategy. You can be too early, for example, when you're not yet able to answer some basic questions about the strategy. But you can also be too late, especially if you want feedback or need to keep the people you pitch to involved in the strategy generation process. The right time to pitch will depend on the reasons you are pitching. If you're pitching for feedback this can be early in the strategy development process. But if you need to convince a potential investor, it should be as crystalized as possible. Maybe you can't schedule the pitch yourself, but a date is given to you. In that case you have a clear deadline and you know when you need to be ready to pitch.

STEP 2. KNOW WHO TO PITCH TO

A second step is to be clearly aware of the people you're pitching to. You want to know their goals and interests and understand how the new strategy can help them personally. Also, you should know what you want from them, and thus why you are pitching your strategy to them. Possible panels include the following.

1. An informal "friendly" panel of critical insiders and/or outsiders. This is the safest kind of panel you can pitch to. It's mainly meant to further improve the strategy or as a test run for a more formal pitch later in the process. Unlike in the other pitches you may want to show unresolved problems or ask targeted questions so that you get the feedback that you need.

2. The board of directors of your organization. Maybe you're part of a strategy team or business development team concerned with developing a new strategy. To continue with the strategy you may first need the support, approval, or resources from the board of the organization. This pitch is more formal than the previous one and should be more convincing.

3. One or more potential investors such as venture capitalists, business angels, banks, or other investment funds. In this case, there should be no problems or lack of clarity anymore and the pitch should be as convincing as possible. You should make sure that you're pitching to the right kind of investors (for example, do they invest in your kind of organization?) and that you know whether

they want to maximize their profits (such as venture capitalists) or get their money back (banks).

STEP 3. PREPARE AND DELIVER THE PITCH

The third and main step is to turn the strategy you've developed into a convincing pitch. In addition to what you've already seen in this chapter about how to formulate your strategy, it's useful to include the following elements in your pitch.

1. What the product, service, or strategy is and how it's unique. It's fatal for a pitch if people don't understand what you intend.
2. What it does for your audience. You should show how the strategy helps the people you're pitching to (see step 2 above).
3. Who you are and why you'll be successful. If pitching to people outside the organization, you especially want to show the strengths of your organization or team so that your audience believes you can do it.
4. What you want from your audience. Your pitch is not a pitch for the sake of pitching. You want something and you should clearly express that. For example, be clear about whether you want them to make an investment, give approval, or provide feedback.

> *"A strategy pitch is just as much or even more about you than about the strategy itself."*

When preparing and delivering the pitch it's furthermore useful to pay attention to the following guidelines.

- *See it their way and sell to them.* Put yourself in their shoes and think about what would convince you. Don't do a neutral pitch that could have been given anywhere.
- *Create excitement.* Strategy seems primarily rational, but that is a misconception. Many crucial strategic decisions

are made based on emotions. Make sure you excite your audience.

- *Be honest and stay grounded.* Don't exaggerate and certainly don't lie. Modesty often works more convincingly, and don't think you can fool your audience.
- *Use facts and figures.* Although market research might not give you the kind of certainty that you want as a basis for your strategy, the facts and figures produced work very convincingly. Use this.
- *You are also presenting yourself.* A strategy pitch is just as much or even more about you than about the strategy itself. You are part of the package, and your audience judges whether they believe you can make the strategy happen.
- *Learn and persist.* It's unlikely you'll get a standing ovation for your pitch. You'll probably get critical comments, rejections, and the like. Politely thank your audience and improve your strategy and your next pitch.
- *Use your time wisely.* You probably have a fixed amount of time that you can use. Don't pitch for any longer, and if you're running out of time, select what you still want to say rather than speaking faster.

Once you've done all of this you've done everything you can to generate a good strategy. There is, of course, no guarantee that it will all work out as expected. However, you have significantly increased your chances.

PART III

STRATEGY
EXECUTION

STEP 6:
BRIDGING GAPS

After having completed the steps for strategy generation in the previous five chapters, this chapter explains the first step of strategy execution: bridging gaps. In this step, you identify the main gaps between your current and your aspired strategy using two categories: information gaps and implementation gaps. This will lead to a list of projects and tasks—the Strategy Backlog—that will help to close these gaps.

> **Bridging Gaps** = Identifying the gaps between your current and your aspired strategy and defining projects and tasks to bridge them.

THE BRIDGING CHALLENGE

The main outcome of strategy generation is that you have come up with a new or adjusted strategy. The challenge of this first step of strategy execution is to define what needs to be done to get from your current situation to the new strategy. Strategy execution was defined as a process of emergent gap closing. Along those lines, the first step is to identify what these gaps are and to find ways of bridging them. The outcome of this step is the first version of your

Strategy Backlog–a list of all the projects and tasks you'll need to execute to realize your new strategy.

IDENTIFYING GAPS

The starting point for this first step is an analysis of the gaps between your newly-developed strategy and the current, factual strategy of your organization. The most practical way to carry out this gap analysis is to use the Strategy Sketch. If you have followed the strategy generation process outlined in the previous chapters, you've already mapped out your current strategy in the mapping step and generated your aspired strategy in the innovation and formulation steps. With these actions, the gap analysis is straightforward. You simply compare your current factual strategy with your aspired strategy along all ten elements, and you'll identify the gaps to be bridged.

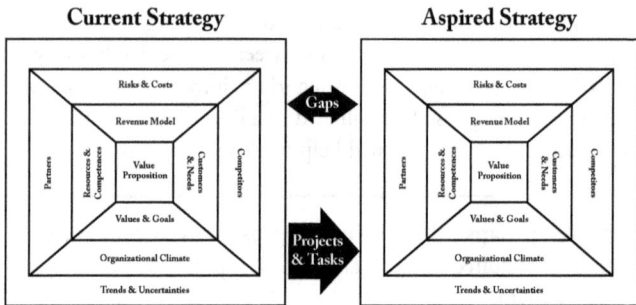

I am not implying here that your strategy should be 100% crystal clear already. As described in Chapter 2, the strategy process is partly linear and partly cyclical. This means that in some cases you can fully specify your new strategy in advance, while in other cases you have to start with execution and further specify your strategy along the way. However, the more precisely both your current and aspired strategy are defined, the more detailed and targeted is your gap analysis–and thereby strategy execution.

The gap analysis is easiest if you have mapped out both your current strategy and your new strategy. This is also why I paid so much attention to the mapping step of strategy generation in Chapter 4. However, there are situations in which there is no such thing as a current strategy. This is the case, for example, when you generated a strategy for a new business unit or start-up venture. Also in those cases, identifying gaps can be relatively straightforward: you simply define what you are still missing–resources and competences, partners, customers–to execute that strategy.

INFORMATION & IMPLEMENTATION GAPS

When you carry out your gap analysis you will probably face two types of gaps, information and implementation gaps.

1. **Information gaps**: gaps between what you know and what you need to know to execute your new strategy successfully.
2. **Implementation gaps:** gaps between where you are now and where you want to be along the ten elements of strategy.

Information gaps refer to a lack of information or confidence about one or more elements of your strategy. Even though you have done your best during strategy generation to gather evidence about whether your new strategy can work, there are things you cannot know in advance, and that may require further inquiry at this stage. For example, you might have assumptions about particular customer needs or the uniqueness of your resources, but you are not sure whether you are right. Therefore, you want to define projects and tasks that are specifically targeted at bridging those information gaps.

"Some of the tasks that you will define will be targeted at bridging more than one type of gap."

Implementation gaps refer to the things that need to happen to turn your strategy into reality. For those gaps, you are relatively sure that you are right and you have sufficient confidence in them to start bridging them. You know, for example, that you need to invest in particular resources, find a particular supplier, or approach a particular group of potential clients. As such, the projects and tasks that you define for bridging implementation gaps indicate how you plan in practice to turn your strategy into reality.

Some projects and tasks will be targeted at bridging more than one type of gap. Interacting with a set of prospective customers, for example, can help bridge information gaps and implementation gaps at the same time. However, it's useful also to keep in mind why you primarily do something: for gathering information or for implementing your strategy.

DEFINING PROJECTS AND TASKS: THE STRATEGY BACKLOG

Once you have identified your information and implementation gaps, your next step is to define projects and tasks that can close them. A *task* is an action that needs to be executed to close a particular gap; a *project* is a collection of tasks that belong together. In this step, you don't need to worry yet about prioritization and planning. The main goal is to come up with a list of projects and tasks that you will later on, in Step 8, prioritize and turn into planning. The goal is now first to create a *Strategy Backlog:* a list of projects and tasks that need to be executed to realize the strategy.

"Create a Strategy Backlog: a list of projects and tasks that need to be executed to realize the strategy."

The idea of the Strategy Backlog is taken from the "product backlog" and "sprint backlog" that we find in the "scrum" approach to software development. Both these backlogs and the Strategy Backlog offer an overview of what it takes to get a complex job done. While a product backlog and sprint backlog typically are lists of software development tasks written from the perspective of the user, the Strategy Backlog is the list of projects and tasks that need to be executed to realize your strategy. Most likely this is going to be a long list, especially if your new strategy is a big change compared to where you are now. Don't get overwhelmed by this–the point is just to get everything on the table that needs to be done.

Maybe you have software-based or physical "scrum boards" or "Kanban boards" (see page 305) that you use in your organization. In that case, you could use those and immediately create your Strategy Backlog there. If you don't have such software or boards, or if entering a list of tasks immediately requires assigning responsibilities, dates, etc., then spreadsheet software like Microsoft Excel, Apple Numbers, or Google Sheets is suitable to do this. Traditional planning software might be useful too, but only if it doesn't immediately draw you into complicated project planning. So, keep it simple.

At this stage only four columns are relevant: one referring to the element of your strategy, one describing the gap, one defining the project(s) for closing the gap, and one listing the task(s) that need to be executed to close the gap. Later on, you'll add some more columns to facilitate the planning process. Your growing Strategy Backlog will look like the example below (in which VP stands for value proposition, RE for resources and competences).

PART OF A STRATEGY BACKLOG

Part of a Strategy Backlog

Element	Gap	Project	Task	...
VP	We assume customers are willing to pay price X for our new product but are not certain enough.	Willingness-to-pay study.	Try selling the product at price X to 10 potential customers.	
			Study prices of 3 main competitors.	
RE	We lack a large enough production hall for housing the necessary growth.	Find new production hall.	Check available buildings within 10 km range.	
			Ask company X for their empty hall.	

BRIDGING INFORMATION GAPS

Bridging information gaps is not about general information gathering or answering open-ended questions such as "What are our unique competences?", "What are the important trends?", or "What are the key risks that we are facing?" Such questions belong to the strategy generation stage and should be answered there. Once you've generated a new strategy, the only information gaps that should be left are your untested assumptions. If you've already tested or validated the main assumptions underlying your new strategy during strategy generation, this is great. In that case, you can skip this section and move on the next one, on bridging implementation gaps. In other cases, you should start here.

MAKE ASSUMPTIONS EXPLICIT

Your entire new strategy can be seen as a set of assumptions. You assume, for example, that a customer has particular needs, that you have particular competences that your competitor does not, or that a particular trend is going to disrupt your industry in the next two years. But you don't know this for sure. There may, of course, be substantial parts about which you are quite sure. However, insofar as your strategy is new, you most likely don't really know whether your assumptions are right.

You may already be aware of some of these assumptions. Others you may have made less consciously, which means they remain implicit. You should make them explicit, though. To do this, you can ask the following four questions for each of the ten elements of strategy.

1. *How certain are we about this element of our new strategy?* By assessing how certain you are about the elements of your new strategy (e.g., on a five-point scale from very uncertain to very certain) you force yourself to think explicitly about possible doubts. So, maybe you score a three on customers and needs, indicating that you are medium-sure whether you are right about them.

2. *What are we still uncertain about with respect to this element?* This question makes you consider what it is about a particular element that makes you less certain. Asking the question directs you to the aspects of this element about which you have made assumptions. So, maybe your medium score of three stems from the fact that you don't know sure enough whether the needs that you assumed your to-be customers to have are in fact their actual needs.

3. *What needs to be true to make it work as expected?* By asking this question, you think about the conditions under which your new strategy would work with respect to a particular element. So, maybe for your to-be customers to have need X, it has to be true that they run into problem Y. This means that you have implicitly assumed that they have problem Y.

4. *So, what are the assumptions that we are making about this?* Based on the answers to question 3, you can now write out your assumptions one by one. It can be useful to state them explicitly in the form of "We assume that …." Examples are:

- "We assume that organizations of type A run into problem Y, which costs them X amount of money on average per day."
- "We assume that adding feature X to our product will make sure that customers are willing to pay price Y."
- "We assume that competitors will respond in manner X in reaction to our price cut Y."

ASSESS THE NEED TO TEST ASSUMPTIONS

Not all assumptions are worth testing. If you're relatively certain about an assumption or if you can bear the costs of being wrong, it's preferable that you leave it alone and focus on the more important ones or on bridging implementation gaps instead of information gaps. To decide which information gaps you will try to bridge, ask yourself the following two questions for each assumption.

1. Are we confident enough to assume we are right?
2. Can we bear the costs if we are wrong?

For every assumption for which your answer to these two questions is "no," you may want to define an information-bridging task. If your answer is "yes" to one of them though, there is probably no need to define a task because you're either confident enough to take the gamble or have relatively little to lose.

> *"This step should not result in a perpetual certainty-seeking cycle that prevents you from taking any action."*

I want to emphasize that this step should not result in a perpetual certainty-seeking cycle that prevents you from taking any action. The purpose of this step is to avoid making costly mistakes. Certainty, however, can never be achieved. In deciding whether or not you need to define an information-bridging task, it's good to keep in mind what the costs are of gathering the information in comparison to the cost of simply proceeding with the execution of the strategy. If they are more or less equal, the latter is preferred. If the potential costs of a mistake are too high, though, you can perform one or more of the following eight types of information-bridging tasks.

1. **Just do it**
To emphasize once more the importance of action and not getting paralyzed by analysis, the first type of information-bridging task is just to start with execution, focus on bridging the implementation gaps, and learn from your experience. The key here is to fail fast and cheap. The sooner you find out that you were wrong about your assumptions, the better. And if you were right, even better, since you have made a head start with executing your strategy. As long as the costs of being wrong are affordable, keep in mind Motto 1: just do it. But don't let this be a reason for mindless execution. Always reflect on the results and adjust where necessary.

2. **Prototype or pilot**

A second way to bridge information gaps is to create a prototype or do a pilot. Like with the first way, the focus here is on action. However, rather than immediately starting "for real," you do a trial run. The first thing you may think of here is a prototype of your product or service or a pilot study to explore a new market. However, you can also prototype or pilot many other things in your organization, like a new process, structure, incentive system, contract, or website. The bottom line is that you create a first mock-up version of something before you make larger investments in terms of money, time, or effort. There are three reasons why you would do this.

- **Viability testing:** finding out what your product or service actually should be. You probably have ideas on this, but often these are still rather vague, or you have no idea whether customers would actually want such a product or service. To test this, you can create a *minimum viable product*. A minimum viable product is an early version of your product or service with just enough features to allow you to learn as much as possible about your customer.

- **Capability testing:** finding out whether the organization is capable of doing something. You can also make a prototype to find out whether you can create a new product that has the required technical features, or whether you can deliver a new service that offers customers what they need. Often, such a prototype is an unfinished product or service that needs further improvement in future versions. What you are testing here is mainly whether the organization is capable of creating the product or service.

- **Convincing:** impressing or convincing a particular stakeholder to work with you. A common example of this is that you create a prototype or model of your product or service to impress a potential customer and convince them to buy your product or service. When made for this reason, the prototype needs to be more finished and have at least the quality that it would have when offered for real. It is still a prototype, which may require adaptations. However, its quality, and especially its look and feel, need to be much higher than in the first two cases.

3. **Gather data**

The third type of task that you can consider for bridging information gaps is data gathering. This includes the use of databases, reports, and the Internet to find relevant information. With its emphasis on analysis, this type of task is traditionally done at the start and throughout the strategy generation stage. In that stage, though, data gathering becomes easily undirected and vast since there is no clear reference point to decide which data to gather—and which not. As a result, one easily falls into the trap of gathering general, marginally relevant data about trends, customers, and competitors.

Data gathering can be more targeted and efficient when you do it to test your assumptions. This is more targeted because, if you have for example estimated that a particular technology will be very useful for your organization, you can gather specific data on whether this is the case or not. You can investigate the possibilities of this technology to find out whether or not adopting it is going to bring you a competitive advantage. This approach is also more efficient because, through the two filtering questions on page 200, you only gather data for testing those assumptions for which the costs of being wrong are too high.

"Data gathering can be more targeted and efficient when you do it to test your assumptions."

4. **Ask**

A fourth way of bridging information gaps is to ask people. These could be your customers, suppliers, employees, or any other stakeholders that are important in executing your strategy. Asking in an explorative way what people need or what they think about your product is usually not such a good idea. It often just leads to casual wish-lists, general, and polite answers that you already expected, or people say what they think they should say because everyone else is saying it. None of that is particularly helpful.

A more effective approach is to ask people concrete questions about things they are trying to accomplish. The trick is to ask them to describe specific events or things they did or experienced. When asking them, you should focus on issues and irritations since you want to know how you can make it easier or otherwise better for them. If you have done strategy generation well, you have asked such questions already (for example along the lines of the Empathy Map on page 78). If there are still important information gaps at this stage, you can ask additional questions in this same way now.

An even more effective approach at this stage is to propose something specific to people and ask them to commit. If they don't, you know your assumption was wrong; if they do, you have immediately started to realize your strategy. If for example, your assumption is that your pricing should change from a high fixed initial fee to a lower but recurring fee, you can put two offerings in front of current or potential customers and let them choose, to find out which option they prefer. In this way, you don't ask people just for their opinions, ideas, or feedback, but you probe them to commit for real. Such commitments are more reliable than mere answers.

5. **Observe**

Asking can be notoriously unreliable. People make things up, over-rationalize, and answer what they think they should answer. Often, they don't do this intentionally to fool you. They do it because they are people. Even though the ways of asking described above can help overcome such problems, observing people rather than asking them works even better.

> *"Asking can be notoriously unreliable."*

The main advantage of observation is that it captures the real action, not reported or hypothetical behavior. Thus, rather than rely on what people say they do or would do, you rely on what people actually do. Observation is also richer than asking. You can see people's emotional responses and the things they do unconsciously. It's also more natural. Rather than interrupting people with all kinds of questions, you simply let them do things and observe them. Observation forces you to *listen* rather than talk. Instead of steering a conversation towards what you want to hear, observation let the facts speak as much as possible for themselves.

Like the other information-bridging tasks, observation may already have been part of your strategy generation. But it can also play an important role in execution. You can use it to test assumptions about your products or services and how these are supposed to improve what customers are trying to achieve. To do this, you give your product or service to a number of (potential or actual) customers and observe how they engage with it, whether they use it as expected, or whether things are clear to them.

Observation can also be used to test other parts of your renewed strategy and whether your organization is fit to execute it. You can observe, for example, whether a redesigned process is really an improvement for how employees do their work, whether people actually have the capabilities that they will need, or whether the systems in place are suitable for the new strategy. Basically, you can observe anything people are doing.

6. Attack the assumptions

What the first five approaches have in common is a focus on obtaining more information that's as realistic as possible. You can also test your assumptions in a more subjective way by attacking them and finding reasons why you would be wrong.

A way to do this is to put together a team with the explicit assignment of proving that your assumptions are wrong. This could be the strategy team you are working with already or another team, as long as it includes critics. You ask them to convince you and give as many reasons as possible why the assumptions would be incorrect, irrelevant, or faulty in any other way. For example, you might assume that your new strategy is going to save you an X amount of money. When you ask a team to attack this assumption and prove that it's not going to happen or that the new strategy will even cost you more money, they might point you to additional costs that you had not thought of or that some savings that you anticipated are just not realistic.

There are four possible outcomes. First, if the team succeeds in attacking the idea and convinces you that it's wrong, you may have saved yourself from making expensive investments or misdirected commitments. Second, if the team fails to find reasons why you're wrong, you'll gain confidence that your assumptions are right and thereby reduce the information gap. Third, the team may have pointed out some weak spots in your assumptions that you can learn from and use to improve. Finally, it *is* possible to disagree with the team's conclusions and choose to ignore them. This is a risky strategy but sometimes justifiable if you're strongly convinced your vision is right. The risk is yours though.

> *"If the team fails to find reasons why you're wrong, you'll gain confidence that your assumptions are right."*

7. Make a basic business case

Some information gaps are not caused by a lack of information, but by a yet-to-do analysis. Such gaps cannot be closed by any of the approaches above. Instead, you need to combine the data that you have in a proper manner. One way to do this is to make a business case. This is a realistic and concrete scenario that shows whether or not the new strategy can be financially feasible or attractive.

Making a business case, in the way I use it here, is not about making accurate projections of how much money you're going to make or lose. The point of a business case at this stage of the strategy process is to get a realistic idea of whether your strategy adds up if the assumptions are right. So, rather than testing the assumptions themselves, you test whether the assumptions make sense together. In other words, a business case doesn't tell you whether you *will* make money. Instead, it shows you whether you *could* make money with your new strategy in the first place.

With doing a business case, I don't mean writing an extensive document by, for example, following PRINCE2 guidelines or the numerous business case templates circulating on the Internet. What I mean are relatively simple calculations of your revenues and costs in what you think is a realistic scenario of what could happen. I say "relatively simple" here because making such calculations is never really simple. It takes the following four steps.

a. Specify the *boundaries*. Define the scope of the business case (e.g., whether it only concerns in a particular region or product) and set a timeline (e.g., does it concern half a year, a year, five years).

b. Define the main *variables* that influence your revenues and costs. These include, for example, the number of customers, how much they pay, your fixed and variable costs.

c. Define how you calculate your revenues and costs. This means building the main *formulas* that define how the variables should be combined, multiplied, added, etc., to calculate revenues and costs.

d. Create realistic *data* to work with for each of the variables. Define, for example, the number of paying customers you expect, what they will pay, and how much this will cost you.

With these boundaries, variables, formulas, and data you have all the ingredients for your basic business case. An easy way to create it is to put it in a spreadsheet. When you do this, you should make sure that you clearly distinguish between input cells that require manual input and outcome cells that are automatically filled by your formulas. This will make sure you only touch the input cells when you play with the data that you enter.

Example of a Basic Business Case

Boundaries:	Scope: a single product line | Timeline: 3 years				
Variables:	One-time investment in equipment (I), variable costs per product (C), # of products sold per year (N), sales price per product (P)				
Formulas:	Cumulative profit Year X = Cumulative profit Year X-1 + (N*P) - (N*C) - I				
Data:	I = € 200,000, C = € 23, N = 10,000, P = € 30				
Input Data:	Investment in equipment € 200,000.00 Variable costs per product € 23.00 # of products sold per year 10,000 Sales price per product € 30.00				
Outcomes		Spendings	Earnings	Profit/Loss	Cumulative Profit
	Year 1	€ 430,000	€ 300,000	-€ 300,000	- € 130,000
	Year 2	€ 230,000	€ 300,000	€ 70,000	- € 60,000
	Year 3	€ 230,000	€ 300,000	€ 70,000	€ 10,000

8. **Simulate**

Making a business case is a kind of simulation. Rather than testing the assumptions themselves, you simulate what the outcome will be if they are correct. Simulations can be used more broadly and in different, non-financial ways as well. Their main purpose is to understand the dynamics and mechanisms that would be triggered if you executed your new strategy. As such, they inform you about possible or likely effects and responses to the choices that you make in your strategy. Two useful types of simulations are the thought experiment and software simulations.

- **Thought experiment.** With a thought experiment, you try to deduce the consequences of the assumptions underlying your new strategy in a chained, step-by-step manner. You ask yourself questions like "If I do X, what happens to Y?" and "If that happens to Y, what will happen to Z?" For example, you think through how your competitors will respond to a change in the price of your product, how customers will respond to that, and how you will respond to that again. To facilitate your thinking here, it's useful to visualize these inferences in a causal map–a map with boxes and arrows showing how one thing leads to another. Of course, rather than just thinking the simulation through in your mind, you can also do this together with others–e.g., with the strategy team suggested on pages 36-38. This will most certainly give you better insights than if you do it on your own.

"The main purpose of simulations is to understand the dynamics and mechanisms that would be triggered if you executed your new strategy."

- **Software simulations.** You can also simulate your new strategy using software. For this, you need to codify your strategy into a digital format and run it in a software program. On the one hand, software simulations can be very valuable because they allow for much more complexity than the other two forms, and so can give you deeper and more accurate insights into how your strategy would work. Also, they allow for trying out more and quicker variations. On the other hand, creating an accurate enough software simulation can be costly. Off-the-shelf (educational) business games are often too generic. This means that you will likely have to invest a lot of time and money to create a suitable, tailor-made simulation. Although powerful, software simulations are only recommended if your answer to the two questions on page 200 is a clear "no."

BRIDGING IMPLEMENTATION GAPS

Once you feel confident enough, or when you can take the risk because the potential loss is affordable, you can define projects and tasks for bridging the gap between your current and your aspired strategy. If you have mapped out both in a Strategy Sketch, this is a straightforward thing to do. As visualized on page 194, you simply compare both along the ten elements and identify the gaps that need to be closed.

For some gaps, it will be obvious what you need to do to bridge them. For example, if you need a new resource that you currently don't have, you can buy it, and if you need to make a change to your product, you can do that. This doesn't necessarily mean that doing these things is easy. However, *identifying* what must be done is relatively easy.

It could also be that even though the gap is clear, coming up with suitable projects or tasks is still difficult. In such cases, you know what is needed, but you don't know yet how to achieve it. To stimulate and facilitate your thinking about this, you can use the Action Maps on the following pages. An Action Map is a mind map containing a set of verbs that suggest the kind of tasks you could use to bridge the gap for a particular element. You should read them inside-out in the following way:

"If your current *{element}* is/are *{implementation gap}* for realizing your aspired strategy, then you can *{action}*."

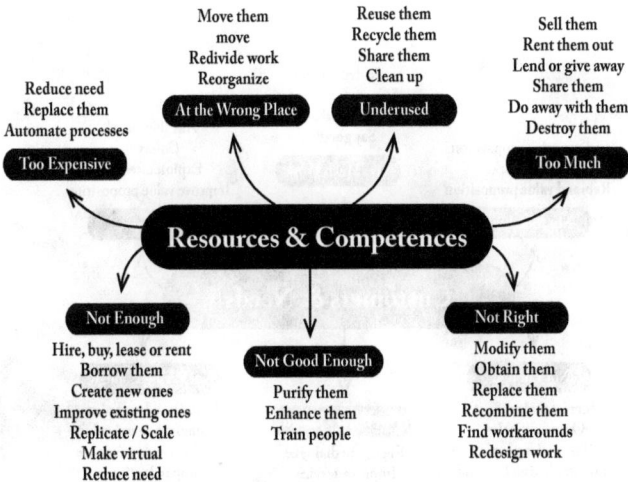

Move them
move
Redivide work
Reorganize

At the Wrong Place

Reuse them
Recycle them
Share them
Clean up

Underused

Sell them
Rent them out
Lend or give away
Share them
Do away with them
Destroy them

Too Much

Reduce need
Replace them
Automate processes

Too Expensive

Resources & Competences

Not Enough

Hire, buy, lease or rent
Borrow them
Create new ones
Improve existing ones
Replicate / Scale
Make virtual
Reduce need

Not Good Enough

Purify them
Enhance them
Train people

Not Right

Modify them
Obtain them
Replace them
Recombine them
Find workarounds
Redesign work

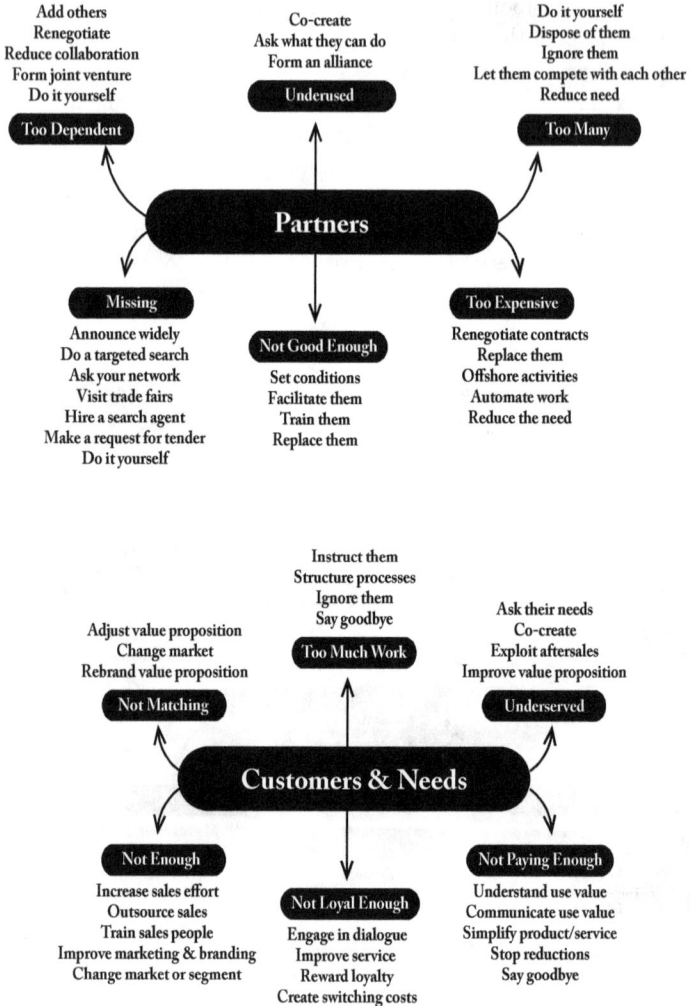

Partners

Too Dependent
- Add others
- Renegotiate
- Reduce collaboration
- Form joint venture
- Do it yourself

Underused
- Co-create
- Ask what they can do
- Form an alliance

Too Many
- Do it yourself
- Dispose of them
- Ignore them
- Let them compete with each other
- Reduce need

Missing
- Announce widely
- Do a targeted search
- Ask your network
- Visit trade fairs
- Hire a search agent
- Make a request for tender
- Do it yourself

Not Good Enough
- Set conditions
- Facilitate them
- Train them
- Replace them

Too Expensive
- Renegotiate contracts
- Replace them
- Offshore activities
- Automate work
- Reduce the need

Customers & Needs

Too Much Work
- Instruct them
- Structure processes
- Ignore them
- Say goodbye

Underserved
- Ask their needs
- Co-create
- Exploit aftersales
- Improve value proposition

Not Matching
- Adjust value proposition
- Change market
- Rebrand value proposition

Not Enough
- Increase sales effort
- Outsource sales
- Train sales people
- Improve marketing & branding
- Change market or segment

Not Loyal Enough
- Engage in dialogue
- Improve service
- Reward loyalty
- Create switching costs

Not Paying Enough
- Understand use value
- Communicate use value
- Simplify product/service
- Stop reductions
- Say goodbye

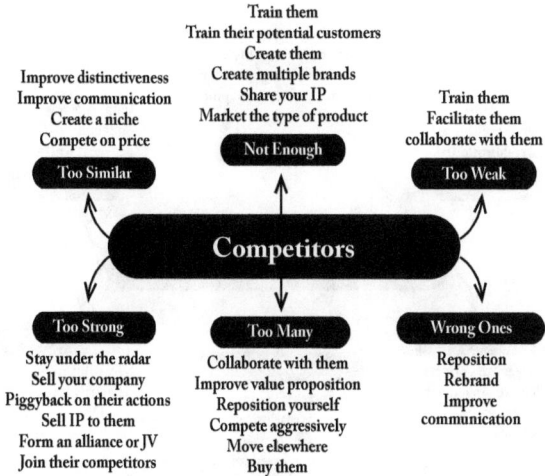

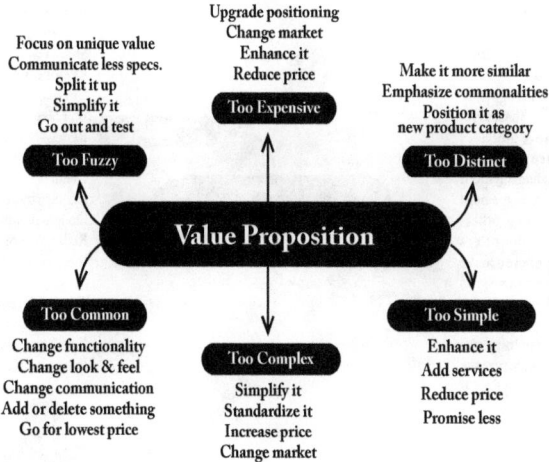

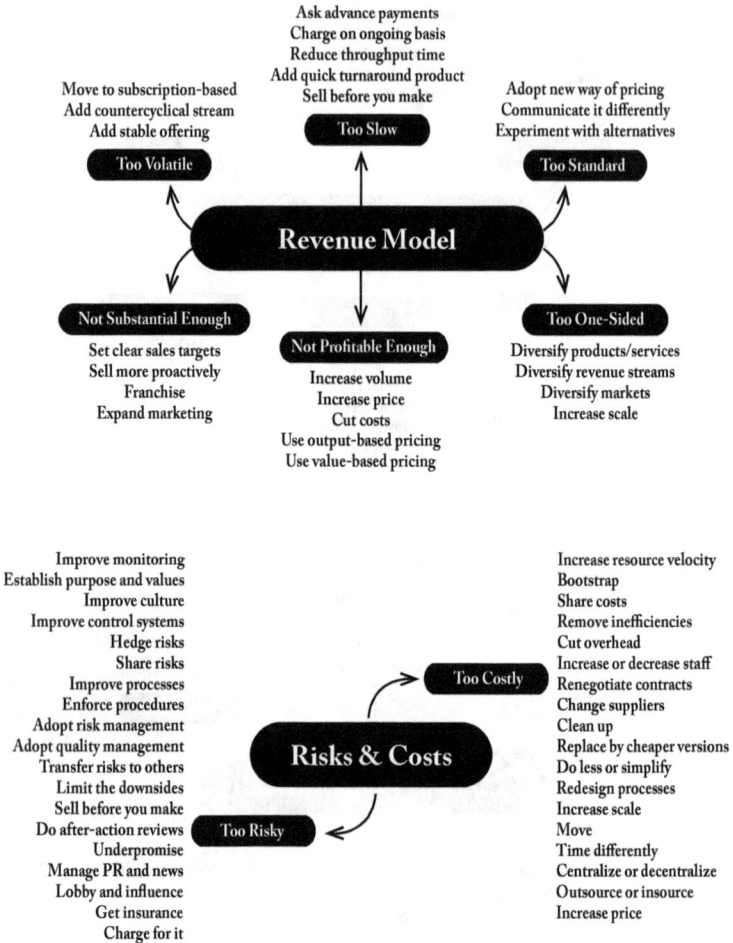

Ask advance payments
Charge on ongoing basis
Reduce throughput time
Add quick turnaround product
Sell before you make

Too Slow

Move to subscription-based
Add countercyclical stream
Add stable offering

Too Volatile

Adopt new way of pricing
Communicate it differently
Experiment with alternatives

Too Standard

Revenue Model

Not Substantial Enough

Set clear sales targets
Sell more proactively
Franchise
Expand marketing

Not Profitable Enough

Increase volume
Increase price
Cut costs
Use output-based pricing
Use value-based pricing

Too One-Sided

Diversify products/services
Diversify revenue streams
Diversify markets
Increase scale

Improve monitoring
Establish purpose and values
Improve culture
Improve control systems
Hedge risks
Share risks
Improve processes
Enforce procedures
Adopt risk management
Adopt quality management
Transfer risks to others
Limit the downsides
Sell before you make
Do after-action reviews
Underpromise
Manage PR and news
Lobby and influence
Get insurance
Charge for it

Too Costly

Risks & Costs

Too Risky

Increase resource velocity
Bootstrap
Share costs
Remove inefficiencies
Cut overhead
Increase or decrease staff
Renegotiate contracts
Change suppliers
Clean up
Replace by cheaper versions
Do less or simplify
Redesign processes
Increase scale
Move
Time differently
Centralize or decentralize
Outsource or insource
Increase price

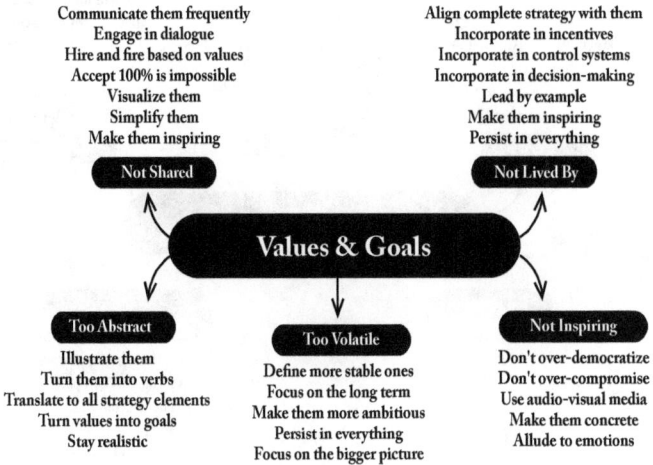

Communicate them frequently
Engage in dialogue
Hire and fire based on values
Accept 100% is impossible
Visualize them
Simplify them
Make them inspiring

Not Shared

Align complete strategy with them
Incorporate in incentives
Incorporate in control systems
Incorporate in decision-making
Lead by example
Make them inspiring
Persist in everything

Not Lived By

Values & Goals

Too Abstract

Illustrate them
Turn them into verbs
Translate to all strategy elements
Turn values into goals
Stay realistic

Too Volatile

Define more stable ones
Focus on the long term
Make them more ambitious
Persist in everything
Focus on the bigger picture

Not Inspiring

Don't over-democratize
Don't over-compromise
Use audio-visual media
Make them concrete
Allude to emotions

Trust and show trust
Reward, don't punish
Engage in open dialogue
Fail by example (but small)
Allow risk-taking

Too Fearful

Simplify procedures
Reduce paperwork
Get rid of rules
Decentralize
Reduce hierarchy
Focus on outcome, not on process

Too Rigid

Focus on values and goals
Fucus on the long-term
Create structure
Create and enforce processes
Adopt team-based working
Use control mechanisms

Too Ad Hoc

Organizational Climate

Too Relaxed

Set challenging targets
Follow-up with consequences
Hold people accountable
Create pressure

Too Demanding

Offer support
Allow failure
Allow free time
Relax demands

Too Negative

Engage in a dialogue
Solve problems
Celebrate achievements
Restrict time for complaining

Too Confident

Correct hubris & arrogance
Celebrate modesty
Acquire more difficult work
Challenge people

Gather more relevant data
Learn more about them
Monitor them systematically
Visualize and quantify

Too Unclear

Monitor more accurately
Influence and lobby
Focus on what you can control
Reduce need for prediction
Focus on internal strengths
Redirect attention elsewhere

Too Uncertain

Focus on few factors only
Focus on what you can analyze
Redirect attention elsewhere
Rely on intuitive decision-making
Identify patterns
Look at the bigger picture

Too Complex

Trends & Uncertainties

Too Dynamic

Decentralize
Split up
Divest
Invest in flexible solutions
Outsource
Shorten time to market
Shorten strategy / planning cycle
Redirect attention elsewhere

Too Threatening

Redirect attention elsewhere
Turn threats into opportunities
Use it against competitors
Redefine your business
Ignore and focus on value creation
Move elsewhere

CLOSING THE BRIDGING STEP

Your efforts to identify projects and tasks for bridging information gaps and implementation gaps can lead to a long Strategy Backlog. This is expected, and there is no need to be concerned. It just shows how much work it can take to execute a new strategy. And when you take the next step—Organizing Strategy—the list of projects and tasks is going to be longer anyway.

However, to close the bridging step, there is some point at which you need to stop. There is no particular number that you can use as a rule of thumb or a set of criteria that you can use to decide this. It will depend on how different your new strategy is compared to where you are today. But usually, the moment of closure will come naturally. At some point, your Strategy Backlog dries up, and you will feel that this is a good moment to stop. After you experience this moment, sleep on it, and if you still can't come up with any additional important projects or tasks the next day, then consider the Strategy Backlog complete for now.

After completing your Strategy Backlog at this stage, it's useful to do two additional things. First, review it critically and delete the projects and tasks that you're not going to execute anyway. Even though you listed them, thinking once more about them might make you realize that they don't belong on the list after all. Second, you might want to perform some or even all information-bridging projects and tasks before moving on. If you followed the guidelines above, these projects and tasks would refer to assumptions about which you are not confident but which would be too risky to get wrong. You might want to test them first to gain confidence that your strategy will work. Once that has been done, you can move on to the next step.

THE FOUR EXAMPLES

As summarized on pages 176-181, the execution of the aspired strategy involves many challenges for all four examples. Rather than listing their entire Strategy Backlogs, I illustrate this chapter with different types of outcomes that result from this first step of strategy execution. They are:

- **Macman**: defining projects and tasks for bridging implementation gaps with respect to their resources and competences.
- **Hospicare**: their approach for bridging information gaps relating to the new type of self-paying customers they envision.
- **GoforIT**: defining projects and tasks for bridging implementation gaps with respect to their revenue model.
- **Comcom**: a Strategy Sketch summarizing the main gaps between the current and the aspired strategy.

BRIDGING AT MACMAN

One of Macman's main gaps between their current and aspired strategies is their lack of customer and service orientation. They are hard-working, loyal, and highly-skilled engineers, but not very adept at putting themselves in the shoes of their customers. The main gaps that relate to this reside in their resources and competences. They are:

1. Moving from a product orientation to a customer orientation. They do not have the competences to understand and address customer needs.
2. Their attitude towards service is that they still see it as a costly nuisance rather than as a value-added product.

Using the resources and competences Action Map (page 209) led to the following two projects and tasks:

1. Develop customer and service awareness:
   a. Go on a site visit to a customer-centric organization to learn.
   b. Let the sales department present to the rest of the organization the issues they face when interacting with customers.
   c. Organize meetings between engineers and three loyal customers to learn by seeing customers as real people.
2. Develop a customer and service orientation:
   a. Find appropriate training.
   b. Select a first group of engineers to do the training as a pilot.
   c. Follow the training and evaluate.

Of course, more projects were necessary, particularly for those employees who could not change sufficiently. However, before thinking about replacing or repositioning them, the company first wanted to try the two projects above. Bridging the gaps also required substantial organizational changes. We return to this on page 267 in the next chapter on organizing.

BRIDGING AT HOSPICARE

Hospicare wants to move to a hub-and-spoke model with a general hospital at the core and privatized specialized centers around it. One of the main assumptions behind this new strategy is that there is a large enough group of patients willing to pay for health care themselves rather than via insurance. This, however, is an assumption that requires further scrutiny. To bridge this information gap, they did the following.

Step 1. Make the assumptions explicit.
In a session with a team of five, going through the four questions on pages 198-199 led to a set of assumptions regarding their customers and needs and value proposition. Three key ones include the following.

1. We assume that only people with at least an income of twice the middle income will be interested.
2. We assume that people will be interested in this when it concerns less severe or contained psychiatric problems associated with a) burnout, b) ADHD, and c) Asperger syndrome.
3. We assume people will not be interested in this when it concerns more significant psychiatric problems such as, for example, depression and mental disorders.

Step 2. Assess the need to test them.
After reflecting on the assumptions, it was clear that 1 and 2 needed to be tested. Assumption 3 was less important to test because they decided not to focus on these more serious psychiatric conditions in the first instance anyway. They wanted to try the easier ones. Assumptions 1 and 2 did require serious testing because setting up a specialized psychiatric health care center is costly.

Step 3. Define projects and tasks for testing them.
To test the assumptions, the following projects and tasks were defined and added to their Strategy Backlog.

1. Estimate the total addressable market (customers and needs).
   a. Gather data on the number of people with officially diagnosed burnout, ADHD, and Asperger syndrome in a radius of 50 km around their core location.
   b. Gather data on the estimated number of non-diagnosed people in that same region.

      c.   Gather data on the percentage of people with at least twice the middle income in that same region.

2.   Do a real-life pilot for burnout (value proposition).

      a.   Define a contained treatment that could be offered commercially to people experiencing a burnout (a "minimal viable product") and price it.

      b.   Offer it via the current hospital as an additional product to the normal path via insurance.

      c.   Create a low-cost marketing campaign.

      d.   Gather responses, learn, and pivot.

BRIDGING AT GOFORIT

GoforIT faces many challenges if they wish to realize their ambition to triple in size in the very short time of two years. An obvious gap that appeared was a lack of cash. Without a significant investment of at least half a million euros, they cannot make it happen. In terms of the ten elements of strategy, this is a gap concerning their resources and competences and it clearly needs to be solved by means of a partner–an investor. Based on the Action Map for partners, they outlined the following projects and tasks.

1.   Carry out a targeted search for a suitable investor.

      a.   Define a profile for the kind of investor sought.

      b.   Search online, including via online startup platforms.

      c.   Ask two friendly (small-scale) investors whether they know suitable investors.

2.   Announce that we are looking for an investor.

      a.   Inform partners and contacts that we need €500k+.

      b.   Talk to a nearby business incubator.

While it quickly turned out that there was a lot of money available, after talking to one of their two friendly investors, it immediately became obvious they also had to be more organized and make a plan for how to do that. Otherwise, no investor would be willing to invest in them. Thus, they immediately moved on to the next step—organizing.

BRIDGING AT COMCOM

As formulated on pages 180-181 of Chapter 7, Anisha's new strategy for Comcom is to standardize and automate her communication services so that she saves time and gets better margins. Her old strategy was summarized in a Strategy Sketch on pages 106-107 of Chapter 4. A comparison of the two strategies highlighted a number of gaps that Anisha needs to bridge. These are summarized in the Strategy Sketch below. This Strategy Sketch does not contain her current strategy or her new strategy, but the gaps between them and some clear pointers for projects and tasks that she can define.

GAPS TO BRIDGE FOR COMCOM

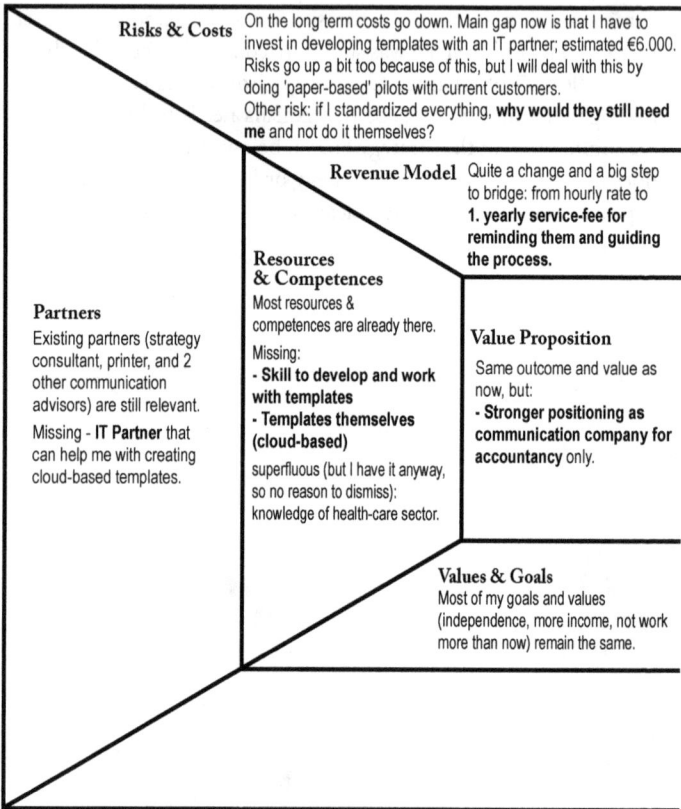

Risks & Costs On the long term costs go down. Main gap now is that I have to invest in developing templates with an IT partner; estimated €6.000. Risks go up a bit too because of this, but I will deal with this by doing 'paper-based' pilots with current customers.
Other risk: if I standardized everything, **why would they still need me** and not do it themselves?

Revenue Model Quite a change and a big step to bridge: from hourly rate to
1. yearly service-fee for reminding them and guiding the process.

Resources & Competences
Most resources & competences are already there.
Missing:
- **Skill to develop and work with templates**
- **Templates themselves (cloud-based)**
superfluous (but I have it anyway, so no reason to dismiss): knowledge of health-care sector.

Partners
Existing partners (strategy consultant, printer, and 2 other communication advisors) are still relevant.
Missing - **IT Partner** that can help me with creating cloud-based templates.

Value Proposition
Same outcome and value as now, but:
- **Stronger positioning as communication company for accountancy** only.

Values & Goals
Most of my goals and values (independence, more income, not work more than now) remain the same.

Trends Trend of **increasing price competition can become and opportunity:** competitors will have a hard time beating me with my standardized services.

Uncertainties
New uncertainties: **how will customers respond** to my new offering?

2. fixed price per communication product (newsletter, report, etc).

Customers & Needs
No big change, but: **Focus on accountancy firms only.** So far, this was 60-70%, this should move to 100% of turnover. Thus, **need to sell €20.000 more in this sector.**

Additional needs served;

- Further cost saving

- **Support with the process too.** They want someone to take the lead and contact them pro-actively when a new message or report should go out.

Competitors
Existing competitors (other communication advisor + marketing companies) remain the same, but by my positioning as niche specialist, they should become less relevant.
On the other hand, other services targeting accountancy will become more important. These include **coaches and trainers** that help accountancy firms communicate better themselves.

- **Structured process** in which I take the lead rather than them contacting me.
- **More standardized,** less flexible and tailor-made communication products.

Also my dream to make a living from a food blog remains. However, I will first give priority to renewing my communication services and make it more efficient.

Organizational Climate
Bigger changes will be 1) more structured and predictable way of working and 2) more efficient. This will make my job more relaxed and predictable and give me the better work-life balance that I need.

Trend that becomes increasingly important: everything related to the accountancy sector, since I will 100% depend on it.

STEPPING BACK AGAIN

After this first step of strategy execution, you'll have a substantial list of projects and tasks that need to be executed to bridge information and implementation gaps. This is the start of your Strategy Backlog. This Strategy Backlog shows the projects and tasks that you need to perform to feel confident about your strategy and to execute it. Now that you have this backlog, this is a good moment to step back again and ask yourself the following question:

"Do we still want the strategy that we generated?"

It's important to ask this question because, through the process so far, you have enhanced and refined your insights by thinking in more concrete terms about what it takes to realize your strategy. Based on these insights, you may have changed your mind. Or maybe you now understand that you were too ambitious and that it takes too much to realize your strategy. As emphasized various times, strategy making is an iterative process. Asking the question above makes sure that it remains iterative and that you avoid the trap of just pressing on with the strategy that was formulated. There are three possible answers to the question.

1. **Yes, but** you expect that getting there is going to demand some changes to the organization too. In this case, you should move on to Chapter 9, "Step 7: Organizing Strategy" (page 225).
2. **Yes, and** you don't expect any significant organizational challenges when realizing your new strategy. In this case, you could skip the next chapter and move on to Chapter 10, "Step 8: Planning Strategy" (page 275).

3. **No, or** at least you already know that you need to make changes to your strategy. In this case, you should go back to Chapter 6, "Step 4: Innovating Strategy" (page 139).

9

STEP 7: ORGANIZING STRATEGY

This ninth chapter explains the second step of strategy execution: organizing strategy. In this step, you identify which projects and tasks are needed to make your organization fit for executing the strategy. Like strategy, "organization" is a black box; therefore, the chapter starts with opening it and decomposing organization into its core elements. It then discusses these elements one by one in more detail and offers information and tools to identify and close the deficiencies that are there.

> **Organizing Strategy** = Identifying the most important organizational deficiencies and defining projects and tasks to solve them.

THE ORGANIZATIONAL CHALLENGE

Successfully executing a strategy almost always requires changes in the organization. Making such changes is difficult and is responsible for a lot of the failure in strategy execution. An important reason that change is so difficult is that organizations are complex; they consist of many different parts, including people, processes, structures, and systems, that are divided over different departments, business units, or locations. The complexity is further increased by the fact that these parts are constantly moving and changing. New people come in, processes are improved, systems are replaced, and so forth. And to make it even more complex, the parts are also interrelated, implying that a change in one part also has consequences for other parts.

The result of this complexity is that it's hard to achieve a strategic change as planned. Changing just one part may already be difficult, let alone changing many of them at the same time. Just think how difficult it is just to change your own habits and multiply that by the number of people working for the organization. Results of change efforts can also be unexpected. In a system with so many interrelated and moving parts, the result of a particular action can be very unpredictable. This is called the "butterfly effect": what starts with a small action in one part of the organization (for example, firing one employee), may cause a chain reaction with unexpected and sometimes extreme consequences elsewhere in the organization (such as an organization-wide revolt against the leadership). Furthermore, there can be resistance by people who don't like the change and disagree with it. Within their own sphere of influence, they will actively or passively make the change more difficult to realize.

> *"It's perfectly normal if you find strategy execution difficult."*

So, accomplishing any change in organizations can be a real challenge. And since realizing a new strategy is mostly associated with many, substantial changes, it's easy to see why strategy execution can be so arduous. This is not to discourage you. On the contrary, it shows why it's perfectly normal if you find strategy execution difficult–and why all the steps outlined in this book are necessary.

THE ORGANIZATIONAL MAP

In Chapter 2, I decomposed strategy into its ten core elements. I did this to make strategy more concrete and tangible so that you can talk about it and work on it in a practical way. For the same reason, I decompose the term "organization" here into its core elements. This leads again to a framework with ten core elements: the Organizational Map.

The Organizational Map

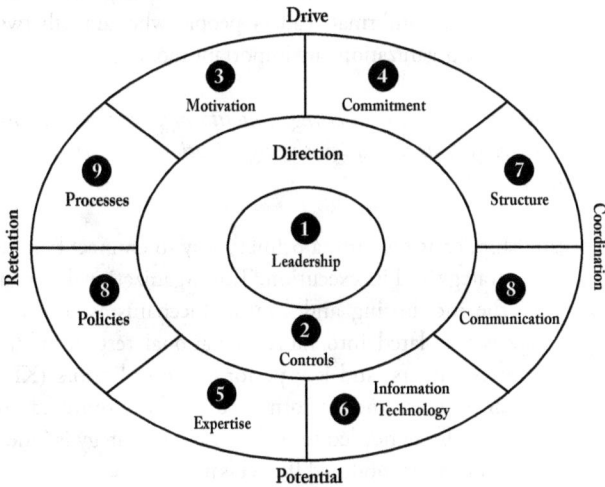

At the center of the Organizational Map, we find leadership and controls. These two elements form the connection between strategy generation and execution by setting the *direction* of the organization. The next two elements, motivation and commitment, refer to people's *drive* to follow that direction. Expertise and information technology, then, concern the *potential* of the organization to achieve the strategy. Subsequently, structure and communication refer to the *coordination* of the work that needs to be done. And, finally, processes and policies concern the *retention* of all of this so that the changes that have been made are turned into the new normal way of working. More precisely, these ten elements are defined as follows.

1. **Leadership.** *Key people who influence, promote, and empower others in the organization to achieve a collaborative outcome.*

Leaders are the main connection between strategy and execution. They personify the strategy and are needed to activate and guide the organization in the right direction. Without leaders, strategy execution is impossible, since there will be no one in the organization taking responsibility. The most obvious people to look at here are the organization's formal leadership–its CEO, management team, or board. However, informal leaders–people who are otherwise influential in the organization–are important too.

2. **Controls.** *The target-setting, monitoring, evaluation, and corrective systems that align the organization's activities with its strategy.*

Like leadership, controls form a primary way to connect between the aspired strategy and its execution. This organizational element consists of the monitoring and control mechanisms by which the strategy is translated into more operational responsibilities, accountabilities, targets, and key performance indicators (KPIs) against which progress and performance can be monitored and managed. Controls are needed to make sure the strategy is indeed executed as planned or modified if necessary.

3. **Motivation.** *The ways and means used to inspire, incentivize, and get people to perform effectively.*

While leadership and controls direct the organization in line with the aspired strategy, the strategy will only be realized if people are motivated to do what is necessary. Ideally, we might want everyone to be intrinsically motivated so that they care about the strategy and purpose of the organization and are personally excited about their value. However, in real organizations, we also need conditions in place that motivate people in a more extrinsic way through rewards or repercussions.

4. **Commitment.** *The sense of community within an organization along with the willingness to do what it takes to ensure collective success.*

Having people motivated to do their work is a good start. However, to make the organization function properly there also needs to be a sense of community and commitment so that people don't just care about themselves or their department but also about others in the organization. I'm not implying here that there should be complete harmony or that everyone is thrilled about collaborating with everyone else. However, some shared values and culture with which people identify and a willingness to do things for others are necessary.

5. **Expertise.** *The knowledge, skills, and experience of employees and the mechanisms to manage these.*

Next to knowing where to go and having the mechanisms and willingness in place to realize that together, the organization also needs the ability to do it. Therefore, a fifth element is expertise, which refers to the people in the organization and how these are managed. This concerns people in every role and rank in the organization. Particularly, it involves making sure that people have the knowledge, skills, and experience to do what is necessary for the organization to prosper.

6. **Information technology.** *The tools and applications that are used to enable and enhance the functioning of the organization through data.*

In addition to having the right people, organizations also rely on information technology to function properly. It concerns all the local and networked hardware and software that are used to process any form of data, from traditional paper-based systems to artificial intelligence. Information technology has become so prevalent today that even traditional "non-tech" service companies rely on information technology at their core. Therefore, it's another key element of the organization.

7. **Structure.** *The allocation and coordination of responsibility, accountability, power, and reporting relationships in the organization.*

With the first six elements, we have an organization that knows in which direction it should go, and that has the requisite drive and ability. Structure, then, refers to how the work is divided and coordinated in the organization. It concerns defining who is responsible and accountable for what and how power is divided and dealt with in the organization. Thus, structure refers to the "horizontal" division of the work to be done in different parts of the organization and the "vertical" division of control and power over levels of the organization and the choice of coordination mechanisms.

8. **Communication.** *The ways and channels by which information is shared both informally and formally throughout the organization.*

Structuring the organization is primarily a matter of dividing work and responsibilities. This creates an immediate need for communication in order to collaborate effectively. The eighth element of the organization refers to the formal and informal communication in the organization and between the organization and its environment. The importance of communication can hardly be overestimated. As research on strategy shows, a lack of effective communication is one of the key reasons why strategy execution fails.

9. **Processes.** *The formal and informal procedures, habits, and routines that define the way things are done in the organization.*

Next to organizing the structure and communication, the way of working also needs to be addressed. This is done through the formal and informal processes in the organization. These processes define which actions need to be taken, how they should be performed, in which order, and how they are dependent on each other. Processes include deliberate and formal procedures and working instructions, but also informal habits and ways of working that develop over time.

10. **Policies.** *The rules, guidelines, agreements, and contracts that define what is expected of everyone in relation to the organization.*

The final element of the organization is its policies. These are the written and unwritten rules, guidelines, agreements, and contracts which define how the organization is supposed to work. They express the rules of the game for everyone involved, both internally and externally. As such, they are an important mechanism to glue together all the other elements in an organized manner.

A QUICK ORGANIZATIONAL FITNESS SCAN

To find out in which elements your organization has the most important issues, it's useful to start this second step of strategy execution with a quick organizational fitness scan. Based on the outcomes of this scan, you can decide which elements to focus your attention on–most likely the *no's* and *maybe's*. For these elements, you can use the more detailed information and tools in the remainder of this chapter to identify gaps and add projects and tasks to your Strategy Backlog.

ORGANIZATIONAL FITNESS SCAN

	YES	MAYBE	NO
Leadership Does the organization have the right leaders in the right place?	●	●	●
Controls Are there effective control mechanisms for steering progress and performance in line with the strategy?	●	●	●
Motivation Are people sufficiently motivated to do their job?	●	●	●
Commitment Do people look sufficiently beyond their job and contribute to the rest of the organization?	●	●	●
Expertise Do people have the right knowledge, skills and experience to do what is needed?	●	●	●

	YES	MAYBE	NO
Information Technology Is the information technology that is used effective, up to date, connected, and complete?	○	○	○
Structure Are roles, responsibilities, and power clear and divided in an effective manner?	○	○	○
Communication Is there enough and effective communication within the organization and with the outside world?	○	○	○
Processes Are the processes in the organization clear, effective, and followed by people?	○	○	○
Policies Are the organization's policies effectively guiding and supporting the work that should be done?	○	○	○

HOW TO USE THE TOOLS

The Organizational Map can be used for diagnosing the organization along its ten elements and defining what gaps there are and what changes are needed. As mentioned, the goal of this second step is to complete your Strategy Backlog with the projects and tasks that are needed to get your organization in shape. To facilitate this step and help you in defining projects and tasks, this chapter contains a rich set of information and tools that you can use. For each element, you will find the following.

- **Quotes.** An outline of the element in three inspiring quotes. These help you grasp the essence of the element and the way you should look at it.
- **Summary**. A brief explanation that provides you with some key insights into the element and tells you which aspects are most relevant.
- **20 Questions.** A list of 20 questions that can be used to identify gaps and define projects and tasks for your Strategy Backlog.

- **To-dos.** A simple step-by-step approach that suggests the kind of projects and tasks that you can define to deal with that element.

Using these tools, you can expand your Strategy Backlog with those projects and tasks that will close the gaps between your current and aspired organization. Thus, in the same way as you identified the gaps between your current and aspired strategy, going through the ten elements below should help you identify the gaps between your current and aspired organization and define the projects and tasks needed to organize your strategy. You can simply add these gaps, projects, and tasks to your Strategy Backlog, and you still don't need more than the four columns described on page 197.

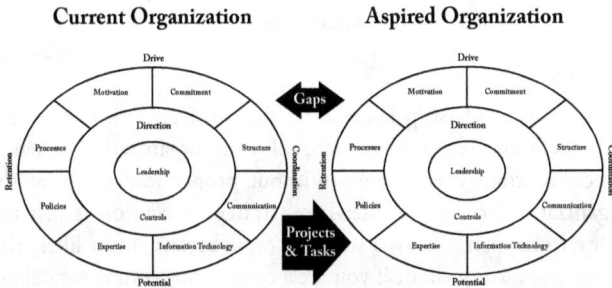

Current Organization   **Aspired Organization**

It's important to emphasize here that not all gaps that you identify will need to be closed. If you use, for example, the 20 Questions, you might answer many of them with "no," but this does not necessarily mean that immediate action is required. In many cases, a "no" may be perfectly acceptable. Accordingly, you should make sure that you don't use the tools below to identify all gaps, projects, and tasks that you can possibly come up with, but to select and define those that are important enough for executing your strategy.

You should also keep in mind that more is not always better and that you can also have "too much of a good thing." Too much commitment, for example, can impede openness towards new ideas or people, too much control can hinder innovation, and too much communication could easily lead to a communication overload. Along the lines of Motto 2 ("Perfect is the enemy of good"), your goal should be to optimize the ten elements, not to maximize them.

1. LEADERSHIP

> "A good leader is a person who takes a little more than his share of the blame and a little less than his share of the credit." – *John Maxwell*

> "If the highest aim of a captain were to preserve his ship, he would keep it in port forever." – *Thomas Aquinas*

> "A leader is best when people barely know he exists, when his work is done, his aim fulfilled, they will say: we did it ourselves." – *Lao Tzu*

I start with leadership because it's the most crucial, but usually also the most sensitive element of your organization when it concerns strategy execution. Without proper leadership, at the organization's center or elsewhere, strategy execution is just not going to happen. This is a sensitive topic because most likely this concerns you as well, or if you are a consultant, your direct client. And unfortunately, problems in strategy execution are more often than not a result of inadequate leadership.

Although it may concern you, leadership should not be *about* you. It's about the organization. A good leader does whatever it takes to make their organization successful, even if that means stepping back or leaving the organization when other qualities are needed than the ones they have. I am not assuming they do this because they are so altruistic. No, good leaders acknowledge it's also in their own long-term interest to step back from situations for which they don't have the right skills.

From the quotes above and Mottos 9 and 10 on pages 33-34, you get an idea of the kind of leadership that I think is required: humble, courageous, and focused on empowering people. This does not only concern leadership at the top of the organization, but also at all other places where a group of people needs to get things done together. Whether you call them managers, team leaders, heads, or bosses is not relevant. In all cases their role is similar. And so are the requirements: a good dose of humility to get egos out of the way, the courage and persistence to differ, decide, and act, and an emphasis on facilitating people.

> *"Good leaders do whatever it takes to make their organization successful, even if that means stepping back or leaving the organization."*

20 QUESTIONS

To assess the leadership currently in place or improve it, you can use the following list of questions. Every "no" points at a gap that may need to be closed for successful strategy execution. Ask yourself: as leaders in our organization, do we sufficiently…

1. …envision an inspiring future for the organization?
2. …plan ahead and define a suitable path forward?
3. …instigate new initiatives, innovation, and change?
4. …set an example by being a role model for behavior?
5. …make decisions and choices, especially hard ones?
6. …listen to people and hear what they say?
7. …encourage, persuade, and influence people?
8. …hire and (re)place people for the roles that are needed?
9. …inform people clearly, also about good and bad news?
10. …shape the rules and conditions by which work is done?
11. …acquire resources and negotiate good deals?
12. …allocate time and resources for the work to be done?
13. …get out of people's way so that they can do their work?
14. …promote, represent, and defend the organization?
15. …keep the organization to its values and goals?
16. …check progress and make sure there is follow-up?
17. …reward and penalize behavior?
18. …put things in perspective and keep them in proportion?
19. …enjoy, laugh, and approach everything with a bit of humor?
20. …serve as back-up and last resort for everything else?

TO-DOS

To improve the leadership in your organization and define projects and tasks for your Strategy Backlog, you can take the following steps.

Reflect	Reflect on leaders' abilities (including your own) and assess realistically what they can do and what they cannot.
Develop	Train, coach, and mentor leaders to develop the mindset, knowledge, and skills they lack.
Share	Reallocate tasks that leaders are not good at or have no time for to others in the organization.
Replace	If developing or sharing does not work, replace leaders by ones who can do the job. This concerns you too.

2. CONTROLS

> "Setting goals is the first step in turning the invisible into the visible." – *Tony Robbins*

> "Every line is the perfect length if you don't measure it." – *Marty Rubin*

> "Trust is good, but control is better." – *Vladimir Lenin*

To make sure that a strategy is executed, you need mechanisms to allocate resources and to monitor and control whether the organization is doing what it's supposed to do. I am certainly not suggesting total control-seeking performance management here. Generally, empowering people, trusting them and keeping out of their way are far superior mechanisms for getting things done than tight monitoring and control. In that sense, you must see Lenin's quote above with a good dose of skepticism. However, there is no value in being naïve or in a "laissez-faire" style of managing by which you just let things go and hope for the best.

"You need a 'minimum viable' set of controls."

Control does not have to be top-down. Often it is, but there are other control mechanisms too. Peer-to-peer control, for example, is a horizontal control mechanism where equals form each other's checks and balances to make sure the work is done. And control can even be bottom-up in the form of voting or other democratic mechanisms. This happens, for example, when managers are evaluated by their employees or when budgets are decided through voting.

A big risk of control is overdoing it. Especially when uncertainty is increasing, our primary response is usually to try to get more control. Everywhere around us we see this happening: increased security, tighter quality management, obsessive information gathering, and so forth. While such measures may make us feel more in control, it's questionable whether they actually make a difference. Therefore, the control function of organization also means accepting that not everything can or should be controlled. At the end of the day, you don't want to control your organization. You want to be in control without controlling it. This means that you need a *minimum viable* set of controls: a set of control mechanisms that is comprehensive enough to be effective, but not more than that.

Another risk is that you control the wrong things. This happens, for example, when you set targets and define KPIs that are not really relevant for realizing or improving your strategy or when you pick them because they are easily measurable. The bottom line is that your strategy is about building a unique way of achieving sustainable value creation, and that your controls should focus on measuring whether you are achieving this aim. Thus, you should make sure that your KPIs are derived from your strategy, and the customer journey that comes with it, and not from the organization chart, job profiles, or from what others are using.

20 QUESTIONS

To assess the current control mechanisms in place and improve them, you can use the following list of questions. Ask yourself: do we sufficiently...

1. ...understand the ten elements of our strategy and how they relate?
2. ...understand the ten organizational elements and how they relate?
3. ...derive our targets, objectives, and KPIs from our strategy?
4. ...allocate budgets in line with the organization's strategy?
5. ...ask what information people need, to be in control of their work?
6. ...define measures and KPIs that are relevant for people?
7. ...choose measures and KPIs that people can influence?
8. ...quantify measures where possible to make them concrete?
9. ...simplify and reduce to what we really need to measure?
10. ...define which information should be gathered and how?
11. ...check whether what we measure covers what we want?
12. ...gather the required information on a regular basis?
13. ...assign who are responsible and accountable for which tasks?
14. ...promote peer-to-peer accountability between people?
15. ...agree on consequences and actions if targets are not met?
16. ...have the means and power to enforce consequences?
17. ...actually follow-up and take action if targets are not met?
18. ...stay abreast of changes and update KPIs?
19. ...resist the inclination to measure more or micromanage?
20. ...put trust first and control second?

TO-DOS

To improve the controls in your organization and define projects and tasks for your Strategy Backlog, you can take the following steps.

Understand	Understand how the elements of your strategy and your organization affect each other in a cause-effect manner.
Choose	Determine what you measure and how. Focus on "hotspots": few, simple factors that say a lot about the performance.
Design	Define how to gather, process, report and follow-up information and who is responsible for what.
Operate	Measure and act upon the information that is measured.
Update	Refresh and improve your control mechanisms to keep them up-to-date with your strategy and organization.

3. MOTIVATION

"What you lack in talent can be made up with desire, hustle and giving 110% all the time." – *Don Zimmer*

"Happiness is the secret ingredient for successful businesses. If you have a happy company it will be invincible."
– *Richard Branson*

"When one must, one can. " – *Charlotte Whitton*

Motivation is a strong element of organizing because it can compensate for a lot of things. Individually, it can compensate for lack of skills or talent; organizationally, it can compensate for deficiencies such as a lack of structure, inefficient processes, or outdated information technology. An organization with strongly-motivated people can get away with weaknesses in any of the other nine organizational elements.

Motivation is not just about the intrinsic motivation to do a job, important though that is. Not everybody likes their job and certainly not all the time, and this means that you have to rely on other mechanisms to motivate people. These mechanisms include giving money or other rewards, penalizing people with negative consequences, using your power, or simply giving attention to people and the work they do. Which of these mechanisms works best depends on the precise context of your organization. However, all of them can be used to motivate people.

As science has found out, motivation consists of a rational, conscious part and an emotional, subconscious part. For the rational part, people need to be convinced of three things to be motivated to do something.

1. They need to like the outcome of what they do. Whether it's the money, the work itself, or the impact they make, if they think the outcome is no good, there is no reason for them to be motivated.
2. They need to believe that what they are expected to do actually leads to that outcome. If not, they're probably more motivated to do other things that will lead to that outcome.
3. They need to believe they are capable of doing what is expected. If they don't believe this, they will be frustrated rather than motivated.

Thus, to motivate people along this rational path, you need to make sure that all three conditions are met.

The emotional, subconscious part of motivation works very differently. As research on persuasion shows, people respond very much to psychological and social factors. People are more likely to do something if they see others do it, feel pressure from others, or get confirmation from others that they are doing the right thing. Convenience is another factor; people will be more inclined to do something if it's easy. This is only the tip of the iceberg. For more factors, refer to the list of 20 questions below. In any event, it's crucial to pay ample attention to this emotional, subconscious side of motivation.

Not everyone in the organization will be highly motivated, no matter what you try. Whatever you do, you will find that there are three groups: progressives, pragmatists, and conservatists.

- **Progressives** are a relatively small group of people who are highly motivated and eager to execute the new strategy.

- **Pragmatists** are a large group of people, usually the majority, that will just go with the flow and do what is expected of them.
- **Conservatives** are a small group of people that will actively or passively resist the new strategy.

The progressives and the conservatives typically have your immediate attention. However, in the long run, you should not forget the large group of pragmatists, since they are responsible for the lion's share of the work. While they are less visible, don't forget to pay them sufficient attention too.

20 QUESTIONS

To assess the way people are currently motivated and improve on this, you can use the following list of questions. Ask yourself: do we sufficiently…

1. …assume people are generally motivated to do what is needed?
2. …clarify purpose and explain to people why something is needed?
3. …show the urgency and consequences of doing what is needed?
4. …act in line with what we say and set an example?
5. …treat people kindly so that they want to do stuff for us?
6. …make sure that the organization is fun to work for?
7. …give people attention by telling them regularly they are doing well?
8. …hear what people really say about their concerns and wants?
9. …take away simple barriers or problems that irritate people?
10. …give people more influence on their own working situation?
11. …make sure that people can learn and develop through their work?
12. …give people something before we expect them to do something?

13. ...emphasize to people the personal benefits of doing what is asked?
14. ...appeal to herd-behavior by referring to others as examples?
15. ...shape conditions so that people naturally do what is needed?
16. ...persist and repeat continuously what needs to be done and why?
17. ...use our power to enforce the behavior that is needed?
18. ...penalize people for their behavior if they consistently misperform?
19. ...offer team-oriented and performance-based financial incentives?
20. ...share profits and make transparent how people have contributed?

TO-DOS

To improve people's motivation in your organization and define projects and tasks for your Strategy Backlog, you can take the following steps.

Listen	Listen and know what really motivates people and what is demotivating them now.
Direct	Use rational forms of influence including explanation, incentives, and persuasion to direct people's behavior.
Excite	Tempt people emotionally or subconsciously by triggering their psychological and social needs.
Shape	Create the conditions that make doing what is required easy and doing other things hard or impossible.
Enforce	If none of the previous steps work to motivate people, then enforce decisions so that they have to do what is needed.

4. COMMITMENT

> "If men were actuated by self-interest, which they
> are not–except in the case of a few saints–the whole
> human race would cooperate."
> — *Bertrand Russell*

> "Empathy is about finding echoes of another person in yourself."
> — *Mohsin Hamid*

> "If you're talking about how you promoted synergy
> in an organization, that could mean you just got everybody
> together for donuts twice a week."
> — *Erin McKean*

Having people motivated to execute the strategy, and to do their
work more generally, is an important step for driving your strategy.
However, you also want people to look beyond their silos and
be committed to the organization more broadly. Without such
commitment, people will just care about their job, and this creates
a lot of inefficiencies and tensions in the organizations. Smooth
strategy execution also requires commitment.

Commitment doesn't mean sect-like unanimous excitement
about the organization's purpose. While sometimes sold as the
ideal, such commitment is seldom realistic or real. And, personally,
I find such a level of commitment quite spooky. What I do mean
is that there is a basic level of:

- **like-mindedness,** so that people support a common
  purpose.
- **trust,** so that people can rely on each other.
- **empathy**, so that people can put themselves in the shoes
  of others.
- **kindness**, so that people respect and treat each other
  well.
- **pride**, so that people defend the organization to the
  outside world.

Paradoxically, creating commitment asks for setting clear boundaries, both internally and externally. For external boundaries, this is intuitive. By making a clear division between "us" and "them," you foster a strong group identity focused on distinguishing the organization or beating the outside world. Internally, however, setting clear boundaries seems, at first sight, to lead exactly to the kind of silo-behavior that we want to avoid: every department for themselves. However, such boundaries are necessary since they create clarity about who is responsible for what. Imagine an organization where no such boundaries are defined. Everyone would mingle in each other's work, possibly ending up in chaos. That is not commitment but a mess. I will return to this topic in the "structure" section later in this chapter.

> *"Paradoxically, creating commitment asks for setting clear boundaries, both internally and externally."*

20 QUESTIONS

To assess the current level of commitment and improve it, you can use the following list of questions. Ask yourself: do we sufficiently…

1. …create a safe environment allowing failure and disagreement?
2. …take people seriously, treat them as adults and trust them?
3. …engage with them: show interest, do stuff for them, and be proud?
4. …talk about what makes people proud of their organization?
5. …discuss the organization's identity and create a "who we are" story?
6. …create common "enemies" which people can refer to as "not us"?
7. …build a unique organizational habit that reinforces the identity?

8. ...let people visit or work at other units to foster understanding?

9. ...do as we say so that people can trust us and depend on us?

10. ...do things together and have fun, also outside the office or factory?

11. ...collaborate for a common cause, such as a charity or fund-raising?

12. ...organize open days for family so that people can show their work?

13. ...organize internal networking events and be active connectors?

14. ...let people shine and present their successes to the organization?

15. ...celebrate achievements regularly and point out who contributed?

16. ...encourage people to voluntarily and publicly commit to actions?

17. ...define roles and responsibilities for teams rather than individuals?

18. ...give incentives based on team rather than individual performance?

19. ...involve people in decisions and ask for ideas and objections?

20. ...make people consult all key stakeholders before making decisions?

TO-DOS

To improve the commitment of people in your organization and define projects and tasks for this element, you can take the following steps.

Identify	Discuss and define what is unique about the organization that makes people proud to be different from others.
Open up	Foster empathy by dialogue, involvement, and making people experience each other's jobs in the organization.
Organize	Define team-based roles and responsibilities and make sure people focus on those rather than on those of others.
Reinforce	Build unique habits and make people exhibit their pride within the organization and to their social network.

5. EXPERTISE

> "Train people well enough so they can leave, treat them well enough so they don't want to." – *Richard Branson*

> "Executives owe it to the organization and to their fellow workers not to tolerate non-performing individuals in important jobs." – *Peter Drucker*

> "Slow down and remember this: Most things make no difference. Being busy is a form of laziness–lazy thinking and indiscriminate action."– *Tim Ferriss*

To execute your strategy, it's crucial that you have the right people with the right expertise. Strategy execution is also very much about managing your people. It involves both bringing in the right people as well as using their full potential to the organization's advantage. When you do this, it's important that you see people not just as human "resources" with valuable expertise, but as complete human beings. This means two things:

1. People's "organizational me" and "private me" are one and the same person. This is easily overlooked, thereby ignoring important skills that someone might have. Think about a production worker who is at the same time chairman of a local soccer club. Just using his production skills would be a serious missed opportunity.

2. You should look at the complete package people bring. This includes their experience, knowledge, and skills. But it also includes their mindset, character, ideas, passions, and concerns. This is what makes them human and also affects what they can contribute to the organization and how they should be managed.

> *"Good people management requires being soft on people, but at the same time hard on performance."*

Good people management includes what we may see as "soft" and "hard" tasks. On the soft side, it means understanding people's emotions and needs, listening to them, and taking care of their well-being. On the hard side, it also means evaluating, moving, demoting, or firing them if they consistently underperform in their job. Thus, it requires being soft on people, but at the same time hard on performance.

These two sides are not as opposite as they may seem, especially if we look at the organization as a whole. Being "hard on performance" means that people are put in a place where they can contribute most, or they are asked to leave. It also means avoiding the "Peter Principle" so that people are not promoted beyond their competence. Even though an individual may not like to be treated this "hard," it's fair to others in the organization and good for the organization's long-term health. And there is a big chance that the person is secretly relieved that they don't have to disappoint themselves and others anymore.

20 QUESTIONS

To assess the way of managing people and expertise and improve it, you can use the following list of questions. Ask yourself: do we sufficiently…

1. …search for and be open to new talented individuals?
2. …advertise the organization so that good people want to work there?
3. …select people based on their expertise, ideas, values, and mindset?

4. ...create contracts that are mutually motivating?
5. ...on-board people so that they become part of the organization?
6. ...train people for their jobs and for their future?
7. ...mentor and coach people in their job and development?
8. ...put people in the right role and at the right place?
9. ...tap on people's full repertoire of knowledge and skills?
10. ...get out of people's way so that they can do their job?
11. ...give people the time and resources needed to do their work?
12. ...evaluate whether people function as well as they can and need to?
13. ...monitor people's satisfaction, ambitions, concerns, and well-being?
14. ...build up personal records and ensure all paperwork is correct?
15. ...give talented and ambitious people the room to develop?
16. ...spot people with leadership talent and help them to lead?
17. ...move people in the organization to roles where they fit?
18. ...stimulate people to learn and take new roles and responsibilities?
19. ...enable and motivate people to share their expertise with others?
20. ...demote, don't promote, or lay off people if they don't perform?

TO-DOS

To improve the way you deal with people in your organization and to define projects and tasks for your backlog, you can take the following steps.

Place	Put the right people in the right place. This means hiring, moving, and firing people in the interest of the organization.
Facilitate	Create conditions so that people can use their full potential. Empower and equip them and get out of their way.
Develop	Challenge, train, and coach people to help them develop themselves for future roles in or outside the organization.
Evaluate	Assess people's well-being, fit and contribution to the organization and take the necessary actions.

6. INFORMATION TECHNOLOGY

"Every company is a technology company." – *Peter Sondergaard*

"Information technology and business are becoming inextricably interwoven. I don't think anybody can talk meaningfully about one without the talking about the other." – *Bill Gates*

"The number one benefit of information technology is that it empowers people to do what they want to do. It lets people be creative. It lets people be productive. It lets people learn things they didn't think they could learn before, and so in a sense it is all about potential." – *Steve Ballmer*

Next to people and their expertise, information technology is the second major element determining what an organization can and can't do. It includes hardware such as computers and mobile phones, classic information systems such as financial or planning software, traditional paper-based systems and forms, as well as more recent developments in digitalization, online business, Internet of things, big data, artificial intelligence, computer-generated imagery, and blockchain technology.

Information technology can be a source of competitive advantage for an organization and at the core of its strategy. Along these lines, you might have included some forms of information technology already when thinking about the "resources and competences" element of strategy during strategy generation. However, information technology is also an essential part of an organization itself, and increasingly so. Without it, hardly any organization today can function properly. And with it, you can change the way organizations work, make them more efficient and reliable, and do things that were never possible before. Information technology has made many organizations and industries that we would never have thought of technology-focused, relying on information technology to their core.

20 QUESTIONS

To assess the way you use information technology now or improve on this, you can use the following list of questions. Ask yourself: do we sufficiently…

1. …digitalize text, images, audio, and video for internal or external use?
2. …automate and robotize processes for efficiency and reliability?
3. …offer products and services online and mobile?
4. …virtualize and simulate experiences for learning and excitement?
5. …make things more entertaining or rewarding through gamification?
6. …monitor and control processes, people, machines, and so forth?
7. …protect and secure the organization against data threats?
8. …follow developments inside or outside the organization?
9. …gather, use, or sell large amounts of detailed data–big data?
10. …use artificial intelligence for analysis, learning, and problem solving?

11. ...connect employees, customers, and suppliers locally and globally?
12. ...connect machines or equipment so that these can communicate?
13. ...enable people to work remotely for the organization and clients?
14. ...empower people by providing them the information they need?
15. ...circumvent intermediaries (e.g., via blockchain or online sales)?
16. ...shift activities to customers so that they can do these themselves?
17. ...interact, listen, and talk to customers through social media?
18. ...improve and customize our offerings to individual customers?
19. ...present and market our organization in more targeted ways?
20. ...reach new types of customers that could not be reached before?

TO-DOS

To improve the use of information technology in your organization and define projects and tasks for this element, you can take the following steps.

Tune in	Stay abreast of technological developments and make sure that you know what is available, possible, and coming.
Embrace	Adopt new technology that will come anyway as soon as possible and tcertainly not later than major competitors.
Discard	Do away with old technology as soon as you can but also be a bit skeptical about any new technology trend.
Integrate	Think of the bigger picture and always consider how new technology fits into the rest of the organization.

7. STRUCTURE

"Clutter is the physical manifestation of unmade
decisions fueled by procrastination."
– *Christina Scalise*

"The trouble with organizing a thing is that pretty soon folks
get to paying more attention to the organization than to what
they're organized for." – *Laura Ingalls Wilder*

"Research shows that the climate of an organization influences
an individual's contribution far more than the individual
himself." – *W. Edwards Deming*

Changing an organization's structure is an invasive measure. When done properly, it can substantially aid the execution of a strategy. However, it can also seriously disturb the organization–especially when changes are made frequently and with every new leader who comes in. As a rule of thumb, you might want to leave the organizational structure alone as long as it does not seriously impede the execution of the strategy.

Obviously, changing structure does not just mean drawing a new organization chart. It means changing or redefining how the work that needs to be done is divided. It has four key dimensions that you can influence, including location, roles and responsibilities, resource allocation, and coordination mechanism.

1. **Location:** defining where work should be done. This is about physical location–the place within the building, town, country, or the world–but also about what to put together in a department or business unit, what to centralize and decentralize, and what to outsource to others.
2. **Roles and responsibilities:** defining who is doing what. This means defining who is responsible for doing something, who is accountable for ensuring it gets done, who should be involved or consulted in decisions about it, and who should verify and decide whether the work is done.
3. **Resource allocation:** allocating and organizing resources. This includes defining where resources should be located

and whether they are dedicated to one specific task or unit or shared with others. It also includes defining who owns the resources–whether a resource is on the balance sheet of a business unit or the organization.

4. **Coordination mechanism:** making things work effectively as a whole. There are five basic mechanisms here that can be used individually or combined.

   a. **Hierarchy:** a top-down blueprint describing how everyone has a boss to listen and report to and who should oversee what is going on.

   b. **Democracy:** bottom-up coordination by people choosing and evaluating their leaders and making decisions based on voting.

   c. **Network:** peer-to-peer coordination by equals who consult and inform each other and who evaluate each other's performance.

   d. **Sociocracy:** coordination by "consent," a process in which people can propose things which are accepted if there are no major objections.

   e. **Market:** coordination through internal competitive markets where demand and supply of tasks, people, and resources meet.

With these four key dimensions, you can (re)design the organizational structure in a way that best fits your strategy. In doing so, you can look at existing standardized forms of organizing such as the traditional functional, divisional, and matrix structures and at more modern forms such as "flatarchies," "holacracies," and "agile." These forms offer ideas for how you could structure your organization along these four dimensions. However, if you adopt one of these forms, it's important to adapt it to the specific situation and needs of your organization.

If you redesign your organization's structure, you should realize that this does not just change the way the organization works, but also people's jobs and their position in the organization. In particular, it affects the power relationships in the organization. People who get more responsibility will gain power and people with fewer responsibilities will lose power. When not accepted, such changes may seriously frustrate implementation of a new organizational structure that otherwise looks great on paper, so be aware.

20 QUESTIONS

To assess the way your organization is currently structured or to change that, you can use the following list of questions. Ask yourself: do we sufficiently…

1. …define what needs to be done and how precisely to specify this?
2. …define and assign roles, responsibilities, and accountability?
3. …put people in roles and give them responsibilities that suit them?
4. …make sure people don't meddle too much with the tasks of others?
5. …decide how to combine or split up work, resources, and people?
6. …split up large units and teams into smaller ones?
7. …locate things at the right place in the building, country, or world?
8. …put activities inside or outside the organization?
9. …think about ownership and allocation of resources?
10. …define who should listen and report to whom?
11. …decentralize what you can and centralize what you must?
12. …give people autonomy and make them accountable for their actions?
13. …minimize the number of layers and roles to what we really need?
14. …use peer-to-peer or inverted accountability ("boss" to employees)?
15. …create internal markets of supply and demand of work to be done?
16. …stimulate serendipity via coincidental encounters between people?
17. …organize in a modular way by defining interfaces between units?

18. ...balance stability and flexibility for an ambidextrous organization?
19. ...balance organizational and individual interests in the structure?
20. ...take into account the changes in power relationship that occur?

TO-DOS

To improve the structure of your organization and define projects and tasks for adjusting the organization's structure you can take the following steps.

Specify	Know what to organize for: define the work that needs to be done to realize the strategy and get what you want.
Locate	Define where work needs to be done in terms of location, organizational unit, organizational level, and inside or outside.
Assign	Assign roles and define who is responsible and accountable for what, who should be involved, and who should verify.
Enable	Allocate resources so that people can do their work. Locate the resources at the right place and allocate ownership.
Coordinate	Choose suitable coordination mechanisms: hierarchy, democracy, network, sociocracy or market mechanisms.

8. COMMUNICATION

"A good communicator does not think only of himself: he also thinks about what the receiver has in his head."
– *Tor Nørretranders*

"The most important thing in communication is hearing what isn't said." – *Peter Drucker*

"I like to listen. I have learned a great deal from listening carefully. Most people never listen." – *Ernest Hemingway*

Communication refers to all communications that take place in an organization and between the organization and others. This includes formal communication such as meetings, reports, newsletters, website, corporate social media, and so forth, as well as informal communication such as coffee talk, emails, phone calls, and personal tweets. Furthermore, it concerns horizontal communication between colleagues, units and departments; vertical communication between employees and leaders; and external communication with suppliers, customers, and other stakeholders.

It's frequently argued that strategy execution is all about communication. That's as true as it is exaggerated. It's exaggerated because, as you see in this book, strategy execution concerns more than just communication. It's also true, however, because lack of clear communication is one of the key inhibitors to successful strategy execution, or to change more generally.

Good communication has two parts: inquiry and advocacy. Inquiry means listening, or better, *hearing* what people are saying. It asks for truly getting to know people's needs, intentions, and concerns. This involves asking questions to get the actual message behind what they are saying, being receptive to what they are not saying, reading their facial expressions and attitude, and trying to understand their emotions. Advocacy, on the other hand, refers to what you want to say and how you are saying it. The term advocacy emphasizes that you are communicating with a purpose and not just for the sake of communicating. There is something you want to achieve, a behavior, answer, or any other kind of response from the people with whom you are communicating.

Just like motivation, communication has a rational side and an emotional side. The rational side is the side where we can explain things to people and try convincing them with reasons and evidence for what we say. In organizations, we often assume that people are rational and therefore lean towards this side of communication. There is also an emotional side, however, that is at least as important. In situations where the message is unpleasant and involves bad news, a big change or uncertainty, communication easily becomes emotional. In such situations, it's important to give emotions a place and not respond with more reasons and evidence. Saying nothing for a while is usually the best advice in this case.

> *"The trick is to move the focus away from the person to the situation and from blaming each other to finding solutions."*

Because communication has this emotional side and because strategy execution often comes with bad news, change, and uncertainty, communication easily gets personal. And before you know it, you end up in fruitless "you versus me" and "yes, but" discussions. In such cases, it's important that you realize you're in a shared situation in which all parties have an interest in finding a solution. The trick is to move the focus away from the person to the situation and from blaming each other to finding solutions. This is easier said than done, but much more productive (see also pages 38-40).

20 QUESTIONS

To assess the way communication currently takes place or to change that, you can use the following list of questions. Ask yourself: do we sufficiently…

1. …listen to and hear what employees truly are saying and not saying?
2. …do the same for customers, suppliers, and other stakeholders?
3. …know why we communicate—what kind of response we want?
4. …express this clearly so that people also know what is expected?
5. …make sure that messages are consistent with each other?
6. …send messages and briefings on a need-to-know basis?
7. …brief when there is a new initiative, an issue, or a relevant update?

8. ...invite all people who are needed in a meeting and only them?
9. ...keep meetings focused in terms of time, agenda, and action points?
10. ...reserve time in meetings for someone to pitch a success?
11. ...avoid cc-ing or informing people when information is not relevant?
12. ...keep doors open and lower the threshold for people to enter?
13. ...give bad news directly and give people the time to process it?
14. ...turn "you versus me" fights into dialogues focusing on the situation?
15. ...tell the world about the organization and what it can do?
16. ...focus external communication on the unique value we add?
17. ...make friends with the media and feed them useful news?
18. ...help employees and customers to become our ambassadors?
19. ...start communicating when this is needed?
20. ...stop communicating when this is needed?

TO-DOS

To improve the internal and external communication in your organization and define projects and tasks, you can take the following steps.

Listen	Understand what people truly are saying and not saying and what are their needs, concerns and intentions.
Know	Know why you communicate, what you want to achieve with it, from whom you want something, and when.
Compose	Design your message, how you will deliver it, when, to whom, in which format and through which channel.
Deliver	Actually deliver your message and monitor whether it lands and whether you get the response you are looking for.
Wait	Be silent, go away, or wait in another way to give people the chance to process and come up with a response.

9. PROCESSES

"If you can't describe what you are doing as a process, you don't know what you're doing." – *W. Edwards Deming*

"The first rule of any technology used in a business is that automation applied to an efficient operation will magnify the efficiency. The second is that automation applied to an inefficient operation will magnify the inefficiency." – *Bill Gates*

"Quality is not an act; it is a habit." – *Aristotle*

The ninth element of an organization is its processes. This concerns the organization's formal processes and procedures and also the more informal habits and routines of people in the organization. It includes operational processes such as purchasing, production, and sales, and also financial processes, human resource processes, innovation processes, and decision-making processes–and thus also the strategy process. Furthermore, it includes the learning and adaptation processes by which other processes and the organization as a whole are improved and changed.

A process implies that there is a certain order and routine in the way the work is done. Along those lines, processes have three key functions.

a) They create predictability and reliability so that everyone knows how to work and what to expect, so similar outputs are created in similar ways.

b) They are a way to capture and replicate the best and optimized ways of working. They standardize the organization's best practices and thereby ensure quality and efficiency.

c) Once optimized, the repetitive nature of processes facilitates automation and robotization and so enables further improvements in quality and efficiency.

While processes help to create predictability, optimization, and automation, there is also a limit to the variety they can handle. It's not desirable or feasible to capture all activities in the organization completely in predefined processes. The following six rules of thumb are useful to take into account.

1. Develop processes for how the majority–say 80%–of the work should be done. Don't try to capture every exception and variation.
2. Allow room for flexibility and interpretation in your processes, so that people can adjust them based on their insights and experience.
3. If such flexibility is undesirable, automate the process because machines are much better in exact repetitive work.
4. Make processes modular. Define interfaces, inputs, and outputs so that you can connect and change a process without disturbing others.
5. Start with the processes that involve the customer and work backward. Your main output is what you create for customers, and the rest is derived from that.
6. Install learning processes for all processes so that they are improved and updated regularly.

20 QUESTIONS

To assess the current processes in place or to improve them, you can use the following list of questions. Ask yourself: do we sufficiently...

1. ...define processes for work that has some degree of repetitiveness?
2. ...improve processes and not just push more work through them?
3. ...allow freedom in processes so that people can optimize them?
4. ...treat exceptions as exceptions and not adjust processes for them?
5. ...create flexible processes that allow customization and small series?
6. ...simplify processes and find out which ones we can discard?
7. ...automate processes after we have optimized them?
8. ...automate processes that require or allow exact standardization?
9. ...keep other processes humane so that people can perform them?
10. ...reduce and simplify interdependencies between processes?
11. ...define the outputs that processes should produce for others?
12. ...start with outputs for customers and work backward from there?
13. ...start and finish processes as late as possible and early as needed?
14. ...minimize overall throughput time, not time per process?
15. ...build habits so that processes are routinely executed correctly?
16. ...make clear who is responsible and accountable for a process?
17. ...install a learning and improvement process for every process?
18. ...regularly check whether processes are still needed and up to date?
19. ...create a process for introducing new products or services?
20. ...create and optimize a strategy process for our organization?

TO-DOS

To improve the processes in your organization and define projects and tasks for your Strategy Backlog, you can take the following steps.

Understand	Understand what processes should produce, how they relate, and what is standard and what is an exception.
Design	Reduce, optimize, create, simplify, automate, and align processes so that they produce what they should.
Enforce	Make sure that work is done as specified in the processes and build habits so that they are executed routinely.
Update	Review, improve and update processes regularly and install a process to do also this on a routine basis.

10. POLICIES

> "From now on it is only through a conscious choice and through a deliberate policy that humanity can survive."
> – *Pope John Paul II*

> "If you have poor management that's not doing the right job, you end up with unions filling the void and… page after page of work rules and thicker and thicker contracts." – *Eli Broad*

> "Any system was a straitjacket if you insisted on adhering to it so totally and humorlessly." – *Erica Jong*

The last element of organizing is policies. These are the written and unwritten rules, guidelines, agreements, and contracts that define how the organization should function. Policies are important because they express the organization's rules of engagement for all internal and external stakeholders. They are an important mechanism to explicitly define and glue together the other nine elements in an organized manner. We can identify two broad types: rules and contracts.

Rules refer to all norms, standards, guidelines, and regulations setting out how things are organized and defining what can and should or should not be done. These include the following.

- Articles of association, defining responsibilities of directors, the kind of business undertaken, and how shareholders exert control.
- Dividend policies, expressing when and how dividends are paid.
- Decision-making principles, saying who can make which decisions and according to what rules (e.g., majority vote, veto, or by consent).
- Codes of conduct, expressing what is seen as right, ethical behavior.
- Quality systems, defining quality standards and rules to make sure that the right level of quality is realized.
- Security policies, defining how to realize virtual and physical security.
- Job profiles, expressing which tasks and compensation belong to which job or role in the organization.
- Human resource policies, saying how and on what criteria recruitment, selection, promotion, etc., take place.

Contracts refer to the formal and informal agreements between two or more people or organizations reflecting their mutual rights and responsibilities. These include the following.

- Employment contracts with your permanent, temporary, or flexible employees.
- Sales contracts between you and your customers, or between a supplier and you.
- Alliance contracts between you and key partners expressing mutual responsibilities in a formal collaboration.
- Memoranda of understanding or letters of intent expressing a willingness to cooperate–usually preceding a more formal contract.

- Non-disclosure agreements stating that you will keep particular information private for yourself.

There's a reason why policies are the last of the ten organizational elements that are discussed. Before defining them, it's usually a good idea first to have the other elements clear. This will make sure you know what you want to support or enforce through the policies and that you don't see them as solutions in and of themselves. Policies are powerful organizational mechanisms–for good or bad. A lack of appropriate policies might result in serious chaos or in people hiding behind overly-rigid rules (think "I'm not allowed to do that"). On the other hand, strong policies can make the organization efficient and resilient–think about the Army, for example, where clearly-defined policies are a powerful mechanism to make sure everyone acts as they are supposed to.

20 QUESTIONS

To assess the current policies in the organization and improve them, you can use the following list of questions. Ask yourself: do we sufficiently…

1. …work on the other elements first before we touch our policies?
2. …see policies as complementary to trust, not as replacements?
3. …avoid capturing every little detail in our rules and contracts?
4. …try to fix our existing policies first before we replace them?
5. …revisit our policies if we are losing business because of them?
6. …establish rules and contracts when things are still going well?
7. …use the drafting of policies as a way to sharpen our minds?
8. …focus on content first, and legal aspects later?
9. …develop policies with the stakeholders who are concerned?

10. ...make sure our policies keep serving their intended purpose?
11. ...make sure policies don't hinder people in thinking for themselves?
12. ...make exceptions to the written policies when this makes sense?
13. ...check whether our policies adhere to legal and ethical standards?
14. ...get rid of unnecessary and harmful policies promptly?
15. ...keep policies simple, short, and modular to stay flexible?
16. ...carefully think through the transition process to a new policy?
17. ...communicate policies to everyone who is affected by them?
18. ...check whether people know and understand the policies?
19. ...enforce policies so that they are followed and take action if not?
20. ...evaluate and update policies regularly so that they stay current?

TO-DOS

To improve the policies of your organization and define projects and tasks for your Strategy Backlog, you can take the following steps.

Identify	Understand the need for policies, what they should lead to, and how they support the other elements of organizing.
Write	Write policies down together with stakeholders before they are needed. This prepares you and sharpens your mind.
Enforce	Make sure that policies are followed and take appropriate action if this is not the case.
Update	Evaluate policies regularly and revise, discard, or add policies when circumstances or viewpoints have changed.

CONNECTING BRIDGING AND ORGANIZING

With the quick scan of pages 231-232 and the above information about the ten elements of organizing, you have all that is needed to identify deficiencies in your organization and to define projects and tasks for them that you can add to your Strategy Backlog. However, the chapter so far gives you little support in establishing which organizational deficiencies you need to solve to execute your strategy. And that is, of course, the point of this entire chapter.

There is no one-to-one relationship between elements of your strategy and elements of your organization. Basically, any gap in one of the ten elements of your strategy might necessitate changes in any element of your organization. A gap in your resources and competences, for example, could be a result of inappropriate leadership, incomplete processes, lack of motivation, or any of the other elements of organizing.

This means that to identify relevant organizational deficiencies, you may need to check each element of your strategy to see whether changes to any of the ten elements of organizing are needed. The most straightforward way to do this is by using the Organizational Deficiency Identification Matrix below. When you use this matrix, you should constantly ask yourself the question below and tick a box for each "yes":

"To realize our strategy with respect to our *{element of strategy}*, should we change something in our *{element of organization}*?"

Organizational Deficiency Identification Matrix

Elements of Organization / Elements of Strategy	Leadership	Controls	Motivation	Commitment	Expertise	Information tech.	Structure	Communication	Processes	Policies
Resources & Competences										
Partners										
Customers & Needs										
Competitors										
Value Proposition										
Revenue Model										
Risks & Costs										
Values & Goals										
Organizational Climate										
Trends & Uncertainties										

For each box in this matrix that you have ticked, you can use the information in this chapter to come up with projects and tasks to solve the organizational deficiencies that you have identified. As you will experience, one and the same organizational project or task defined at the horizontal axis of the matrix will often contribute to resolving more than one strategic issue at the vertical axis.

Like with the bridging step, your aim is not to come up with the longest possible list of organizational deficiencies. At some point, you will recognize that you have identified the most important ones; that is the time to stop and move on to the next step. Before you do so, you may want to do the same final thing as when closing the bridging step: delete projects and tasks that you already know you are not going to do anyway.

THE FOUR EXAMPLES

ORGANIZING AT MACMAN

In Macman's new strategy, offering services plays a key role. Realizing this strategy asks for substantial organizational changes.

As part of their analysis along the elements of organizing, Macman went through the 20 questions for all elements. Here I focus on their answers for the expertise element. For the answers in bold, they added projects and tasks to their Strategy Backlog.

Question: do we sufficiently...	Macman's answer
...search for and be open to new talented individuals?	Not really, but no action required in terms of setting up a process.
...advertise the organization, so that good people want to work there?	Not at all. → **Action required to attract service-oriented staff.**
...select people based on their expertise, ideas, values, and mindset?	No, only on technical skills. → **add service-orientation in vacancies.**
...create contracts that are mutually motivating?	Yes.
...on-board people so that they become part of the organization?	Yes.
...train people for their jobs and their future?	Yes, but only technical. → **Explore service-orientation training.**
...mentor and coach people in their job and development?	A bit. No action required now.
...put people in the right role and at the right place?	Yes.
...tap on people's full repertoire of knowledge and skills?	Not enough for their soft skills. → **Find a way to assess these.**
...get out of people's way so that they can do their job?	Yes.

…give people the time and resources needed to do their work?	Yes.
…evaluate whether people function as well as they can and need to?	Yes.
…monitor people's satisfaction, ambitions, concerns, and well-being?	Yes, although we don't use the word happiness.
…build up personal records and ensure all paperwork is correct?	Not really. → **Build records, especially for low performers.**
…give talented and ambitious people the room to develop?	Yes, although we don't promote it actively. No action required.
…spot people with leadership talent and help them to lead?	No. → **Identify who can lead in shifting to a service orientation.**
…move people in the organization to roles where they fit?	Mostly yes.
…stimulate people to learn and take new roles and responsibilities?	No, but this is more for the long term. Something to remember.
…enable and motivate people to share their expertise with others?	Yes, regular meetings (although not much is said there).
…demote, don't promote, or lay off people if they don't perform?	No, we are too soft. → **Some should actually be demoted. Take action.**

ORGANIZING AT HOSPICARE

Also at Hospicare, executing the strategy required substantial organizational changes. Applying the to-dos for the ten elements revealed that one of Ingrid's core challenges was dealing with the leadership of the organization. Here is an illustration of the four steps for this element.

1. *Reflect: reflect on leaders' abilities (including your own) and assess realistically what they can do and what they cannot.* Ingrid first made a personal assessment of the three other members of the board. Although she preferred an open dialogue with the entire board, she knew this would be too much for them. They wouldn't feel safe being open about their skills or lack thereof. Therefore, Ingrid had a two-hour one-on-one meeting with each of them in which she openly discussed their strengths and weaknesses.

2. *Develop: train, coach, and mentor leaders to develop the mindset, knowledge, and skills they lack.* One of the board members clearly lacked the necessary interpersonal and social skills to lead effectively. He was realistic about this himself and willing to learn. Therefore, they sought training on communication and listening skills.

3. *Share: reallocate tasks that leaders are not good at or have no time for to others in the organization.* Another member lacked the administrative knowledge and skills required to do his job well. While he found this hard to admit, Ingrid managed to sell the idea to him of delegating some of that work to one of his close colleagues who was clearly more capable of doing it.

4. *Replace: if developing or sharing does not work, replace leaders by ones who can do the job. This concerns you too.* The last board member was a problem. He was arrogant, did not consider himself as lacking leadership qualities, and was not willing to learn or make any change. Ingrid saw no other option but to replace him. She knew this was going to be a long and tiresome process, but it was necessary.

ORGANIZING AT GOFORIT

In parallel with the need for an external investment, GoforIT needed to get more organized. Otherwise, it would be impossible for them to realize the aspired growth in a healthy manner. To identify the organizational changes that were required to realize their new strategy, they prepared an Organizational Map. It looks as follows and contains the key organizational deficiencies they needed to resolve.

Organizational Map for GoforIT

Drive

Motivation
Employees are demotivated by the fact that Frank & Liu make big profits, but they don't share this. Willingness to work hard is decreasing. Therefore: create and implement a profit sharing mechanism.

Commitment
Commitment and team spirit are high. There is a real sense of community in the sense that there is a closely collaborating group of people.
No immediate attention required, but keep paying attention to this when the company grows. Could be easily lost in the growth.

Processes
Currently very ad hoc and differs per individual; not tenable when growing further.
Things to do.
- Structure development process
- Structure sales pipeline & process + support with IT.
- Create financial & control processes.

Direction
Control is currently done through direct supervision only. Does not work anymore.

Leadership
Frank & Liu are good at technology & commerce. Lacking is a 'people and organization' person - a COO should be added to the team.

Structure
Major point of improvement because currently there is no clear structure.
Things to do:
- Divide work between Frank, Liu and to-be-hired COO.
- Create two business units + appoint managers + divide people + add new hires
- Define responsibilities + coordination.

Policies
The only policies currently used are contracts with clients and employees. It is unclear what people can and cannot do.
New policies needed for:
- Profit sharing for employees
- Security - online and offline
- HR: training & development policy

Controls
Need to define targets and KPIs + basic monitoring system.

Communication
Currently very informal; and we have been lucky so far we haven't missed out on important information.
To do:
- Adopt messaging tool (e.g. Slack, Fleep, etc.)
- Formalize meeting schedule and agenda for meetings

Expertise
So far this works well. However, for managing the growth finding suitable people is going to be a major challenge. To do:
- Create HR process + HR function
- Decide on functions & number of people
- Create a hiring campaign

Information Technology
Works well. IT is our business, so we can manage this. But we need to expand our IT infrastructure.
- Simple management information system with KPIs etc. (dashboards?)
- Pick CRM system (probably one of the cloud-based ones)

Retention · **Coordination** · **Potential**

ORGANIZING AT COMCOM

Since it is a one-person company, there is not so much organizing going on at Comcom—or so it seems. Especially with respect to processes, though, Anisha needed to organize her company much more. She decided to redesign her primary process completely from scratch from a customer perspective. So, she asked herself: which process is needed to serve the customer optimally? To answer it, she went through the following steps.

1. Identify current problems: what are all the customer's irritations, delays, and errors appearing in the current customer journey? This created a list of things-to-avoid in the new process.

2. Map out the primary yearly processes of clients (accountancy firms). This told her when they needed to communicate and about what.

3. Define the main communication products that clients need plus a list of their main content plus information required from the client plus timing.

4. Define processes reflecting the timing, input, activities, and output for each communications product.

5. Discuss the processes and products (including price) with two current and two new clients to check and align with their needs.

6. Create, test, and improve templates for all communication products.

7. Do a pilot with three clients, reflect, and improve.

STEPPING BACK
ONCE MORE

A fter mapping (step 2) and bridging (step 6), I recommended you step back for a moment and ask yourself whether you still want the strategy that was generated. Now, after the organizing step, is a good moment to ask this again. You have a more complete understanding of what it takes to execute your strategy, including the organizational changes that are needed. This means that your Strategy Backlog is longer now and showing you the total effort it will take. At this point, you should ask yourself once again:

"Do we still want the strategy that we generated?"

Asking this question once again makes sure that you remain committed to your strategy, or that you revise it if needed. This avoids finding out at a later stage that you should have changed direction, and it limits the risk of incurring unnecessary costs. It also avoids the "sunk cost" and "consistency" traps that would keep you working on something just because you have started it. In any case, it's better to understand that you want a change now than when you've made substantial investments in time, money, or effort. There are three possible answers.

1. **Yes, but** you found out that some projects or tasks take too much effort to execute. In this case, you should rework your Strategy Backlog and find alternative ways of achieving the same result.
2. **Yes, and** you are committed to your strategy and to doing what it takes to realize it. In this case, you should move on to step 8: planning strategy (page 275).

3. **No**, **or** at least you know that you would like to make changes to your strategy. In this case, you should go back to step 4 of strategy generation: innovating strategy (page 139).

STEP 8: PLANNING STRATEGY

In the first two steps of strategy execution, you defined the projects and tasks that need to be executed to realize your strategy and listed them in your Strategy Backlog. After these two steps, you know what it takes to realize your strategy. This tenth chapter focuses on the third step of strategy execution: planning your strategy. In this step, you turn your Strategy Backlog into a dynamic and prioritized course of action to which the organization commits, and you establish a way of working for strategy realization.

> **Planning Strategy** = Developing and committing to a dynamic, prioritized course of action and a way of working for closing the gap between the actual and the aspired strategy.

THE PLANNING CHALLENGE

Planning doesn't mean that you try to turn your strategy into comprehensive project plans and programs. Those will be outdated as soon as you start—or earlier. Such plans will also easily become so complex that they become unmanageable. On the other hand, some planning is needed, for without it strategy execution becomes unguided. If you only adapt to circumstances, you change course and priorities all the time, which is ineffective too. This means that you need to find a balance between planning and adaptation.

Finding such a balance doesn't mean that you do "a bit" of planning. That's as useless as, or worse than, overplanning or no planning because it creates vagueness about what is planned and what is not. What it does mean, though, is that you need to separate the short term and the long term. In the short term, things don't change that much, and so you can plan accurately; this is what this chapter focuses on. In the long term, however, things can change a lot, which means that your planning has to be adaptive.

Up to this point, strategy execution was mainly about making an inventory of everything that *could* or *should* be done to realize your strategy. You've identified all the gaps between where you are and where you want to be and have turned those into projects and tasks in your Strategy Backlog. And if you've done this as suggested with a team in a participative manner, the people whose commitment is needed most are likely to agree that this is what needs to happen.

> *"In the planning step, you make the transition from what could or should be done to what* will *be done."*

In this third strategy execution step, you make the transition from what could or should be done to what *will* be done. This is a crucial difference that needs your attention. So far, things have largely been hypothetical and noncommittal; all projects and tasks on the Strategy Backlog are still ideas or suggestions. As explained on pages 38-40, this was important because separating ideas from decisions makes people more likely to come up with good ideas. Now is the time to turn those ideas and suggestions into a plan that people commit to for real. To achieve that, your challenge is to develop collaboratively a plan that fulfills the following three criteria.

- The plan should be *relevant* in that it needs to take a substantial step forward in the realization of your strategy. Any plan that doesn't progress your strategy further is not really worth considering.

- The plan should be *sound* in that it makes sense and is achievable by the organization. This means that the plan should be realistic, coherent, and detailed enough so that it can actually be executed.
- The plan should be *appealing* in that people are motivated and energized to execute it. Without people being motivated, the plan won't be executed. Therefore, the plan should also appeal to people.

How to keep your planning relevant, sound, and appealing over time during the realization of your strategy is described in Chapter 11. How you create such planning in the first place is covered below by discussing the *what*, *who*, *when*, and *how* of planning.

COMPLETING THE STRATEGY BACKLOG: THE *WHAT* OF PLANNING

The first step in planning your strategy is to complete your Strategy Backlog, and this includes completing the list of projects and tasks and estimating the effort these require. Of course, it will never be "complete" in the literal sense, and it will keep on changing. However, as the starting point for your planning, it should be as complete as reasonably possible. This means that:

- Everything needed to realize your strategy is in the Strategy Backlog.
- Everything in the Strategy Backlog is needed to realize your strategy.

Having a complete as possible Strategy Backlog at this stage is important because you need to be able to rely on it. So long as you still have doubts about whether everything is listed or whether everything listed is really necessary, you won't arrive at a plan that is relevant, sound, and appealing. Furthermore, so long as your Strategy Backlog is incomplete, you can't get your head clear, and you won't be focused enough through the rest of the process because you're still thinking about the Strategy Backlog.

COMPLETING THE LIST OF PROJECTS AND TASKS

Based on the first two steps of strategy execution–bridging and organizing–your Strategy Backlog consists of three types of projects and tasks covering information, implementation, and organizational gaps. Now that you have all these projects and tasks listed, you should look at the Strategy Backlog as a whole and see whether it makes sense. Although you never can be sure, double-checking it now can avoid wasting time, effort, money, and frustration later on in the process. When checking your Strategy Backlog, you should ask the following questions–and in this order.

1. *Can any project or task be dropped?* Because you had different routes to come up with projects and tasks, you might have listed some of them more than once. Or you might have defined different projects and tasks that target the same result. Such redundant projects and tasks can most likely be dropped. The more you can drop, the better.

2. *Can any projects or tasks be combined?* So far, you looked at projects and tasks per gap. Now that you look at the whole, you might find out that some projects or tasks are better combined because they belong together, or because they are so small that it makes sense to turn them into a combined bigger project. Thus, combine projects and tasks where possible because it will reduce overall complexity.

3. *Should any project or task be split up?* Some projects or tasks may be so big that it makes more sense to split them up into smaller, more manageable ones. This can make your Strategy Backlog more balanced since the size of projects and tasks on the list will differ less. So, split projects and tasks up if they are too big.

4. *Should any project or task be revised?* It can also be that, now you see the whole Strategy Backlog, you want to

change a particular project or task because it doesn't make sense anymore in the light of the other projects and tasks. Therefore, revise projects and tasks when that makes more sense.

5. *Should any project or task be added?* Even though you have done your best to come up with a complete list, you might find that important projects or tasks are missing now that you see the entire Strategy Backlog. Therefore, add projects and tasks if needed.

ESTIMATING EFFORT

Once you have completed the list of projects and tasks that need to be executed, you should estimate how much time and budget will be needed to execute them. This is useful for three reasons.

1. It gives you a sense of the total amount of time and resources required for realizing your strategy. This indicates the feasibility of your strategy and whether you can commit to realizing it while at the same time running your daily business.
2. It gives you extra input for completing your Strategy Backlog. While estimating the required time and resources, you might find out that some projects or tasks are so substantial that they can better be split up. Others might be so small that they are better combined.
3. It helps with prioritizing projects and tasks. Even when effort is not itself a criterion in your prioritization, adding time and resources allows you to estimate the critical path for realizing your strategy.

> *"Resist the temptation to make very precise estimations and calculations."*

In estimating effort, you can assess the required time and budget. Generally, the advice is to keep this process as simple as possible. So, if an estimation of time is enough, then stick to that. But if you need more details, you can also add required budget.

- **Time:** the total number of estimated hours, days, or weeks required for executing a particular project or tasks. Generally, hours or days are preferred since tasks that take more than a working week in terms of effort, should probably be split up into smaller tasks.
- **Budget:** depending on how precise you want to be, you can add an estimated amount of out-of-pocket costs that are associated with a particular project or task. You could also list specific resources that are required for executing it.

You should resist the temptation to make very precise estimations and calculations. This will be a waste of time since, while you are on your way, things will change, which means you will be wrong anyway. What is important here is that you get a sense of the total effort it will take in terms of time and money to execute your strategy. Whether, in the end, it will be 10% or 20% lower or higher should not be your primary concern. You should factor that in. What you want to avoid though, is that you have no clue what you are getting yourself into or that you totally underestimate or overestimate what it takes.

CLOSING THE WHAT OF PLANNING

Once you think you have completed your Strategy Backlog you and the team should ask the following question to come to a closure:

> ### "Do we trust our Strategy Backlog well enough to proceed?"

This is more a gut-feeling question than a brain question. If you really start thinking about it, you might get stuck as the list of projects and tasks might be too overwhelming to answer this question rationally. The clearest signal that your Strategy Backlog is complete enough is that your mind gets clear and that you feel calm and confident about it. So, closing this step doesn't just mean stopping. It also means closing it mentally.

"Closing this step doesn't just mean stopping. It also means closing it mentally."

ASSEMBLING THE REALIZATION TEAM: THE *WHO* OF PLANNING

Completing the Strategy Backlog is a natural moment to think about the team that is going to take responsibility for realizing the strategy. This team might not be very different from the team that you have worked with so far. However, if you want to make changes, this is a good time to do so because here the transition takes place from a list of projects and actions that *could* be executed to a prioritized action plan to which you *actually* commit. Putting together the realization team means that you define the roles that are needed and select the people who will fulfill these roles.

STRATEGY EXECUTION ROLES

To make strategy execution work, you most likely need three types of roles in your organization.

- **Coordinators** are the persons in charge of the entire strategy realization effort. They lead and coordinate the strategy realization process to make sure that it keeps going in the right direction. Two specific roles are needed that are best taken by two people.
  - A **progress manager** is a dedicated person who is responsible for checking progress, setting up meetings, arranging communication, and signaling problems. This person is the linchpin of strategy realization. This may not be a full-time job, but it takes substantial time every day and week.
  - A **business leader** is someone who actively supports the execution process and has the final authority to make and enforce decisions. If everything works well, this person can stay in the background, but their weight is crucial.

- **Organizers** take individual responsibility for the realization of specific projects and tasks and collaborative responsibility for strategy execution as a whole. Together with the coordinators, they form the strategy realization team. Most of them probably have been part of the strategy team throughout the process already; they meet regularly with coordinators and producers.
- **Producers** are people who actually deliver the projects and tasks. Organizers may deliver a large share themselves. Other projects and tasks though, might be delegated to other people in the organization. I call them producers because, in the end, they're the ones producing the actual results.

SELECTING TEAM MEMBERS

With the possible exception of the progress manager, the roles above are preferably fulfilled by internal people working for the organization. This means that the pool of people you can source from is limited and that you don't always have much choice. Nevertheless, it's crucial that you establish a well-functioning team, or otherwise all efforts so far have largely been a waste of time.

"The progress manager should be painstakingly meticulous, tirelessly persistent, and patiently empathetic"

If you have selected a productive team for strategy generation along the lines of the suggestions on pages 36-38 you probably have a large part of your strategy realization team already. In general, the realization team has similar requirements as suggested there (heterogeneous, people who are influential and vocal, etc.). There are a few more specific criteria though that you may want to take into account when selecting people.

1. **Drive:** strategy execution requires much more persistence than strategy generation. Therefore, people should have a strong drive to succeed in realizing the strategy. While some level of intrinsic drive should be there, there are

things you can do to increase this; see pages 239-246 on motivation and commitment.

2. **Qualities:** next to the drive to achieve, the people in the strategy realization team obviously also need to have some qualities. Generally, because they all take leadership roles, both coordinators and organizers need the kind of leadership qualities summarized on pages 234-236 and pages 329-331. It doesn't make sense to look for more specific qualities since your choice will be limited anyway because you're selecting from a subset of your employees. However, you want to be pickier when selecting the progress manager because this person is the linchpin of strategy realization. The primary qualities that he or she needs are to be:
    - ○ a) painstakingly meticulous (so that important details are not overlooked),
    - ○ b) tirelessly persistent (so that progress is being made, no matter what), and
    - ○ c) patiently empathetic (so that the human side of strategy is never forgotten).

3. **Power:** both the coordinators and the organizers in your team need to have the power to get stuff done by others. This was already important for strategy generation, but is much more so for strategy execution. Power could come from people's position, experience, age, or other individual characteristics. It could also be mandated power. Business leaders, for example, can give progress managers a mandate for making certain decisions or taking certain actions.

4. **Time:** people need to have the time to fulfill their role in strategy realization. Too often, this role is just added to people's existing responsibilities. The result is that they won't be able to give strategy realization enough priority, which leads to delays or failure. It's key that people either have or get the time to fulfill their roles–which usually means spending less time on other things.

Even though I used the word "selecting" above, this does not mean that the people in the strategy realization team need to be selected in a top-down manner. As described on page 253, there are at least four alternative mechanisms to this hierarchical model: democracy, network, sociocracy, and market. All these mechanisms can be used to select team members as well. Accordingly, people could be selected based on voting, peer-to-peer evaluation, decision-making by consent, and by signing up themselves.

PRIORITIZING AND SCHEDULING: THE *WHEN* OF PLANNING

Once you've completed your Strategy Backlog and put together the realization team, it's time to turn the Strategy Backlog into a more manageable package that you'll start executing. The first step to do that is prioritizing projects and tasks so that you know which ones you want to focus on first and which ones can be postponed. Subsequently, you start scheduling the first set of projects and tasks, so you know what to do and when, and commit to it.

The main purpose of this step is that it focuses your attention. The previous steps should give you the confidence that you know what it takes to realize your strategy and that you have a team in place that can make it happen. In this third planning step, you channel this confidence toward a focused action plan. Attention is key because, as the saying goes, what you put your attention on grows. Research supports this with broad evidence that the best way to make sure that something happens is to give it undivided attention. That's what we aim for here.

PRIORITIZING

The main reason why you prioritize is to rank-order projects and tasks so you can select those that you want to execute first. It's important to keep this in mind and make your way of prioritizing no more complex than is necessary. There are many criteria that you can use. The following ones are generally the most useful.

- **Urgency.** A simple criterion that could be used on its own for prioritization. For this criterion, you simply ask: what is the first thing that needs to be done? What is the second? So on and so forth. It's not very precise, but quite effective.

- **Criticality.** Also, a criterion that can be used on its own. It's focused on identifying the "hotspots"–those projects or tasks that really should be executed because otherwise, the strategy will fail. For this criterion, you ask which projects and tasks are critical for realizing the aspired strategy.

- **Effort and impact.** A variation of the previous two, but then combined into two complementary criteria. When you prioritize on effort and impact, you look at both projects and tasks that offer quick wins (low effort) and those that are big hits (high impact).

- **Path dependency.** Path dependency means that one project or task cannot be started or finished before another one is completed. As such, it dictates the order in which some projects or tasks should be performed. Using this criterion, you give higher priority to those projects and tasks on which others depend.

- **Possibility.** This is a more pragmatic criterion that should preferably be used in combination with one of the other criteria. For this criterion, you ask not so much what is necessary to do, but what the organization can realistically do, taking into account that it also has to keep on running its daily business. So, rather than prioritizing based on what *should* be done, you prioritize on what *can* be done.

"Focus on just one or two criteria and use them loosely while relying on your intuitive judgments."

This list of criteria is incomplete, and there is also some overlap between them. But in practice that's no problem. When you prioritize the projects and tasks in your Strategy Backlog, you'll find that it's not necessary to use criteria rigidly. You should avoid complex algorithms with many criteria and precise weightings. That takes too much work and only offers artificial accuracy. Instead, it's recommended that you focus on just one or two criteria and use them loosely while relying on your intuitive judgments. For this, simply add a column to your Strategy Backlog in which you assign the priority. You can use, for example, a five-point scale ranging from one (very low priority) to five (very high priority). In this way, prioritization can be done relatively quickly.

SCHEDULING AND ESTABLISHING A REALIZATION RHYTHM

By prioritizing projects and tasks, you have made a first step in creating focus in your Strategy Backlog. The next step is to plan *when* you'll execute projects and tasks. The traditional way would be to turn your entire list of projects and tasks into a complete project plan; I advise against such an approach. There are simply too many uncertainties and changes that will happen, which means that your planning will soon be outdated. On the other hand, precise planning is needed in the short term to make sure that you do the right stuff and don't end up with unguided action. Furthermore, even though you can't plan strategy execution in the long term, you can plan systematically when you will update your planning and make plans for the next short term.

> *"Create a realization rhythm and choose one that matches the rhythm of the organization."*

A practical solution is establishing a 30-day *realization rhythm* in which you continuously plan what you'll do in the first 30, 60, and 90 days. Looking further ahead than 90 days is usually too far, because of the changes that might occur in between. And having a time frame of less than 30 days is often too short since executing your strategy usually takes time and cannot be done in just a couple of weeks. Another advantage of the 30-60-90 scheme is that it fits the monthly and quarterly meeting and reporting schedules that many organizations have. In this way, strategy realization can be naturally woven into the existing meeting and reporting rhythm of the organization. This is crucial, for without such rhythm it's unlikely that the strategy will be systematically executed, or executed at all, because it doesn't get the continuous attention that it requires. It's recommended that you create a realization rhythm and choose one that matches the rhythm of the organization.

To get your 30, 60, and 90-day planning (or any other rhythm that works for your organization), you simply select, from your prioritized Strategy Backlog, those projects and tasks that you plan to execute in the first 30 days (or month), in the following 30 days, and in the subsequent 30 days. In this way, you create three 30-day Backlogs.

Once you've selected the projects and tasks that you'll focus on in the first 30, 60, and 90 days, there are a few more things to do to make your planning effective: defining when a task is considered done and assigning responsibilities and dates. In this way, it's very clear what should be done, who should do it, and when it should be done.

Defining "done": depending on how precisely you have defined your projects and tasks, it can be useful to define explicitly when you consider them done. For some projects and tasks this will be clear, but for others, you need to think about this and specify what you mean. When, for example, have you really "tested" a new product: when you have asked two people what they think of it or when it has been used for half a year in at least five pilot projects? Or when have you attracted enough customers in a new market: when they have said they would order your product or when they have actually ordered it? Providing such definitions of "done" gives clarity to everyone involved about what exactly is required to complete particular projects and tasks. This avoids discussion later on and makes sure that people focus on the right things.

Assigning responsibilities: while composing your Strategy Backlog and prioritizing the projects and tasks it contains, you probably have implicit thoughts about who should do what. That should be made explicit. A plan only works if it's clear who is responsible for doing what. For every project and task that you have selected for the 30, 60, and 90-day Backlog, you should now specify who is responsible.

Assigning dates: the last thing to do to complete your planning is to assign start dates and due dates for the projects and tasks in your 30, 60, and 90-day Backlog. This is not always necessary. By creating these three backlogs, you already have indicated roughly when things should be done. However, it can be useful to plan a bit more precisely and define when a project or task should start and when it should be done. The resulting 30, 60, and 90-day Backlog will look something like the example below.

Example of a Comprehensive 30-day Backlog

Element	Gap	Project	Task	Priority	Depends on	Definition of done	Time	Resources	Who	Start	Due
LE	We lack a competent leader for our R&D department.	11. Find new R&D leader.	11.1 Identify the desired job profile.	VH	3.4, 5.6	2 pages, following company standard	1d	-	*John, Rita*	1-4	25-4
			11.2 Write and publish a vacancy on LinkedIn.	H	11.1	Published in company profile + shared on site X, Y, and Z	4h	-	*Rita*		
			...		...	...	...	...	...	...	...
PR	Our process for new product introductions is inefficient and ineffective.	12. Improve NPI process.	12.1 Redesign the process in a meeting with production, engineering and sales.	H	1, 2, 3.4	Flow-chart + 15-minute presentation for board	1d	Meeting room	*John, Team members t.b.d.*	4-4	8-4
	...		...								

This example reflects a comprehensive backlog with many columns. As such, it contains all information for accurate planning. If you can, though, I recommend simplifying it by removing columns that are not strictly necessary. In its simplest form it should at least contain the following:

1.   **What** needs to be done (the project and/or task).
2.   **When** it should be done (the start and/or due date, or an indication of when work will be done).
3.   **Who** is responsible (the person(s) responsible for executing or managing the project or task).

MEETINGS AND BRIEFINGS:
THE *HOW* OF PLANNING

With the "how" of planning, I don't mean specifying exactly how each project and task should be executed; that should be left to the people responsible. You do need to establish an effective way of working though. Primarily, this means establishing an effective way of communicating through meetings and briefings during strategy execution.

MEETINGS

Many people resist meetings because there are too many, with too many people and too little focus. Meetings, however, can be effective and efficient because they enable interactive communication between two or more people at the same time. To make sure you have effective meetings during strategy realization, here are five things to consider before every meeting.

1. *What to talk about?* If there is nothing to talk about, there is no need for a meeting. Also, remember the importance of focused attention and make sure there is an agenda that is sent out in advance so that everyone knows what the purpose of the meeting is. Make sure you stick to it and don't end up in broad discussions.

2. *Who should be there?* Everyone necessary for making a decision or taking action should be there. No more and no less. Additional people will lose interest, while meetings with fewer people will remain inconclusive. It's not always required to habitually meet with the entire realization team.

3. *When should it be?* The timing of meetings is important. If held too early, not all the necessary information might be available and, if held too late, much of the usefulness of the meeting is lost since decisions have already been made elsewhere. So, time well and plan ahead.

4. *How long does it last?* Decide upfront how long the meeting will last and stick to it. Manage time well, and preferably don't plan meetings longer than one hour because you'll lose focus and pace.

5. *What to deliver?* Make sure every meeting ends with clear action points with a date and designate someone to be responsible. In the end, the purpose of the meeting is not meeting, but doing something.

It's primarily the progress manager's job to make sure that these guidelines are followed. However, it's *everyone's* responsibility that this way of having meetings becomes the normal way of working.

BRIEFINGS

The other form of communication that you'll need are briefings: internal and external mainly one-way messages in any form, be it a presentation, video message, email, newsletter, or other. Because of the ease of sending out messages of one sort or another, "communications clutter" can easily occur, even if well-intended– think of cc-ing groups of people in email messages.

To keep briefings focused, it's first of all key to be selective in choosing the audience. Briefings are sent out because you want something from people. And sending out messages that are not relevant to people just creates communication overload. Think carefully about who should receive your message–inside the team, within the organization, and outside of it.

You also want to make sure that you don't send too few or too many messages. Too few is not good because people are ill-informed, while too many is not good because they'll be over-informed–and thereby also ill-informed. As a rule of thumb, it's useful to send out a briefing:

a) when something new starts so that people are aware that something is going on,
b) when there is a question or issue that needs an answer or solution, or
c) when there is a relevant update, for example a change or an important task that's finished.

These rules apply to everyone involved, and the progress manager should keep an eye on whether people apply these rules.

COMMITTING TO THE PLAN

By creating your 30, 60, and 90-day Backlogs, you have turned your new strategy into concrete actions in a transparent way. It's clear now what needs to be done in the first few months, and you can trace back why a particular project or task was defined and how it contributes to realizing your aspired strategy. Of course, a lot might still change once you're on your way and have made further progress. However, at this point, you've done the best you can to create a concrete short-term plan for realizing your strategy that is relevant, sound, and appealing.

> *"Create a document, poster, or brown*
> *paper that everyone signs."*

This is a good moment to commit explicitly to the action plan. Of course, you have shown your commitment already during strategy generation by formulating your new strategy, and also by stepping back a few times and confirming that you still want this strategy. But those commitments have mainly been implicit and preliminary. Commiting explicitly to your strategy can be powerful in turning the strategy into action and motivating everybody involved.

Research has revealed that there are various things you can do to make the commitment as strong as possible. The five most important are noted below.

1. **Make it explicit.** Make it clear exactly to what you are committing. This can, for example, be to the new strategy, to solving the gaps, or to the specific 30, 60, and 90-day Backlog. The advantage of the latter is that it's very concrete. It should, however, not lead to the dogmatic execution of the plan. The advantage of committing to the strategy itself is that it's more flexible, but it also remains rather vague as to what people are committing. The most effective approach might be to commit to doing whatever it takes to solve the gaps between the current and aspired strategy.

2. **Make it collective.** It's not just important that you commit. Everyone involved and affected, or even the whole organization, should commit. Executing your strategy is a collective effort and can only work if everyone who needs to contribute commits to doing what it takes.

3. **Make it voluntary.** Commitments that are forced are not real commitments. Of course, there always will be some pressure, but it should be clear that people are not forced into it. The commitment and its effectiveness will be much stronger if people have voluntarily committed.

4. **Make it public.** People respond to social pressure and want to stay consistent with what they promised, especially in front of their peers. Therefore, having people commit openly to realizing the new strategy is a very strong mechanism to make it happen.

5. **Make it stick.** Finally, you want to make sure that the commitment stays alive during its implementation. This requires that you actively and regularly remind people during the realization process to what they committed; it also helps to display the commitment, in some form, visually in a place where people see it frequently. Furthermore, to ensure that people still see it after some weeks, it's best to change the way it's displayed often.

Based on these insights, you can choose whatever form works best to make people commit to the new strategy or its execution. You could, for example:

- Prepare a document that everyone involved signs. This signing is symbolic and it should, therefore, be clear that the document is not a contract and that people are not legally bound by it. A letter of intent or manifesto can work well.

- Create a poster or brown paper that everyone signs. Give it a nice title that summarizes the overall change that's going to be made and let everyone sign it, preferably in a public meeting.

While you could also use voting or oral commitment, written commitment is much stronger and therefore preferred. It also makes it easier to create something that lasts and that people can be reminded of easily.

THE FOUR EXAMPLES

PLANNING AT MACMAN

At Macman, one of the key challenges regarding planning was the prioritization of projects and tasks. Not being used to any substantial change over the last decade (or, actually, throughout their 52 years of existence), they were overwhelmed by all the changes that were needed. After having completed their list of projects and tasks, they wanted to reduce this list substantially and focus on the absolute core of what needed to be done. They applied the following criteria.

1. **Possibility**. They liked this criterion and went through their list of projects and tasks to see which ones were most feasible and could be executed while at the same time keeping the business running. This made sure strategy execution would not disrupt their operations too much.
2. **Urgency**. The second criterion used was urgency. To apply it, they arranged all the possible projects and tasks in order of urgency. Then, for the first period of 30 days, they simply picked the top ten and focused on executing those.

Note: My personal recommendation would be to inverse the order of these two criteria: urgency first, then possibility.

PLANNING AT HOSPICARE

Hospicare's new strategy was a major deviation from their current one. Making the transition involved a lot of interdependent projects and tasks. To smoothen the transition, they paid substantial attention to path dependencies. When doing this, they identified three types of path dependencies.

1. **Straightforward dependencies:** simple, time-related dependencies telling them that some things simply needed to be done before others. For example, setting

up one new privatized center contained the following series of projects and tasks: a) find a suitable building, b) renovate it, c) obtain new equipment, etc., etc.

2. **Compromising interdependencies:** situations where two or more activities need to be done at the same time so that a compromise needs to be made. An example was that when moving treatments to the new privatized center, treatments still needed to continue at the hospital too. Solutions that were identified included moving during the night and no treatments for three days.

3. **Catch-22 interdependencies:** situations where A has to be done before B, but B before A. An example of this was that they first needed new (privately-paying) patients before they had money to invest, but needed to invest first before they could serve patients. Also here, the typical solution was to find compromises, such as starting small without investment.

Based on these interdependencies, they had to change some of the projects in their Strategy Backlog. After that, they were able to turn it into a workable 30, 60, and 90-day plan.

PLANNING AT GOFORIT

After completing their Strategy Backlog, removing duplicate tasks, and combining some tasks into projects, GoforIT estimated the time and budget required to realize their strategy. They soon discovered that they had been too ambitious and that there were some gaps that seemed impossible to bridge. The most difficult gap was finding the people who would be needed to achieve their growth ambitions; their original idea was just to hire the software engineers they needed. That sounded nice; the only problem was these engineers are simply not available, or at least not in the country. Therefore, they looked for ways to solve this gap.

1. Define alternative tasks that also focused on bridging the expertise gap. Instead of hiring experienced software engineers nationally, they identified two possible alternatives: a) hire inexperienced people with an interest

in software and/or technology and train them, and b)
hire people from abroad through specialized agencies.
They decided to start by trying the second approach.

2. Counterbalance with tasks for other elements. Focusing
on the motivation element wasn't an answer because
people already worked very hard. However, instead of
simply hiring new software engineers, another possibility
was to change the structure and processes so that they
could hire less experienced software engineers. Only
some of the programming work required the high-level
skills of their current engineers. By restructuring the
work into basic and advanced work, they could hire less
capable engineers too.

3. Revising the strategy was not (yet) an option they were
willing to consider. Even though realizing their growth
ambitions was extremely challenging, they were not
ready to give up or lower this ambition. Therefore, they
insisted on the strategy as generated, and rather looked
for other ways to obtain the required growth. If 1 and 2
did not work, they would consider buying another firm
or outsourcing non-core activities to others.

PLANNING AT COMCOM

At Comcom, generating the complete Strategy Backlog and
prioritizing it went pretty smoothly. However, when specifying
projects and tasks, Anisha found it difficult to provide a definition
of "done" and to assign dates. She simply wasn't used to working
in such a planned manner. Nevertheless, she found it a good
experience to do so—not least because she had to start working in
a much more structured way because that was the core of her new
strategy. This is how she defined "done":

1. *For the communication products:* three out of the four
clients that she was going to test these products with
should approve them.

2. *For her primary process with clients:* in the two pilots she
would do, none of the irritations, delays, or errors from
her "things-to-avoid" list should return, nor should any

new ones appear–neither for her nor for the two pilot clients.

3. *For her complete offering:* in April, she should have at least two paying customers. She preferred to measure satisfaction after a year, but this was too long term for now. This should, however, return in the monitoring during the realization step of strategy execution.

11

STEP 9: REALIZING STRATEGY

Y ou've arrived at the last step of the strategy process: strategy realization. It's in this step that you turn your strategy into reality. If you've done the previous steps well, you should be ready to go. As you'll see though, there are some things you need to do to ensure that the strategy is fully realized and that the process keeps on going in a relevant and productive way. This will be the topic of this eleventh chapter.

Realizing Strategy = Effecting the aspired strategy by putting the execution plan into action and managing relevance, progress, and emotions over time.

THE REALIZATION CHALLENGE

During strategy realization, there are three key aspects that you need to check and manage to keep your strategy relevant, sound, and appealing.

1. *Managing relevance* concerns making sure that the strategy you're executing is still the right strategy. As such, it refers to keeping track of what's happening within and outside the organization that could affect the relevance

of your strategy and to dealing with the information gaps that you identified in Chapter 8.

2. *Managing progress* refers to making sure that you stick to your planning and regularly update it so that you keep on making progress. This is obviously important and the most operational part of this last step.

3. *Managing emotions* refers to keeping track of people's moods and motivation. While your strategy might still be relevant and you're making good progress, you want to find out whether people are still committed, or whether problems are to be expected in this respect.

Below I discuss these three challenges and offer tools and tips on how to deal with them.

MANAGING RELEVANCE

The first thing you want to do on a regular basis (for example every month or quarter) is to check whether the strategy you generated is still the right one. In a month, or even in a couple of days, important things could have changed that force you to "pivot": to repair, adjust, or even completely renew your strategy. This means that you have to monitor the relevance of the strategy regularly and take action if important things have changed. Managing relevance has three key parts: reviewing information gaps, identifying changes, and defining new possible information gaps.

1. REVIEWING YOUR INFORMATION GAPS.

As part of the bridging step, you may have identified few or even many information gaps that needed to be bridged to be certain enough about your strategy. The respective projects and tasks that you've included in your Strategy Backlog are crucial for managing the relevance of your strategy. You have defined them because you don't want to take the risk of being wrong. The first thing you want to do is focus on those tasks and evaluate whether the information you've gathered confirms or rejects the ideas that you had. After all, if you're wrong, you want to know as soon as possible. Reviewing the information gaps means that, for every question you've sought to answer and for every assumption that you've tested, ask yourself:

"Do our findings confirm the strategy that we generated?"

There are three possible answers:

1. **Yes.** Great, you're on the right track and you can continue executing your strategy in the way you anticipated. You can: a) cross this task from your Strategy Backlog and mark it done, b) briefly revisit your Strategy Backlog and see whether, based on your findings, any projects or tasks should be added, deleted, or changed, and c) move on to the next project in your Strategy Backlog.

2. **No.** Not the outcome you hoped for, and this means that you have to pivot. This could be a small pivot that just requires a change of the tasks in your Strategy Backlog (e.g., you found out that you need to change the product a bit which doesn't affect any of the other elements of your strategy), or a bigger pivot in which you have to revisit your strategy (e.g., you found out that the market you assumed was there does not exist, or at least you haven't found it yet). In the first case, you do the same as 1b above: you revisit your Strategy Backlog and add, delete, or change projects and tasks. In the second case, you have to go back to the innovation step of strategy generation: you're facing a new situation now, which most likely means that you have to adjust your strategy. And to start with that, you revisit the strategy as you generated it there.

3. **Undecided.** It can also be that the information isn't clear. If this is because you haven't gathered sufficient information, the follow-up is simple: gather it as soon as possible. If the answer is undecided because that's what the information shows, you'll have to force it into a "yes" or a "no" because you have to move on. You should not go on with information gathering since that will easily

end up in an endless quest for certainty, thereby delaying the process too much. So, decide for yourself: am I confident enough that I'm right, or shall we play it safe and assume we're wrong? In the first case, you proceed as in 1; in the second case, you proceed as in 2.

> *"Ask yourself regularly whether the strategy is still in line with reality as you experience it today."*

2. IDENTIFYING INTERNAL AND EXTERNAL CHANGES.

Since you formulated your strategy and created your Strategy Backlog, time has passed. This means that, next to the information gaps that you have identified, the relevance of your strategy can also be affected by any changes within or outside the organization. To manage the relevance of your strategy, you need to stay abreast of such changes and ask yourself regularly whether the strategy is still in line with reality as you experience it today. To do this, you use the Strategy Sketch and the Organizational Map as checklists to see whether anything substantial has changed on any of their ten elements. So, for each element of your Strategy Sketch and Organizational Map you ask:

"Has anything changed since the last time we worked on it?"

You have three possible answers:

1. **No.** You can just go on and work through your Strategy Backlog.
2. **Yes.** The next question then should be: does this affect other elements of our strategy or organization? If not, you can probably go on with executing your strategy. If the answer is "yes," however, you need to revisit your strategy and go back to the mapping step of strategy generation.

3. **Don't know.** You're not monitoring what is going on inside and outside your organization well enough. If this is the case, you need to do two things. First, you need to define the new information gaps that have appeared and gather the information along the lines of Chapter 8 (pages 198-208). Second, you need to improve the way you're monitoring. This probably requires changes in one or more of the elements of your organization. You may need to define additional projects and tasks, for example, to install or improve particular controls and processes in the organization.

3. IDENTIFYING NEW INFORMATION GAPS.

The final thing you want to do to make sure that your strategy is still relevant is to ask yourself whether any new questions have come up or if there are new assumptions that need to be tested. Over the past period, you've executed a variety of tasks. From doing so, you've learned, meaning that you now know more than you did when you started. However, you also know more about what you don't know. You might have thought you were sure or not even realized that you had made assumptions, but your experience while executing your strategy has given you new insights. Therefore, you should ask yourself:

"Are there any new questions or assumptions that should be answered and tested for executing the strategy?"

Your possible answers are:

1. **No.** You can just go on and work through your Strategy Backlog.
2. **Yes.** You need to formulate the new questions or assumptions explicitly and add projects and tasks for them to your Strategy Backlog. Chapter 8 told you how to do this.

KEEPING TRACK OF RELEVANCE: THE CONFIDENCE CHART

The realization step of strategy execution can be messy. It will probably go on for a long time, consist of several iterations, and concern all the elements of your strategy and organization. Keeping track of what is happening is both important and challenging. Your Strategy Backlog is your backbone and something you can rely on and always return to. However, the Strategy Backlog is very detailed. If you just rely on it, you might easily lose yourself in the details of strategy execution. Therefore, it's helpful if you can visualize the development of relevance, progress, and emotions on a higher level of abstraction so that you maintain an overview. For this purpose, you can use three types of charts: the Confidence Chart, the Burn Chart, and the Mood Chart, the first of which I explain in this section.

"In a Confidence Chart, you ask yourself regularly: how convinced are we that this is the right strategy?"

In a Confidence Chart, you map out your answer to a single question that you should repeatedly ask during the execution process: how confident are we that this is the right strategy? The first moment to ask this is directly when you commit to the strategy (the last part of the planning step, see pages 290-292). Most likely, you're quite confident at that stage because, otherwise, you wouldn't have committed to it in the first place. Subsequently, you should ask this question every time you have a follow-up meeting with the team–for example, every 30 days. In this way, you keep track of the development of confidence and see how it changes over time compared to the initial score. Your Confidence Chart could look as follows.

Example of a Confidence Chart

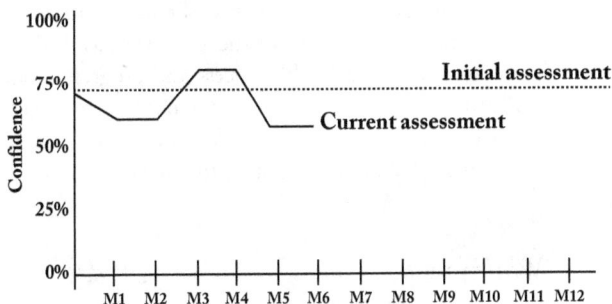

In this Confidence Chart, the solid line reflects your assessment of confidence over time (month 1 to 6 in this case), while the dashed line reflects the initial assessment. In this way, you can easily see whether your confidence in the relevance of the strategy goes up or down in the course of execution. When the score stays more or less the same or goes up, this is a good sign. It shows you're on the right track. If on the other hand, the score goes down too much, this is an indicator that you should revisit your strategy. And if it gets too close to 100% you might check whether your confidence is justified or whether you have become overconfident.

MANAGING PROGRESS

Most of your time during strategy realization is probably spent on managing progress. This involves the day-to-day management of tasks on your Strategy Backlog and primarily consists of monitoring whether you've achieved what you said you would in a particular period and taking action if you haven't. The following pages show you how you can do this.

MANAGING 30, 60, AND 90-DAY PLANNING

During the planning step, you made a plan only for the first 30, 60, and 90 days (or any other rhythm, should that work better for you). As argued there, the core idea behind this approach is that planning can be detailed in the short term, but that the long term comes with too many uncertainties to make planning useful. This also means that, for the first 30 days, you should try to adhere as closely as possible to your plan. In the same way, as during a "sprint" in the scrum approach, the process and progress should be managed ruthlessly and rigidly per 30-day period. In case of a big, unexpected event, such as a calamity, changes can be made but, overall, your goal should be to stick to your plan, whatever it takes.

> *"While you should be rigid within a 30-day period, your flexibility lies in the transition from one period to the next."*

There are three reasons for sticking to your plan. First, sticking to your 30-day plan will keep the strategy realization process manageable, since you make changes from one 30-day period to the next but not within a period; this makes your planning simpler and transparent. Second, it helps in developing a conscientious way of working that's based on delivery rather than excuses; this will increase the effectiveness and efficiency of the realization process and avoids a lousy attitude and unnecessary delays. Third, being forced to stick to your plan also stimulates you to come up with a better plan for the next 30-day period. If you over- or underestimated how much can be done in 30 days, you can learn from this and use these insights to improve planning for the next period.

While you should be rigid within a 30-day period, your flexibility lies in the transition from one period to the next. After every 30-day period, you update your plan. This means that you first assess the progress that's been made, using the following questions.

1. Did the projects and tasks that should have started within this period start?
2. Did the projects and tasks that should have finished within this period finish?

3. Did we stick to the estimated budgets in terms of time and resources?

If your answer to any of these questions is "no," it's useful to ask why this is the case and what this means for the next period. You want to find out the reason you didn't adhere to your plan. Were there, for example, unexpected events, was your planning too ambitious, or did you just not stick to it? Your focus should not be on finding the ultimate cause or a person to blame. That will just lead to endless discussions about the past. Instead, you should focus on learning for the future. Any insight that you gain should be used as input for the next planning round. If you answered all questions with "yes," that's great. It probably means you're doing well–and perhaps that you can increase your ambition for the next period.

Having looked back at the 30-day period that has passed, the next step is to look ahead. Now the question is: are there any reasons to adjust the planning that you made for the next 30 and 60 days? Relevant questions here are:

1. Do you foresee any trouble in realizing the plan that you made for the next 30 and 60 days?
2. Should any projects and tasks on your Strategy Backlog be adjusted?
3. Should any projects and tasks be added to or deleted from your Strategy Backlog?

Based on the answers to these questions, you now can update your plan. This means you adjust your planning for the next 30 and 60 days (remember that you made a 90-day plan, of which the first 30 days have now passed) and add a new 30-day plan to create a complete 90-day plan again. In this way, you always have a 3-month plan, which you update on a monthly basis.

MANAGING PROJECTS AND TASKS: THE KANBAN BOARD

A useful tool for managing progress throughout a 30-day period is a simple *Kanban Board*. It's called a Kanban Board because it's part of a method called *Kanban* (meaning "signboard" in Japanese) which was developed at Toyota to manage efficiency and quality of production. While you don't need to know this method to realize your strategy, the Kanban Board is a handy tool to use.

The Kanban Board is a very simple way to manage your projects and tasks–perhaps too simple to even give it a name, but this is what it's called. You can think of a physical board such as a whiteboard or a software version that you can find in some (free) cloud-based planning software. In essence, it's no more than a three-column board with columns for "to-do," "doing" and "done." In the "to-do" column, you list the projects and tasks selected for the 30-day period that have not yet started. In the column "doing" you list the projects and tasks that have started but that have not yet finished, and in the "done" column you list those that are finished. While making progress, projects and tasks should gradually move from the left column ("to-do") via the middle column ("doing") to the right column ("done"). Once a project or task is finished and doesn't require any more attention, it can be dropped from the Kanban Board altogether. See an example below.

Example of a Simple Kanban Board

To-do	Doing	Done
Project 5: name project	Project 5: name project	Project 3: name project
- Task 5.2: name task	- Task 5.1: name task	- Task 3.1: name task
- Task 5.3: name task	Project 4: name project	- Task 3.2: name task
	- Task 4.2: name task	
	- Task 4.3 name task	
	- Task 4.5 name task	

KEEPING TRACK OF PROGRESS: THE BURN CHART

Your Kanban Board and Strategy Backlog are useful tools to carefully manage the progress you're making in delivering the projects and tasks that you identified. In addition, you may find it useful to keep track of the time and resources you have used. After all, it's not only important that you realize your strategy, but also that you do it efficiently without exceeding your budgets. I borrow a tool from the scrum approach here: the Burn Chart.

A Burn Chart allows you to keep track of how much of your time and/or resources you have used ("burned") so far in the process of realizing your strategy. This shows you whether you're still doing okay, time and resource-wise, and whether you expect to need more or less time and resources for complete realization. It also shows if significant changes have been made that affect the total amount of resources that you expect to use. A typical Burn Chart looks as follows.

Example of a Burn Chart

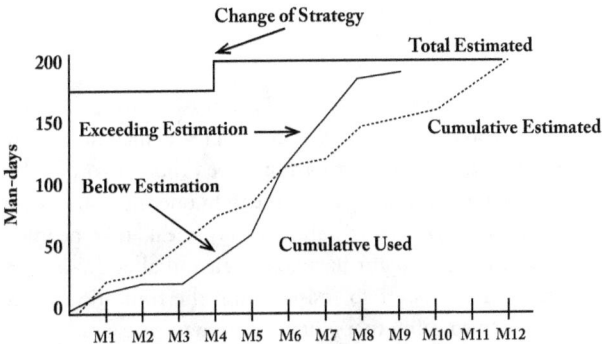

The example above is a Burn Chart for time: the number of man-days estimated and used throughout the project. A similar chart can be made for money or other resources. The bold solid almost horizontal line shows the total estimated number of man-days for realizing the strategy. This is the sum of all the estimated time spent and can be taken from your Strategy Backlog by adding all the values listed in column 8 (see page 288). As shown in the graph above, in month 4, a change was made to the strategy, which was estimated to require an additional thirty man-days.

The dashed line can also be taken from the Strategy Backlog, but only as far ahead as you've planned your projects and tasks, so no more than 90 days ahead of where you are today (in this case month 9). It shows how you have estimated to spend time over the 30-day periods. The relative straightness of the line shows that, in this case, the estimated amount of time required was quite evenly distributed over the various periods.

The final line shows the actual man-days that have been used. In the graph above, it reveals that initially fewer hours were spent than anticipated. However, after a steep increase in month 5, the cumulative time spent in month 9 lies significantly above the estimated amount. Accordingly, the project might be expected to exceed the total estimated amount too. Whether this is a problem or not cannot be determined from the chart itself. However, by visualizing the usage of time and resources in this way, you're stimulated to think about this and take action early on.

MANAGING EMOTIONS

Changing the strategy of an organization can have a substantial impact on people's jobs and lives. It can create uncertainty, stress, frustration, and anxiety. Furthermore, even though you might be convinced that your strategy is still the right one and you're making good progress, this doesn't automatically mean that people are still on board. They might have lost their initial enthusiasm and motivation or may start to resist during the realization process. Therefore, a third thing that you want to manage carefully during the realization of your strategy is people's emotions.

"Resistance is one of the most used and least understood terms when it concerns managing change."

"Managing emotions" seems to be a contradiction in terms. Managing your own emotions is already difficult, let alone managing those of others. However, despite this difficulty, it's crucial to pay enough attention to people's emotions throughout the process. Too often this is forgotten, leading to negative emotions slowly developing under the surface, thereby frustrating strategy realization. Managing such emotions requires both a good understanding of what is happening and a way of dealing with resistance, as well as managing the psychological transitions that come with change.

UNDERSTANDING RESISTANCE

Resistance is one of the most used and least understood terms when it concerns managing change. We easily refer to it to argue that other people fail to see the importance of the change and we blame them for not being willing to change in a way that is obviously necessary. The implicit assumption is that people are either not intelligent enough to see why the change is needed or are actively frustrating the change. This, however, is rarely a correct assumption.

To effectively deal with resistance, you first need to question whether what you're observing really is resistance at all. You might see it as such, but are you sure that, if people don't do as you expect them to do, this is because of resistance? Or is it because it's not at all clear to them what is expected from them? Or because the change is simply a bad idea? Also, do you know for sure that their "resistance" behavior–for example, inactivity or criticism– is, in fact, a sign of resistance? Or are these behaviors emerging because people are seriously thinking about how to incorporate the changes in their work or that they are strongly committed and care a lot about their job and the organization as a whole? Before you call something resistance, make sure you understand what is going on. To do this, you need to:

- Assume that people are intelligent and mean well. Your starting point should be that everyone is smart and reasonable and that they do their jobs as best they can. Some won't, but in general, this is a more valid and more productive starting point than assuming they are senseless and against you or the change.
- Put yourself in their shoes and take their perspective. You need to understand what the new strategy means for them and see how it impacts their work. Then, ask yourself how you would respond in their situation and what would make you more willing to change.

- Listen to people and hear what they say. Engage in a dialogue in which you're open-minded and avoid being defensive. Try to find out what their concerns are and why they're not behaving as you expect.

Understanding resistance also means that you learn to appreciate it. You may initially be annoyed by people's unwillingness to change. Of course, it would be nice if everyone embraced the change and applauded you for initiating it. But that's a Hollywood fantasy that rarely reflects reality. And to be frank, this is also a bit scary. I would be very suspicious if I got only those signals when trying to realize a new strategy that's a significant deviation from the past. Therefore, try to be positive about the resistance you observe. For this, it can be useful to realize that resistance has a number of positive sides.

- It shows that people care about their jobs and are committed at least to some part of the organization as it is now. It would be far worse if people were so indifferent to what they do that they didn't even resist anymore. See resistance as a sign of committed people who want to have a voice in something important to them.
- It helps to create a focus on the fundamentals. By resisting the suggested change, people help you think again about the reasons behind the change. Are the projects and tasks that were defined really contributing to the new strategy, and are they in line with the reason for changing the strategy in the first place?
- It helps to clarify the strategy and its execution. Often, resistance means that things are not clear enough. People, for example, don't know what to do if you tell them to translate the strategy for their units or jobs. This is not resistance, but lack of clear communication.
- It helps improve the strategy and the strategy process. Resistance is a great source of feedback and learning. Maybe the strategy, the action plan, or the process by which they have been generated are not as good as you think they are. Use the signals you get to improve them.

*"Understanding resistance also means
that you learn to appreciate it."*

A third thing that you need to do to understand resistance is to put the blame on yourself rather than on others. You need to reflect on your behavior and ask yourself, honestly, what you might have done that's causing resistance; this might be hard because there are various psychological mechanisms at play that make it easier to place blame outside yourself. Two important ones are named here.

The first mechanism is that people, in general, believe the best of themselves (scientists call this "attribution bias"); we assume that, compared to others, we're more often right and doing the right thing. What goes well must be because of us, and what goes wrong must be because of others. This cannot be true since everyone believes this. Be aware of this bias and be critical of yourself too.

Another strong mechanism is social pressure. People often feel a need to explain mistakes to save face or their own positions. The easiest way to do this is to blame others. And especially with something as complex as executing a new strategy, it's socially accepted to blame others, because there "always will be resistance." Don't fool yourself here; even if others might be the cause of problems, you're responsible for solving them. Therefore, you need to look at what you can do differently.

There are many mistakes that you can make throughout the strategy process that cause resistance. Some of the most widely made are:

1. Overoptimism: thinking more can be done than is actually possible.
2. No focus: trying to achieve too many things at once.
3. Impatience: forgetting that change requires time to digest.
4. Overstating benefits: raising expectations that you cannot meet.
5. Unconvinced: you don't believe in the new strategy yourself.

6. Breaking promises: just not doing what you promised people.
7. Half-truths: breaking trust by not telling the whole story.
8. Unclear communication: people don't know what to expect and do.
9. Lack of purpose: failing to explain why the change is needed.
10. Explaining only: not paying attention to people's emotions.
11. Inconsistency: leaders say different and conflicting things.
12. Bad role model: giving the wrong example in small things you do.
13. Indecisiveness: circumventing and postponing the hard decisions.
14. Pushing too much: creating more resistance by pushing harder.
15. Laissez-faire: leaving it up to people to figure it out themselves.
16. No voice: not giving people a voice in a change that concerns them.
17. Parenting: treating people as kids rather than adults.

The lesson is clear: if you want to reduce resistance, avoid these mistakes.

UNDERSTANDING THE PHASES OF PSYCHOLOGICAL TRANSITION

Next to understanding resistance, managing emotions also requires that you understand the psychological process that comes with strategy execution. Changing an organization's strategy isn't a one-off event. Similarly, changing people's minds and feelings doesn't happen from one day to the next. It requires time and a transition process that includes various steps. Research into psychology has shown that any big change typically goes through a similar process. While the exact number and nature of steps that are defined differ, the process boils down to the following (which is a variation of the "coping cycle" created by Colin Carnall):

1. **Denial.** The first phase of a psychological transition process is usually denial. It means that people deny that change is needed or that change is happening. They don't want to see the urgency and want to keep things as they are. They might simply tell you that you see it wrongly, that you are crazy, or that they have seen it all before and that there is no need to worry. In this phase, it's key that the urgency of the change is made explicit and visible so that people feel it. Since we're dealing with emotions here, simply more explanation will usually not do. You need to give tangible examples of urgency that people recognize and with which they associate. See also Chapter 3 (Activation).

2. **Defense.** In this phase, people start accepting reality and see that you're serious about the new strategy. In response, they may actively resist and defend their past way of working. You will hear a lot of "yes, buts" and all kinds of creative reasons why the current way of working is still the right one or is even superior. You also might face anger and frustration here. For you, this is a phase of persistence. This is probably not the nicest phase, but you need to get through it in order to realize the change that is needed. It's important not to take things personally, but to show that you understand that people defend their current situation.

3. **Discarding.** At some point, people give up their defensive reactions and accept that change is inevitable. They might not agree or like it but accept that things will change. This is an "in-between" period of people losing confidence and feeling uncertain. They know they need to give up their old ways of working, but don't yet know what comes in their place. They may feel lost and complain about the new strategy and "mourn" for all that it "destroys." Although the fight of the second phase and the active resistance associated with it are over, the motivation for executing the strategy is probably at its lowest ebb. Your biggest responsibility in this phase is probably doing nothing: accept it and give people time.

4. **Adaptation.** While the previous phases are primarily about letting go of the past, this fourth phase is future-oriented and focused on creation–on realizing the new strategy. On the one hand, this can create a lot of positive energy since people are looking ahead and working on something new. This may also lead to overconfidence and overoptimism: if something immediately works out well, people may easily think that the change is not such a big deal after all and things will quickly return to normal again. On the other hand, if things don't work out the first time–which they usually don't–it can also cause a lot of frustration and anger.

5. **Internalization.** In this last phase, the transition is completed. Both the organizational change that is needed to execute the strategy, as well as the psychological change that brings people back to the "new normal" come to an end–or at least for a while. People gradually find their place in the changed organization. Things get quieter now, and people may even feel proud and happy with the changes they've gone through. In the light of ever-changing circumstances, your main challenge here is to make sure people don't start to feel too comfortable and too confident. There's always a next change coming, and you probably want it to go a bit more smoothly than the last one.

"Changing people's minds and feelings requires time and a transition process that includes various steps."

The main lesson of these five phases is twofold: patience and perseverance. They are natural phases and rushing through them or trying to skip them usually doesn't work. So, accept that people–including you–need to go through these phases and manage the realization process accordingly. To help you recognize which phase people are in and to choose an appropriate way of responding, you can use the Coping Card below.

Example of a Coping Card

Phase	Signals	Response
Denial	• Overly pretending that things are still normal • Laughing things away • "We have seen that" • BOHICA (bend over, here it comes again)	• Announce that change will occur • Make the urgency visible and tangible • Apply Chapter 3 on activation
Defense	• "Yes, but…" (= "no way!") • Over-stating pros of the status quo and cons of the suggested change • Stop or slow down work • Deliberately frustrating initiatives	• Listen and let people speak out • Wait and weather the storm • Don't argue • Persist, no matter what
Discarding	• Passivity • People asking a lot of questions • Asking for confirmation • Grumbling and "mourning"	• Wait and let people mourn • Don't over-promise to make people feel good • Set a time at which the mourning has to stop • Give clarity about the new direction
Adaptation	• Hope and (over) optimism • New initiatives are taken • People have fun and feel energized • Impatience	• Speed up and get into action mode • Actively manage relevance and progress • Temper high hopes
Internalization	• Things getting quiet • The "normal" complaints return (e.g., about coffee) • Work becomes routine • "Glad it's all over"	• Celebrate the results • Keep challenging people • Install a continuous strategy process • Update your strategy

KEEPING TRACK OF EMOTIONS: THE MOOD CHART

Like with relevance and progress, it's also useful to monitor emotions during the realization process. Doing so helps you make sure you pay explicit attention to emotions. This is important because when focusing on your strategy and the actions needed to realize it, you might easily forget this important aspect of strategy execution. Tracking emotions can help you detect when resistance or frustration are slowly building up. As such, it helps you to take appropriate action on time.

A useful tool for monitoring how emotions develop in the course of the process is the Mood Chart. This chart looks similar to the Confidence Chart and Burn Chart above. In the same way as these charts, you regularly–perhaps every month or week–check the overall mood in the team to find out whether everyone is still on board. Here's an example.

Example of Mood Chart

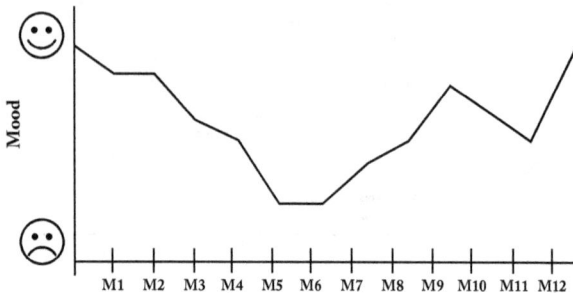

To keep things simple, this Mood Chart just projects emotion as something one-dimensional–ranging from very positive to very negative. Of course, this is a gross oversimplification. However, in practice, this works well since what matters most is whether the mood is generally positive (optimistic, energetic, fun, confident, etc.) or generally negative (pessimistic, passive, unhappy, uncertain, etc.) and that you explicitly discuss the prevailing mood so that you are open about it. In the example above, I have used just a single line. However, if you have multiple teams working on realizing your strategy, you can also include separate lines for each team.

The example above is not uncommon. Often, the realization phase starts off optimistically and full of hope, perhaps because people don't yet appreciate what the impact of the new strategy really is on the organization. Once a few months have passed, negative emotions often start playing a bigger role. The initial tasks did not work out exactly as hoped for, the change is more complex than expected, new tasks have been discovered meaning that more work needs to be done, etc. Further down the process, once substantial progress has been made, moods typically turn more positive again. As shown in the example chart above, this can sometimes lead to overoptimism near completion (month 9).

When using a Mood Chart, you're likely to find out that the development of the team's mood follows the phases of psychological transition described above. Accordingly, it's important to accept that "negative" emotions are normal and not necessarily something that need to be fixed. They require attention and emotions that are too negative can be problematic, but people will require time to digest the change. So, let them be angry, frustrated, and uncertain as long as needed. Furthermore, a situation where emotions are only very positive is equally a bit suspicious. Of course, it may be that you have a fantastic team or are a fantastic leader. However, in this case, you might want to double-check whether you have captured the real mood, or whether there are things going on below the surface.

THE FOUR EXAMPLES

REALIZATION AT MACMAN

A few months into the realization phase, strategy realization at Macman did not go well. They arrived at a point where Ivo and his management team experienced a lot of resistance from employees. It wasn't really clear why, but people complained a lot and didn't make the changes that they were expected to make. Especially with respect to the development of new services, nothing much had happened. Ivo wondered whether his employees were not smart enough (or more accurately: too stupid) to see that a change had to be made quickly or whether they were actively frustrating the change because they had something against it–or against him. So, everyone's moods had reached a point near zero.

When discussing his frustrations with his wife at home over dinner, she asked him a simple question: "Are you sure they are resisting?" After an immediate "Of course!", a "I have tried everything I could!", and a "They just don't get it!" he started to think about this. The next day, after a night's sleep, he had to admit that what he saw in his employees was perhaps not resistance. Actually, now that he thought about it, it looked more like they were lost than resisting. Their constant questions were not even complaints, but requests for more information, asking him to tell them what they needed to do. In other words, they tried their utmost to make the changes but were desperately looking at him to tell them how. How could he have misread these signs so badly?

Reflecting on his and his team's performance, it became immediately obvious they had made various mistakes listed on pages 311-312.

1. *Unclear communication:* not clear enough in explaining what the changes should be and how to make them.
2. *Indecisiveness:* leaving some key issues to be solved by employees which he should have solved himself.
3. *Laissez-faire:* letting his employees figure it out for themselves rather than actively helping them.
4. *Pushing too much:* constantly telling people to perform and thereby make people panic because they didn't know how.

Now that he recognized this, he understood why progress was not as he had hoped. And he also understood that what he had seen as resistance was mainly a reflection of his own counterproductive behavior. Grateful to his wife, he changed his behavior, particularly by giving his employees more direction. And before he knew it, the "resistance" had largely disappeared, and things started to move again.

REALIZATION AT HOSPICARE

The first projects and tasks in Hospicare's Strategy Backlog concerned bridging some information gaps. To test their assumptions about the new privatized centers they were planning to set up, they engaged in data collection and carried out a pilot around burnout (see page 218). The data they collected confirmed their assumptions. The data told them that there were enough people with diagnosed and undiagnosed burnout, ADHD, and Asperger's in the region, with at least two times the middle income. Thus, the market seemed to be there.

The pilot, however, was an outright failure. Even though they had done everything according to plan, there had not been a single client over the past three months. Even worse, no one had even shown interest in the product they created for treating burnout. This meant that, so far, they had to reject their first two assumptions. If they had drawn a Confidence Chart at this point, it would have shown that confidence that their new strategy was right had dropped below zero–and so had their moods.

So, what could have caused this unexpected lack of interest? When discussing this, one of the team members suggested that there was a lot of competition already when it came to treating burnout. Next to the conventional insured treatments, there were numerous commercial alternatives based on mindfulness, light therapy, time management, etc. This explanation made sense to the rest of the team. However, it was still an assumption that they wanted to test. As next steps, they needed to do the following.

1. Test the assumption that people were not interested in their offering for burnout because there were already enough alternatives. They planned to ask 30 people that they had targeted in their lightweight marketing campaign, but who had not responded.
2. Challenge their third assumption (suggesting that people will not be interested in privatized health care for more significant psychiatric problems) by repositioning their burnout treatment as a last resort for people who have already tried other treatments unsuccessfully. They decided to carry out a new pilot with this offering.

Only time will tell whether this change will bring Hospicare the success they are looking for. However, a positioning as a last resort for the more difficult cases of burnout at least better fits the fact that they are a high-quality hospital. And there also seems to be less competition there, since most others focus on the easy cases–many of which might not reflect real burnout in the first place.

REALIZATION AT GOFORIT

GoforIT had made ambitious plans to triple in size over two years. After two months, they carried out a first progress review and had to conclude that nothing much had happened. Their answers to the three progress questions were:

1. *Did the projects and tasks that should have started within this period start?* No. Not even all that should have started in the first 30 days.
2. *Did the projects and tasks that should have finished within this period finish?* No, none of them did.
3. *Did we stick to the estimated budgets in terms of time and resources?* Yes, we used far less, but only because we have hardly done anything.

It was obvious that something needed to change if they were going to make any headway. The reason for the lack of progress was that both Frank and Liu were too busy with all the other stuff that needed to be done. While that was largely a matter of priorities, they also realized more than ever that they urgently needed someone to join their team as COO, someone who could take the lead in making the required changes. Accordingly, they made two changes.

1. They added "finding a suitable COO" as their number one priority to their responsibilities. Together, they made a concrete list of actions they should perform and agreed to reserve at least three hours per week on this. Also, they set up short weekly meetings to discuss progress.
2. They appointed one of their employees as progress manager to make sure that, in the meantime, the change process got moving. After all, they had a concrete plan with projects and tasks that were already agreed. Appointing someone to manage the process and make sure that the plan was brought to life should give a boost to the realization of their strategy.

REALIZATION AT COMCOM

Strategy realization at Comcom went better than Anisha expected. Initially, she was a bit insecure, and she hesitated to get started. But, once she had started, she really got the hang of it and made big steps in a short period. Forcing herself to work in a more structured way (which she had to get used to anyway since that was part of the change), she held a review every last Friday of the month. During this review, she carried out an informal Relevance Check, Progress Check, and Mood Check.

1. *Relevance Check.* With the Relevance Check, she always finished quickly. Although the accountancy sector was in transition, it did not change in a relevant way. If anything, this transition increased demand for cost-efficient communication services. So, changes could not go fast enough for her.

2. *Progress Check.* The main challenge was to give enough priority to making the changes that were necessary. She had plenty of paid work to do for clients, and she had to block one day a week to spend on realizing the new strategy. As long as she did that, progress was largely according to plan.

3. *Mood Check.* After a small initial dip, her mood went up along with the progress she made. After a while, she came to realize that her idea of starting a new business around a food blog had been an escape route. Now that she worked on improving her business and doing something new, rather than being yet another communication company, it became more fun. As a result, she considered focusing on this business alone and letting the whole food blog idea go. And to be honest, in the meantime, so many food blogs had come up that it would be hard to compete anyway, and the trend might have reached its peak already. As a result, she considered focusing on this business alone and letting the food blog idea go.

CONCLUSION

We're at the end of the book and I've done my best to put all that I've learned and experienced about strategy in the past two decades together in one practical and integrated handbook that, I hope, helps you in improving your strategy and making it work. In this final chapter, I'll briefly summarize the approach so that you see once more how it all adds up. I'll also say a few words about how you can implement it in practice. Finally, because getting the strategy process going requires a leader that takes the responsibility for it, I also outline in more detail the kind of leadership that is required to make everything happen.

THE COMPLETE STRATEGY PROCESS

With the steps described in the previous chapters, you now have a complete strategy approach that consists of nine steps: 1. Activating, 2. Mapping, 3. Assessing, 4. Innovating, 5. Formulating, 6. Bridging, 7. Organizing, 8. Planning, and 9. Realizing Strategy. This process was summarized in the figure on page 27 and is accompanied by a variety of tools, checklists, and background information throughout the book. This means that you are now equipped to generate and execute strategy in your organization. For your convenience, I have summarized the complete approach below.

Overall Summary of the Strategy Approach

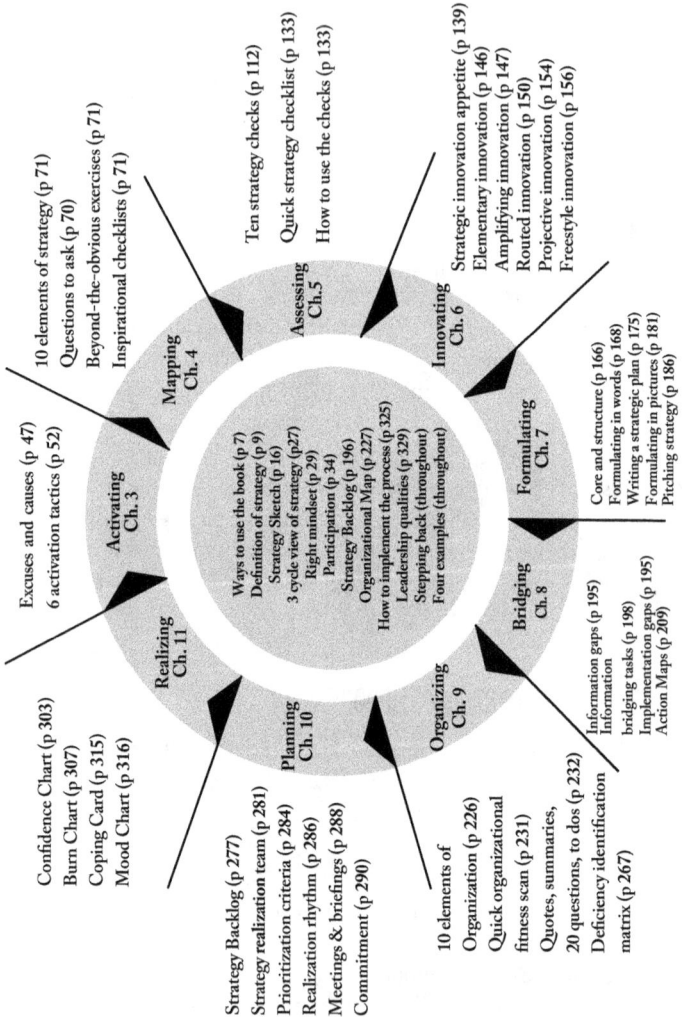

Center:
Ways to use the book (p 7)
Definition of strategy (p 9)
Strategy Sketch (p 16)
3 cycle view of strategy (p27)
Right mindset (p 29)
Participation (p 34)
Strategy Backlog (p 196)
Organizational Map (p 227)
How to implement the process (p 325)
Leadership qualities (p 329)
Stepping back (throughout)
Four examples (throughout)

Inner ring chapters:
Activating Ch. 3
Mapping Ch. 4
Assessing Ch.5
Innovating Ch. 6
Formulating Ch. 7
Bridging Ch. 8
Organizing Ch. 9
Planning Ch. 10
Realizing Ch. 11

Activating (Ch. 3):
Excuses and causes (p 47)
6 activation tactics (p 52)

Mapping (Ch. 4):
10 elements of strategy (p 71)
Questions to ask (p 70)
Beyond-the-obvious exercises (p 71)
Inspirational checklists (p 71)

Assessing (Ch.5):
Ten strategy checks (p 112)
Quick strategy checklist (p 133)
How to use the checks (p 133)

Innovating (Ch. 6):
Strategic innovation appetite (p 139)
Elementary innovation (p 146)
Amplifying innovation (p 147)
Routed innovation (p 150)
Projective innovation (p 154)
Freestyle innovation (p 156)

Formulating (Ch. 7):
Core and structure (p 166)
Formulating in words (p 168)
Writing a strategic plan (p 175)
Formulating in pictures (p 181)
Pitching strategy (p 186)

Bridging (Ch. 8):
Information gaps (p 195)
Information bridging tasks (p 198)
Implementation gaps (p 195)
Action Maps (p 209)

Organizing (Ch. 9):
10 elements of Organization (p 226)
Quick organizational fitness scan (p 231)
Quotes, summaries, 20 questions, to dos (p 232)
Deficiency identification matrix (p 267)

Planning (Ch. 10):
Strategy Backlog (p 277)
Strategy realization team (p 281)
Prioritization criteria (p 284)
Realization rhythm (p 286)
Meetings & briefings (p 288)
Commitment (p 290)

Realizing (Ch. 11):
Confidence Chart (p 303)
Burn Chart (p 307)
Coping Card (p 315)
Mood Chart (p 316)

In this figure, the "donut" summarizes the nine steps of the strategy process. The numbers refer to the chapters in which these steps are described. Outside this donut, you find the main tools and techniques that you can use in each step. The numbers there refer to the part and page at which you find more information about them. Finally, inside the donut, you find the general tools and information that form the basis of the complete strategy approach and that are relevant throughout the strategy process. The numbers there also refer to the pages on which they are described.

HOW TO IMPLEMENT THE PROCESS IN PRACTICE

There are many ways to use the strategy approach outlined in this book. Some you have already seen. In Chapter 1, I discussed three ways of using this book (pp 7-8) and in Chapter 2, I sketched how strategy ideally is a participative process involving people from all over the organization (pp 34-40). Furthermore, after Chapter 4, I laid out a fast and frugal format for strategy generation.

In this concluding chapter I want to give you a better sense of how you can implement the approach in practice, drawing on my own experience. While I most definitely invite you to find your own way of implementation, my own approach has converged over the years and I'd like to share it with you.

In general, I implement the process in the form of a series of 3-hour interactive sessions with a team that is a good representation of the organization. For the ideal characteristics of this team, I refer to the aforementioned section in Chapter 2 on "Strategy as a Participative Process." If possible, I prefer to have these sessions on premise, at the organization, rather than in a hotel or conference center. This is to signal that working on one's strategy is something normal and belonging to people's ordinary work, not something extraordinary. In terms of setting, imagine me sitting (when I use my laptop to facilitate the process) or standing (when I use brown paper and Post-it Notes) in the front, and others sitting in a U-shape behind tables so that they can take notes, have a coffee, and see each other. With that setting in mind, the process typically looks as follows.

1. Draw the Strategy Sketch on a large sheet of paper, the larger the better (e.g., big-sized brown paper). Stick it on the wall at the front of the room so that everyone can see it. Or use a digital form of the Strategy Sketch created in PowerPoint or an online digital whiteboard tool and project it on a screen. While I initially used brown paper, I have completely switched to digital since a couple of years. But both methods work.

2. Map out the existing strategy with the team. While you could ask people to write things down on Post-it Notes themselves, I prefer that they speak out what they want to say while I write it down and put it on the Strategy Sketch. The main reason is that I can immediately ask for clarification and that everyone hears what is being said. This works best if you start doing this element by element. You can encourage people, for example, by asking the first set of "20 Questions to Ask" for each element (see Chapter 4). When I do this, I usually get things that people find good about their current strategy and things that are not so good or that they would still need. To mark the difference, I use green notes for the first and orange notes for the latter. Typically, the mapping phase takes two of these 3-hour sessions.

3. Assess the strategy. Following a similar format as above, the third session typically focuses on assessing the strategy. During the first sessions, mostly a lot is already said about strengths and weaknesses, but it is valuable to include a dedicated session to assess the current strategy as a whole. For this I use the 10 criteria from Chapter 5 and discuss them with the group one by one. I typically start by asking people to give a score (1-5) or color (green, amber, red) to sharpen their minds. After the scoring, we discuss why they gave that score and what are the particular strong and weak points that lead to this score. At the end of this session, there is a comprehensive assessment of the current strategy, providing a solid basis to move on.

4. Now it is time for innovation. Again, using a similar setup, I use one or two sessions to come up with ideas for the new strategy. The previous sessions have given plenty of input in terms of ideas and insights which form a valuable basis for the strategy. In addition, to broaden people's views and come up with even more or better ideas, I typically use one or more of the innovation approaches from Chapter 6. Also, to select the best ideas, I typically use voting or the "sticker method" (give everyone three small stickers that they can put on what they think are the best ideas). The session ends when the flow of ideas dries up.

5. When idea generation is finished, it is time for integration, putting the ideas together into a coherent new strategy. You can use a blank Strategy Sketch for this, put in the selected ideas, and from thereon complete the strategy by drawing the implications for all the elements. This is again a session with the team, where everyone can share their thoughts in the same way as above. If you want to develop multiple scenarios, you can either split the team up into smaller teams, or use multiple subsequent sessions for this.

6. After this part of the process is done, I typically execute the next step–formulating strategy–"offline," without any sessions. Writing down a strategy works best if done by one or two persons, not in a team session. Accordingly, I usually write the strategic plan in close collaboration with the CEO or other executive that has the responsibility for the new strategy. Generally, I write, while the CEO/executive provides his or her feedback and edits.

7. When the CEO and I agree about the draft strategy, we discuss it again in a session with the team. Sometimes I turn the strategy into a presentation format so that we can discuss it. And sometimes I discuss the written strategic plan itself. Both can work. Typically, the team

has various questions and suggestions, which I carefully gather during the session.

8. After the session, the CEO and I revise the strategy and, dependent on the number of comments, we create another draft, or finalize the strategy, and thereby close the strategy generation phase of the process.

For the strategy execution phase, I follow a similar approach combining interactive sessions with the team with "offline" work by me and one or a few others on an individual basis.

- For bridging, you can use a blank Strategy Sketch and use Post-it Notes to define the main gaps, projects, and tasks needed for each of the elements.
- For organizing, you can use the Organizational Map to identify the main changes needed to your organization, again using Post-it Notes in the same way as above.
- For planning, you can create a Strategy Backlog, for example in a spreadsheet, populate it together with the team with the required projects and tasks, and then prioritize.
- The last step, realizing, doesn't really need a session format like above. As explained in Chapter 11, it should better be part of your normal meeting "rhythm" instead of taking place in separate sessions. Therefore, it is recommended you include managing progress, relevance, and emotions in your monthly, quarterly, and annual meeting rhythm.

The exact process and the number of sessions needed depend on the specific circumstances. But overall, I mostly follow a variation of the process above. Assuming that what works for me will also work for you, I recommend implementing the approach in a similar way.

WHAT IT ASKS FROM LEADERS

Strategy generation and execution will only be successful if there is good leadership in the organization. Therefore, in this final section, we discuss the type of leadership that best fits our nine-step approach. As we already saw on page 227, leadership is at the center of the Organizational Map and, without it, nothing will really happen. This applies not only to making the required organizational changes for the new strategy but also to the strategy-making process: without good leaders, it will be an almost guaranteed failure–unless you are very lucky.

In terms of leaders, I don't just mean those at the top of the organization. Leaders are the people who take the lead. This could be at the top, but also anywhere else in the organization–as part of the strategy team, or in any formal or informal leadership position. Probably this includes you, which means that I am getting a bit personal now.

The strategy approach outlined in this book does not fit every type of leader. As you have seen, it is an iterative, participative approach in which strategy is co-created with people across the organization. Such an approach often doesn't fare well with authoritative, directive leaders. Even though the main steps could be followed, this type of leader would not make use of the full potential of the approach. It also doesn't fare well with planning-oriented leaders that prefer extensive and quantitative data, trend analyses, and projections as primary basis for their strategy. The approach outlined in this book does not fully contradict such type of leadership. However, the traditional approach to strategy that we find in many strategy textbooks is probably a better fit for these leaders.

> *"The approach doesn't fare well with authoritative, directive leaders."*

At various places, you have had clues about the kind of leadership that is most successful with the outlined approach. Most clearly, this was the case when I described the mindset needed in Chapter

2 (pages 29-34, especially Motto 10, "No place for HiPPOs") and when I discussed the leadership element of organization on pages 234-236. The kind of leadership that I sketched there and that best fits the approach looks most like what is called "servant leadership" in the literature. To make the strategy approach outlined in this book work effectively, leaders in the organization should have or develop the following six qualities.

1. **Conceptual.** Leaders need to see the big picture and connect the many things that are going on. They need to be able to connect details with an overview and the short term with the long term.

2. **Diligent.** Leaders should be hungry for improvement and not too easily satisfied with how things are. They shouldn't strive for perfection, but always be on the look out for ways to make things better.

3. **Tenacious.** Leaders need to persist until something is done and not give up or give in too soon. They should be determined and able to make tough decisions despite uncertainty and resistance.

4. **Receptive.** Leaders need to be open to subtle signals and listen attentively to what others say. They should be persuadable and change course based on the information they receive.

5. **Communicative.** Leaders need to be able to express themselves clearly and persuade others to do what is needed. They should also be willing to share information and be transparent where possible.

6. **Caring.** Leaders need to care about people and be able to put themselves in their shoes. They should treat people as human beings and take their needs into account wherever possible.

When they have these six qualities, leaders will be able to lead the strategy process effectively. They will be able to balance between thinking big and acting small, between aiming for the best and being pragmatic, between insisting on their own views and listening to others, and between the organization's interest and people's personal interests. Combined with the nine-step approach described in this book, such leaders have all that it takes to effectively generate and execute strategy and achieve daily business success. Do you have what it takes?

A FINAL RECOMMENDATION

I wrote this handbook with the aim that it should improve and ease strategy generation and execution for your organization. You could of course strictly follow my suggestions, stick to the proposed order of steps, and methodically generate a strategy and execute it. What I hope and recommend, though, is that you will use this book as a source of insight and inspiration for developing your own personal approach to strategy. Only in that way will you be able to truly generate and execute your own unique strategy–your way of sustainable value creation.

"Use this book as a source of insight and inspiration for developing your own personal approach to strategy."